100 THINGS
WHITE SOX FANS
SHOULD KNOW & DO
BEFORE THEY DIE

100 THINGS
WHITE SOX FANS
SHOULD KNOW & DO
BEFORE THEY DIE

Bob Vanderberg

TRIUMPH
BOOKS

Library of Congress Cataloging-in-Publication Data

Vanderberg, Bob, 1948– author.
  100 things White Sox fans should know & do before they die / Bob Vanderberg.
    p. cm.
  ISBN 978-1-60078-807-9
  1. Chicago White Sox (Baseball team)—History. 2. Chicago White Sox (Baseball team)—Miscellanea. I. Title. II. Title: One hundred things White Sox fans should know and do before they die.
  GV875.C58V335 2013
  796.357'640977311—dc23

                                    2013049718

This book is available in quantity at special discounts for your group or organization. For further information, contact:
  Triumph Books LLC
  814 North Franklin Street
  Chicago, Illinois 60610
  (312) 337-0747
  www.triumphbooks.com

Printed in U.S.A.
ISBN: 978-1-60078-807-9
Design by Patricia Frey
Photos courtesy of AP Images unless otherwise indicated

This book is dedicated to my son, Brad, who once was a White Sox fan—note the photo of him at age six with Steve Lyons in July 1989, after the ceremonial first pitch. Sadly, though, he long since defected to join fandoms of two teams—the Oakland A's and Toronto Blue Jays—that invariably make short work of the Sox when they meet, whether it's here or on the road.

Not only has he taken great pleasure over the years in the Sox's utter inability to win in Oakland, but at age 10 he came along with me to the Sox-Jays playoff opener wearing a Toronto batting helmet. When Juan Uribe threw to Paul Konerko for the final out of the 2005 World Series, he was saddened at first but then reminded me that the A's had gone 7–2 against the new world champions that season.

My wife and I wonder where we went wrong. Maybe if I had been home at night rather than at work. Well, there is still time for him to "come home."

At least he hasn't become a Cub fan.

Contents

Introduction

They're still the White Sox, and even after 2013's disaster of a season, they're still *our* White Sox. But fans should know that, just three years after the Sox finished last in 1948, they were in first place at the All-Star break in 1951; that two years after they lost 106 games in 1970, they were in first place in August; that in 1977, a year after they finished last, they were in first place in August; that in 1990, a year after they finished last, they went 94–68; and that in 2008, a year after going 72–90, they defeated Minnesota in the "Blackout Game" to win a division title.

The next thing White Sox fans should know before they begin perusing this book is that the White Sox, since they began playing in "New Comiskey Park" in 1991, have had totally different ball-clubs from the ones that played at the old park across 35th Street and dealt with a totally different set of meteorological factors. For whatever reason, there is what amounts to a jetstream at what is now called U.S. Cellular Field that helps take batted balls hit toward right-center field on much longer rides than the baseballs—and those who batted them—had any right to expect.

This "feature" first became obvious on the day the new park opened in April 1991, when the Detroit Tigers hit four home runs—all by right-handed hitters and two of which seemingly were just high flyballs to right field. Instead of being caught 10 to 15 feet short of the warning track, these balls kept going and going until they nestled in among the surprised bleacherites. Soon the White Sox too found the range and ended up hitting 139 long ones that season—74 at "New Comiskey"—compared to a total of 106 in 1990 (and just 41 at the old park).

And so it was that the White Sox, for years derided as Punch-and-Judy hitters playing in a ballpark that humbled slug-gers, suddenly were launching home runs—both at their new long-ball-friendly home park (renamed U.S. Cellular Field, a.k.a. "The Cell" in 2003) as well as on the road. They hit as many as 216 in the division-title season of 2000—after which management decided it would move the bullpens to make them more visible to fans. That, however, meant moving the fences in from 347 feet down the lines to 330 (left) and 335 (right). Later, when the top eight rows of the upper deck were lopped off after the 2003 season to make the climb to the Cell's highest seats less foreboding, almost all well-hit baseballs—not just those driven toward right-center—automatically became home run candidates. (The Sox hit 220 homers in 2003 and 242 in 2004.)

Also, even though head groundskeeper Roger Bossard watched his dad, Gene, create it, "Bossard's Swamp" is a thing of the past, a relic of the '60s, when the muddy home-plate area (and lengthy infield grass) contributed mightily toward making the final score of a Sox game invariably 2–1 or 3–2. The White Sox, furthermore, no longer store game balls in a cold, damp and musty storeroom in the bowels of the ballpark. That was another 1960s stratagem designed to ensure that, since the Sox weren't going to hit home runs, their opponents wouldn't hit any either. So, whereas the Sox club leader in home runs might have hit 15 to 19 in a season during the 1940s, '50s, and '60s, for example, and 25 to 30 during the '70s, nowadays they're routinely hitting 40 and more.

These White Sox, then, are not your grandfather's White Sox. The hallmarks of many of those clubs were pitching, speed, and defense, key ingredients all for success at old Comiskey. The Go-Go Sox hit doubles and triples and ran the bases with abandon, then depended on defense and solid pitching to keep opponents at bay. In this new era, the Sox all too often have played station-to-station ball and depended on the home run—200-plus per season. Used to be that the Sox might hit a home run every other game. Lately it seems like one every other inning.

It will soon become apparent, then, that most of the franchise's big offensive numbers have been recorded since the move to the new ballpark in 1991. Call them the "A" Sox (1901 through 1990) and the "B" Sox (1991 through the present), if you wish. But there is a difference. A big difference.

Maybe someday they'll be the "C" Sox, champions once again. While you're waiting, flip through these pages and read about pennant races and roof shots, legendary players and some not so legendary, stories of cheating scoreboards, oversleeping outfielders, and the biggest home run in club history. Learn about Fox and learn about The Fix, the glory days and the gory days, the Blackout Game and the White Flag trade. The story of the youngest pitcher to ever start a major league game, and the outfield prospect who at 19 clubbed two homers at Yankee Stadium in the 1962 season finale and, three years later, was out of baseball entirely, having launched a career in art. (The chapter is entitled—with apologies to James Joyce—"Portrait of the Artist as a Young Outfielder.")

And my apologies to Mike Joyce, former Sox right-hander, a longtime resident of Wheaton, Illinois, and a grand guy, for my referencing James Joyce in a White Sox book and not him!

1 88 Was Enough

The scene on the field at Houston's Minute Maid Park was almost unimaginable. This wasn't really happening, was it? Men in Chicago White Sox uniforms were jumping on top of each other, hugging each other, celebrating something that the franchise had not accomplished in 88 years: the winning of a World Series. For the first time since 1917, the White Sox—*our White Sox*—were world champions, having swept the Houston Astros in four straight games.

Stop and think of how long ago 1917 was. It was so long ago that Chicago had a Republican mayor, "Big Bill" Thompson. It was the year the U.S. declared war on Germany and sent its boys to France to fight the first of the century's two world wars. It was the year the National Hockey League was formed, with just four teams: one each from Toronto and Ottawa, two from Montreal, and none from Chicago.

Since their 1917 World Series triumph over the New York Giants, the White Sox had won American League titles in 1919 and 1959 and division championships in 1983, 1993, and 2000. There could have been—indeed, *should* have been—more successes along the way to this glorious 2005 postseason, which had ended just moments earlier on the second of two sensational ninth-inning plays by shortstop Juan Uribe. But now, in these moments, previous failures were forgotten. In this 2005 World Series—and also in the two postseason series that preceded it—the Sox were the ones who had delivered the big hit, like Jermaine Dye's eighth-inning, two-out RBI single to center that provided the lone run of Game 4.

It was almost as if the Sox had been awarded the exclusive contract to produce big hits. Hours earlier, former Houston Astro Geoff Blum—in his first at-bat of the Series—had lined a tie-breaking home run into the right-field seats in the 14th inning as the Sox emerged 7–5 winners in the longest game in World Series history to take an insurmountable three-games-to-none lead.

Dye delivered the first big hit of the Series, an opposite-field shot off Roger Clemens in the first inning of Game 1, a blast that let everyone know that these White Sox were hardly World Series impostors. And in Game 2, the heroes delivering the big hits were Paul Konerko, whose two-out seventh-inning grand slam lifted the Sox into a 6–4 lead, and Scott Podsednik, who won the game 7–6 with a one-out solo homer in the ninth off Houston closer Brad Lidge. And neither Scottie Pods nor Konerko was looking for the "big fly"—just the big hit.

"I was just trying to get on base," Podsednik said. "Then we can work from there—then we'll try to get into scoring position. Luckily, I got the count to 2–1, and I said, 'Hey, let's put a good swing on this fastball.' It was a good pitch to hit, and I was able to drive it out." Said Konerko: "In that [bases-loaded situation], a home run is the last thing on your mind. I'm thinking to get a base hit to drive in two and hopefully tie. And then, bang, you get it. That's usually when you get them—when you're not trying to."

There had been huge hits, too, in the division series against Boston—none bigger, perhaps, than Tadahito Iguchi's three-run homer off David Wells in Game 2 in Chicago, the blow that put the Sox ahead to stay at 5–4. There was Konerko's tie-breaking homer in the clinching 5–3 triumph at Fenway. There was Joe Crede's game-winning double with two out in the ninth inning of Game 2 of the ALCS in Chicago, just moments after an alleged dropped third strike by Angels catcher Josh Paul had put the Sox's A.J. Pierzynski on first base instead of in the dugout. There were Konerko's first-inning home runs in the third and fourth games at

Bobby Jenks and Paul Konerko begin to celebrate after the final out of the White Sox's World Series sweep of the Astros is recorded on October 26, 2005.

Anaheim, one a two-run blast and the other a three-run shot. And there was Crede again, coming through with a leadoff home run in the seventh to tie Game 5 and an RBI single in the eighth for the go-ahead run.

And then there was the pitching, incredible by any measure. Jose Contreras, Mark Buehrle, Jon Garland, and Freddy Garcia did a perfect impersonation of Gary Peters, Juan Pizarro, Joe Horlen, and Tommy John, the '60s foursome that was as stingy with runs as Jack Benny was with tips. In the ALCS, the four Sox starters held the Angels to 27 hits and 11 runs in 44⅓ innings and completed all but one start. Thanks in great part to a brilliant relief job by Orlando "El Duque" Hernandez at Fenway Park, Chicago held Boston to nine runs in three games. And, after spotting Houston a 4–0 lead in Game 3 of the World Series, the Sox limited the Astros to one run in the final 19 innings.

It was a dominant performance, the kind that White Sox fans in the past could have only dreamed of. It all came true in 2005, when Sox fans finally got to turn back the clock and party like it was 1917.

2 Be Proud of This

There are times when it seems like being a White Sox fan means you're always in a foul mood. There are the seemingly constant slights, real or imagined—like when an ESPN or MLB Network anchor promotes an upcoming feature on "the Sox" and you stick around long enough to learn that the special piece is about the Boston Red Sox. As your wife rolls her eyes and the dog runs for cover, you yell at the television, "The Sox are the *White* Sox, not the

Red Sox." You continue, "It says 'SOX' on the White Sox's home jerseys; Boston's say 'RED SOX.'"

Then there are those times when the local 10:00 sportscast leads with the Cubs instead of the Sox, even on a day when the fifth-place Cubs lose 13–4 at home and the second-place Pale Hose win 5–2 on the road. Or when you're on vacation and a fellow traveler asks where you're from. "Chicago," you respond, and then hear, "Oh, a Cubbie fan?" And you smile politely and say, "No." And you want to add to that something like, "I've always preferred big-league ball," but then you think better of it when you feel your wife's elbow—the sharper one—in your side.

You eventually come to believe that the only things the nation's sports fans know—or care to know—about the Chicago White Sox are Disco Demolition, the Black Sox scandal, and the fact that three times in 1976 they wore shorts as part of their uniforms. And then you begin wallowing in self-pity, especially during those now thankfully rare rough stretches such as 2007 and 2013.

That's when it's time to remember a remarkable day in White Sox history, to take pride in all that happened that day, and to point it out to as many people as possible, so that they will come to be wary of your approaching footsteps and flee the area rather than hear the message one more time. Here it is:

Even when times seem darkest for White Sox fans, they can still brag that the Sox played in front of the largest crowd ever to see a regular-season or postseason baseball game, 92,706. And not only did they win it, they won 1–0 and they beat Sandy Koufax in the process.

The date was October 6, 1959. Game 5 of the 1959 World Series at the Los Angeles Coliseum (built for track and football but then acting as the National League–champion Dodgers' temporary home until the new ballpark planned for the Chavez Ravine section of L.A. became reality). The Sox, after splitting the opening two games in Chicago, had not found the Coliseum—with its left-field foul pole just 251 feet from home plate—to their liking and had dropped 3–1 and 5–4 decisions. Both Games 3 and 4 had drawn record crowds of 92,000-plus, many fans so far away from the field that the game was just a rumor.

The Sox, though, had to have this one or the Series was not going back to Chicago. Opposing Koufax (not yet the superstar he would become) was Game 2 loser Bob Shaw, who this day matched Koufax zero for zero. Chicago broke through in the fourth inning when singles by Nellie Fox and Jim Landis put runners at first and third with none out. Sherm Lollar then grounded into a double play, Fox scoring what would be the game's lone run.

"They went for the double play," Shaw recalled, years later, "and you can't fault their decision. In that ballpark, you don't figure you're gonna have a 1–0 game, not with that fence in left field. I did a little after-dinner speaking that winter in Chicago, and I used to kid that when I reached real far back for the good fastball that day, I'd scrape my hand on that fence."

Shaw and Dick Donovan made the run stand up, with an assist from Jim Rivera, whose terrific running catch of Charlie Neal's two-out drive to deep right-center in the seventh saved two runs and preserved the White Sox triumph. Two days later, though, the Dodgers romped 9–3 to take the Series four games to two.

Earlier, in May of that year, 93,103 had turned out for a Dodgers-Yankees exhibition game at the Coliseum, an event held to raise funds for paralyzed former-Dodger Roy Campanella. And in March 2008, the Dodgers and Red Sox drew an announced 115,000 to the Coliseum for an exhibition that served to celebrate the 50th anniversary of the Dodgers' move to the West Coast from Brooklyn.

But the postseason/regular-season top crowd remains the 92,706 who watched the Sox edge the Dodgers that afternoon more than 50 years ago.

3 Perfection: 27 Up and 27 Down

Of the three White Sox pitchers who have thrown perfect games, the only one whose feat makes any sense at all is Mark Buehrle.

Charlie Robertson? That's silly. Philip Humber? Come on.

But that's how these things go. It didn't make any sense that Don Larsen would throw a perfect game for the Yankees—in a World Series yet—while New York's Whitey Ford, Bob Turley, Vic Raschi, and Eddie Lopat never got close.

Robertson got his on Sunday, April 30, 1922, in Detroit as a White Sox rookie right-hander making his fourth appearance of the season and his third start. Detroit figured to provide the toughest opposition he'd face thus far. The Tigers had two Hall-of-Fame outfielders in Ty Cobb and Harry Heilmann and another terrific hitter in left fielder Bobby Veach, plus first baseman Lu Blue, he of the .416 on-base percentage the season before.

On this day, Robertson kept the Tigers off balance with slow breaking pitches. Meanwhile, the Sox scored twice against Herm Pillette in the second inning when Earl Sheely singled home Harry Hooper and Johnny Mostil with the game's only runs. By the time the home ninth arrived, the crowd of 25,000-plus was rooting for Chicago's rookie pitcher. Fellow rookie Danny Clark struck out, as did Clyde Manion. Finally, Johnny Bassler batted for Pillette and hammered one down the left-field line. Some years later, Mostil remembered:

"I made a big dive and stabbed it to end the game," he said, also confirming that *Tiger* fans rushed the diamond and carried Robertson off the field. "Some fan snatched the ball out of my hand. In the dugout, [Sox manager] Kid Gleason said, 'Where's the ball?' I told him what happened. He said, 'Go get a ball, any ball.'

I grabbed a practice ball and went to the clubhouse where everyone was making a big fuss over Robertson. We all autographed it. Charlie probably still thinks it's the real ball."

Robertson finished the year 14–15 with a 3.64 ERA, numbers he never again approached. He was out of the big leagues after the 1928 season.

Nor was Philip Humber ever the same pitcher after his surprise perfecto, a 4–0 masterpiece April 21, 2012, in Seattle. He had pitched well for the Sox during the first half of 2011 (8–5, 3.10 ERA) and not so well in the second (1–4, 5.01). But he had shown enough skill to be the club's No. 5 starter for 2012, and this start against the Mariners was just his second of this new season and his 30th in the big leagues.

Humber had been the third player selected in the 2004 draft, taken by the Mets. Injuries messed up his progress thereafter. He bounced around a bit, going to the Twins in a trade and then drifting on waivers to Kansas City, Oakland, and the White Sox. He'd had Tommy John surgery and been nailed by a line drive to the face. He thus was prepared for anything that day in Seattle.

When he got Brendan Ryan on strikes for the 27th out, Humber had become just the 21st pitcher in big-league history to throw a perfect game. "I saw that on TV when I was in the clubhouse, and like I said earlier, I don't know what my name is doing on that list," he told reporters. "It's just so humbling."

Soon Humber was being humbled every time he pitched. He ended the 2012 season with a 5–5 record and 6.44 ERA in a Sox uniform, was picked up by Houston in the off-season and promptly went 0–8 with a 7.90 ERA as an Astro in 2013.

Mark Buehrle's masterpiece, registered against Tampa Bay in Chicago on Thursday afternoon, July 23, 2009, carried with it substantially more importance than the other two White Sox perfect games. These Sox were a game behind Detroit for the AL Central

Mark Buehrle throws the final pitch of his perfect game against the Tampa Bay Rays on June 23, 2009. (Getty Images)

lead; Tampa Bay was third in the AL East, 5½ back of New York, and could not afford to fall further back.

Buehrle (10–3, 3.52) got a huge early lift when Josh Fields, subbing at first base with Paul Konerko in the DH role, drove a grand slam into the seats in left off Scott Kazmir. Back-to-back doubles by Scott Podsednik and Alexei Ramirez made it 5–0 in the fifth. By the sixth, "that feeling" began to course through the stands. When B.J. Upton, Carl Crawford, and Evan Longoria—perhaps Tampa's most dangerous hitters—were easy outs in the seventh, the crowd of 28,036 let out a roar—a confident one. In the eighth, Carlos Pena struck out, Ben Zobrist popped out, and Pat Burrell lined softly to third baseman Gordon Beckham, after which Hawk Harrelson commanded, "Call your sons, call your

This Close to Cooperstown

Billy Pierce could taste it now. As he left the White Sox dugout at Comiskey Park and headed out to the mound for the Washington ninth, the smallish Friday night crowd of 11,300 stood as one to salute the little lefty who had accomplished so much since his arrival 10 years before from Detroit at age 21.

He had started three All-Star Games, won 20 games each of the last two years, and led the American League in complete games twice and in earned-run average and strikeouts once each. He had not thrown a no-hitter, however—let alone a perfect game, which is what he had going this night, June 27, 1958.

The bottom third of the Senators' lineup contained no batters who struck terror into the hearts of pitchers. The dangerous Washington sluggers, Roy Sievers and Jim Lemon, had already gone 0-for-3 and, hopefully, were done for the night. Pierce, then, need only concern himself with second baseman Ken Aspromonte, rookie catcher Steve Korcheck, and a pinch-hitter for the pitcher, Russ Kemmerer.

Aspromonte grounded to shortstop Luis Aparicio for the first out, and Korcheck struck out to give Pierce eight Ks on the night. Now P.A. man Tate Johnson announced backup catcher Ed Fitz Gerald (10-for-32, .313 thus far) as the batter for Kemmerer.

"Fitz Gerald," Pierce remembered, "was a first-ball, fastball hitter. So we threw him a curveball away. And he hit it down the right-field line for a double. It was a good hit."

Billy quickly fanned the next batter, Albie Pearson, his ninth strikeout victim, to end a game that could have been perfect.

daughters, call your friends, call your neighbors—Mark Buehrle is taking a perfect game into the ninth."

Three outs to go. Manager Ozzie Guillen moved Scott Podsednik from center field to left and sent Dewayne Wise, his best defensive outfielder, to center. Now Gabe Kapler, who'd been managing in the low minors when the season began, crushed a 2-2 pitch toward the wall in left-center. Wise raced back, leaped at the fence, brought back what would've been a home run, juggled the ball on the way down, and finally gripped it for keeps with his bare hand. The ballpark shook. "Burls" couldn't possibly lose his perfecto now, not after *that* catch.

"It was probably the best catch I've ever made, because of the circumstances," Wise said after the game. "It was kind of crazy, man, because when I jumped, the ball hit my glove at the same time I was hitting the wall. So I didn't realize I had caught it until I fell down and the ball was coming out of my glove. So I reached out and grabbed it."

Two outs to go. No. 8 hitter Michel Hernandez struck out swinging, and then Jason Bartlett, who wound up the season batting .320, sent a bouncer to Ramirez at short. The throw was perfect, and so, finally, was the game.

"I still don't know what happened," Buehrle said later. What had happened was that the Sox lefty, who had thrown a one-walk no-hitter against Texas on April 18, 2007, joined Sandy Koufax, Cy Young, Jim Bunning, Randy Johnson, and Addie Joss as the only pitchers in big-league history to throw both a no-hitter and a perfect game. "Obviously," Buehrle said, "any time your name gets up there with some of the greats in the game, it means a lot."

4 From Glory to Infamy

Instead of *Eight Men Out,* a better title for Eliot Asinov's all-encompassing study of the 1919 Black Sox scandal might have been *Cheaters Cheating Cheaters* or *The Double-Crossers Get Double-Crossed.*

That is what, in fact, happened. Many of the professional gamblers who had conspired with certain White Sox players to fix the 1919 World Series ended up getting double-crossed and lost a goodly amount of money. The players got double-crossed—most didn't get the money they were supposed to receive—and, much worse, wound up getting thrown out of organized baseball for life.

The club was divided into two groups of players, each with practically nothing to say to the other. Together they formed the best team in baseball—perhaps one of the best teams that ever played the game. One bunch was headed by college-educated second baseman Eddie Collins and the scrappy catcher, Ray Schalk, who both became Hall of Famers. The other faction was essentially made up of the fixers: first baseman Chick Gandil, shortstop Swede Risberg (and his buddy, utility infielder Fred McMullin), center fielder Happy Felsch, and pitchers Eddie Cicotte and Lefty Williams. Joe Jackson and Buck Weaver were said to have friends in both camps, but allegedly chose the "dark side" in 1919.

It was an extremely talented and volatile team. Collins had nothing to say to Gandil, and vice versa. Risberg had nothing to say to Collins, and vice versa. And yet they won and they won and they won. They were world champs in 1917. If World War I had not interfered, the Sox might well have won in 1918 as well. They might well have been going for a fourth straight World Series appearance in 1920 when the scandal story broke during the season's final two weeks.

Yet, even as talented as the players were, they were paid a fraction of what they were worth. Sox owner Charles A. Comiskey paid two of his biggest stars, left fielder Jackson and third baseman Weaver, only $6,000 a year. Comiskey also cut costs by reducing the number of times dirty uniforms went to the laundry, supposedly the practice that labeled his team "the Black Sox" in the first place.

There also was the story of Cicotte being promised a bonus by Comiskey if he were to win 30 games that season. Cicotte won his 28th game on September 5, then mysteriously was idle for two weeks, till September 19, when he beat the Red Sox to go to 29–7. He had two starts after that, one when he was hit around by the St. Louis Browns, the other a two-inning tuneup in the season's final game. Cicotte assumed he was still getting the bonus, but Comiskey reminded him that the extra cash was payable on 30 wins, not 29.

Even so, most baseball historians say Comiskey was probably no worse than most owners—in fact, the Sox had baseball's highest payroll in 1919. In the era of the reserve clause, gamblers could find players on lots of teams looking for extra cash. There was too often a fairly close relationship between player and gambler; some former players had become gamblers, and some players were big bettors. Baseball was in the grip of gamblers. The fix and the cleanup that followed were inevitable, most historians now say. If the conspiring players had not been from the White Sox, they would have arrived on stage from another team.

In any event, Gandil, the ringleader from the players' side, met in Boston with gambler Sport Sullivan during the season's final weeks and told him that his boys would be able to pull it off—for $80,000. Gandil lined up Cicotte, Williams, Felsch, Risberg, McMullin, Weaver, and Jackson—who later said he was promised $20,000 but only got $5,000. Fact is, the gamblers were using money that was to go to pay off the players to place bets on the Reds—previously given no chance—in the Series' first two games, in Cincinnati.

Gandil managed to get $10,000 of the money owed the Sox fixers to Cicotte before Game 1. He assumed the money had come from Sullivan, but things had become confusing. Now he was hearing names of gamblers like "Sleepy Bill" Burns (former Sox pitcher), former pro boxers Billy Maharg and Abe Attell, and even that of "the Big Bankroll," Arnold Rothstein, the most famous gambler of his day.

The Series began on a sunny October 1, and Cicotte's sloppy pitching and fielding along with the butchered plays behind him guaranteed a Reds victory, and Cincinnati rolled 9–1. More of the same came in Game 2, as Williams refused to throw the good curve Schalk knew would be tough on Reds hitters. Mix in a few questionable plays in the field and the Reds were 4–2 winners and on their way to Chicago with a 2–0 Series lead.

But again, the gamblers stalled, saying the money was out on bets. The players were getting tired of this game, but they told Maharg that if they lost behind Cicotte and Williams they surely wouldn't win for Dickie Kerr, the young lefty who was in the Collins-Schalk "camp." So Kerr went out and blanked the Reds 3–0, thus causing a loss of several thousands of dollars on the part of the gamblers.

Cicotte's two fielding errors gave the Reds a pair of runs in the fifth inning of Game 4 and Cincinnati won 2–0. And, in the third game played at Comiskey Park, the Reds' Hod Eller fired a three-hitter and Williams gave up four runs in the sixth and the visitors won again, 5–0. Now, in this best-of-nine series, Cincinnati led 4–1 and needed just one more victory for the world title. But again, not a penny of a $20,000 payment promised to the players for losing Game 5 had reached Gandil or his teammates.

This was getting to be quite annoying. The double-cross was readied. If the Black Sox were going down, without any more money coming their way, they would take the gamblers with them—part of the way, anyhow. Back in Cincinnati, the Sox beat the Reds 5–4 in 10 innings and 4–1 behind Cicotte, and the Series returned to Chicago with Cincinnati's lead in games now down to 4–3 and with both Games 8 and 9 set for Comiskey Park.

But the gamblers couldn't afford to lose anymore. Threats were made, according to some reports, to Lefty Williams (Chicago's Game 8 starter), Joe Jackson, Cicotte, and perhaps others, threats that claimed they and/or their families could well meet with unpleasantness if Williams and the White Sox happened to win Game 8.

They did not; Williams was tagged for four runs in the opening inning and the Reds won 10–5.

The Series was over—but not the story. Newspapermen like Hugh Fullerton and Ring Lardner worked night and day, trying to follow even the slightest lead. Despite official denials, evidence kept mounting. Players started talking. Subpoenas were issued the following September, during the 1920 season's final week, with the Sox and Cleveland fighting for the pennant. With the indictments came Comiskey's suspension of the seven Black Sox (Gandil had quit baseball the previous December). The trial took place during the summer of 1921, and all of the original eight Black Sox were acquitted by the jury.

Baseball's new commissioner, Judge Kenesaw Mountain Landis, however, handed down his own verdict:

"Regardless of the verdict of juries, no player who throws a ballgame, no player that undertakes or promises to throw a ballgame, no player that sits in conference with a bunch of crooked players and gamblers where the ways and means of throwing a game are discussed and does not promptly tell his club about it, will ever play professional baseball."

The great White Sox team was no more. The Sox were to finish in the second division 15 straight years, from 1921 through 1935. They would register winning records only seven times over the next 30 years, 1921 through 1950.

This loss really hurt.

5 Mr. White Sox

Even quite young White Sox fans know that Mr. White Sox is a native of Cuba whose full name is Saturnino Orestes Arrieta Armas Minoso, but is known simply as "Minnie." The first black player in a regular-season game for the Sox, he has been beloved in Chicagoland since May 1, 1951, one day after Frank Lane completed a three-team, seven-player trade that brought Minoso from Cleveland and outfielder Paul Lehner from the Philadelphia A's while sending Sox outfielders Dave Philley and Gus Zernial to the A's.

The deal was announced on April 30, 1951, and the next morning Minoso arrived at Comiskey Park, raring to go. Chicago was facing the defending world champion New York Yankees that Tuesday afternoon, with ace Vic Raschi pitching, and Minnie had seen manager Paul Richards' lineup card: in the No. 3 hole, MINOSO, 3B. He'd also noticed a major difference in this clubhouse compared to that of the Indians: He was the lone black man. In Cleveland, his teammates had included former Negro Leaguers Larry Doby, Harry "Suitcase" Simpson, and Luke Easter. Getting comfortable with these White Sox, and in this city, he thought, might take some time. And how about the fans? How would they react?

It didn't take long for him to get answers. When he was announced as the third batter in the home first, the 14,776 customers on hand gave him a nice round of applause. But when Minnie connected with a Raschi fastball and drove the ball over the center-field bullpen fence, 415 feet away for a two-run first-inning homer, he received far more than a nice round of applause.

And even though his error helped the Yankees win the game 8–3, Minoso knew he was going to like his new address. "The people, the fans, made me feel at home, completely. So after that I figured I had a home here for 100 years."

With Minnie having almost zero knowledge of English, there was some concern with postgame interviews. Richards took care of that potential problem by having Cuban reliever Luis Aloma serve as translator. Things worked out just fine. Minnie even answered one question that day without waiting for Aloma's translation. A writer asked, "Don't you think it's going to be hard to play major league baseball if you can't speak English?" Minoso's classic response: "Ball, bat, glove—she no speak English."

There were others besides Minoso who led the charge of the White Sox, sixth in 1950, to first place by the All-Star Game in July 1951—like second baseman Nellie Fox (hitting .325 at the break), shortstop Chico Carrasquel (.283 with eye-popping fielding), first baseman Eddie Robinson (.306, 16 HR, 70 RBIs), rookie center fielder Jim Busby (.319 and an AL-best 17 steals), and pitchers Billy Pierce and Saul Rogovin. But Minnie (.337 average, AL-leading 12 triples) was the man whose dash and daring rubbed off on his teammates.

The Sox faded to fourth in 1951, but Minoso helped the Sox draw 1 million for the first time in franchise history. He won *The Sporting News* AL Rookie-of-the-Year award by hitting .326 (second in the league to future-Sox Ferris Fain's .344) and posting 34 doubles, 14 triples, 10 homers, and 76 runs batted in—not to mention 31 steals. Over the next six years, with the exception of the sophomore slump season (.281) of 1952, the stats usually were about the same: .313 in 1953 with 104 runs scored and 104 driven in; .288 with 70 RBIs in 1955 after being down at .254 and 28 RBIs at the All-Star break; .316 with 21 homers in 1956; .310 with 103 RBIs in 1957. His greatest year, coming at age 28, was

1954, when he put up these numbers: .320 batting average, .411 on-base percentage, .535 slugging average (.946 OPS), 29 doubles, 18 triples, 19 homers, 116 RBIs, 119 runs scored, and 18 steals. And he struck out only 46 times.

Being traded back to Cleveland after the 1957 season was one of his great disappointments, even though he hit .302 both years there and hit 24 and 21 home runs. "I feel like the whole world was over for me," he said years later. "It was like my city—and you know it's my city because I still live here—had put me out. I never believed it, that I was traded, but it was true."

The deal actually was a key to the 1959 pennant, because the two men who came to Chicago in the trade—Early Wynn and Al Smith—made big contributions. Wynn was 22–10 and won the Cy Young Award, and Smith belted 17 homers, three in July that either won or tied games in the ninth or in extra innings. White Sox boss Bill Veeck, wanting Minnie back in Chicago for the 1960 title defense, gave up top prospects John Romano and Norm Cash to get him, and Minnie celebrated his return with a grand slam and a walk-off homer on Opening Day. He led the AL in hits (184) and batted .311 with 20 homers and 105 RBIs—at age 34. Only in 1961, at 35, did he begin to slip. He went to the Cardinals in 1962 for a top first baseman, Joe Cunningham, moved to Washington in 1963, and finally back to the Sox in 1964, when he got into 30 games before his July release.

But he wasn't through. In September 1976, Veeck activated him off the coaching lines and, at age 50, Minnie lined a single to left off Angels lefty Sid Monge to become the oldest player in major league history to get a base hit. The man was, and is, special.

6 A Night in Cleveland

The White Sox arrived in Cleveland on the afternoon of September 22, 1959, confident that within a few hours they would be flying back to Chicago in possession of the American League pennant, an item that had eluded them since 1919.

"We pretty much thought we had it," pitcher Bob Shaw said, decades later, "but in sports you don't take anything for granted. You know, it's, 'Let's win the damn thing and get it over with.'"

The Sox had beaten the second-place Indians in 14 of the teams' 21 meetings, including eight of 10 in Cleveland's Municipal Stadium. They entered this contest 3½ games ahead of the Tribe, which would close the season with four games at home against Kansas City while the Sox would have three to play—in Detroit. So a Chicago triumph on this Tuesday evening would be the pennant clincher.

Early Wynn, Chicago's 20-game winner and former Cleveland hero, opposed Indians rookie Jim Perry (12–9 with a 2.61 earned-run average). Home runs by Al Smith and Jim Rivera off Mudcat Grant, who had relieved Perry in the sixth, were instrumental in building a 4–1 Sox lead. Rocky Colavito's sacrifice fly scored Tito Francona to make it 4–2 and convince manager Al Lopez it was time for Shaw to relieve his elderly roommate, Wynn. Shaw blazed through the seventh and eighth innings, not so the ninth. One-out singles by Jim Baxes, ex-Sox pitcher Jack Harshman, and Jimmy Piersall—the latter's off the glove of second baseman Nellie Fox—loaded the bases and brought 54,293 to their feet, as well as .300 hitter Vic Power to the plate and Lopez to the mound.

Lopez had a decision to make. He had three pitchers working in the bullpen: hard-throwing Turk Lown, sinkerballer Gerry Staley, and Billy Pierce, who would face the lefty-swinging Francona if needed. "The decision is," Staley said, "do you want a strikeout [Lown], or did you want to take a chance and make them hit the ball [Staley]? A situation like that, a groundball gives you a chance to get a double play and get out of the inning."

That's what Lopez thought, too. In came Staley, who required just one pitch, a sinker, to end it. Power swung and grounded the ball to the left of Gold Glove shortstop Luis Aparicio, who stepped on second base for one out and relayed to first baseman Ted Kluszewski for the second. "The ballgame's over!" WGN-TV's Jack Brickhouse yelled. "The White Sox are the champions of 1959! The 40-year wait has now ended!"

Sox players poured onto the field to begin the Cleveland portion of the celebration. Meanwhile, in Chicago, Fire Commissioner Robert Quinn—longtime pal of Mayor Richard J. Daley and, like the mayor, a rabid Sox fan—ordered the city's air-raid sirens turned on to mark the momentous occasion. Unfortunately, Chicagoans who cared little if anything about baseball—or weren't aware that Chairman Nikita Khrushchev was in Des Moines that night as part of his U.S. tour—were certain that Russian bombers were headed our way and scrambled into bomb shelters. (In the days following, Quinn was scolded by several civic groups, but Daley stood by his friend. "It was no one's fault," the mayor said. "It was all done in the hilarity of the moment.")

The hilarity of the moment also had been evident at Midway Airport, where an estimated 20,000 had gathered to wait for the Sox's plane from Cleveland, scheduled to arrive at 2:00 AM. Thousands more jammed the streets in the Loop, 3,000 alone making merry at State and Madison. It became obvious that Chicago knew how to celebrate pennants. The city just hadn't had much practice.

Back at Midway, the Sox plane rolled to a stop at 2:08 AM. Owner Bill Veeck, wife Mary Frances, plus the mayor and his wife,

Sis, were the first up the ramp to greet the victorious South Siders. The players were stunned by the turnout.

"I remember the crowd at the airport," Bob Shaw said. "I mean, we were exhilarated, we were happy. But when you got off that plane and saw all those people waiting for you, that really gave you goosebumps."

There would be more goosebumps, but not for 24 years.

7 Winning Ugly? Hardly

For reasons known only to Doug Rader, the Texas Rangers manager, after being briefed by his advance scouts on the eve of an August 1983 series with the White Sox, gave reporters this quick summation of the American League West leaders:

"Sounds to me like they're winning ugly."

Rader, who grew up in Chicago's north suburbs and was a sophomore at Glenbrook North High School in Northbrook, Illinois, when the White Sox last were in postseason play (1959), would have been somewhat correct had he said the 1959 Go-Go Sox had won ugly. Certainly the defense up the middle (Sherm Lollar at catcher, Luis Aparicio and Nellie Fox at shortstop and second base, and the brilliant Jim Landis in center) was impressive, and the pitching was far from ugly, but when the Sox came up to bat—well, let's just say that was a good time to visit the facilities.

But this 1983 bunch? Winning ugly? Carlton Fisk begged to differ.

"The assemblage of talent here in Chicago," he said 20 years later, "matches any team that I ever played on."

From the start, this team was designed to contend with an emphasis on power and starting pitching. GM Roland Hemond had decided to let left fielder Steve Kemp escape via free agency, thereby opening that spot for rookie Ron Kittle, who hailed from nearby Gary, Indiana, and had smashed 50 home runs the year before in the Pacific Coast League. Kittle ended up winning the AL Rookie of the Year award by belting 35 homers and driving in 100 runs. The center fielder was speedy leadoff man Rudy Law, who after hitting .318 in 1982 with 36 steals batted .283 with a club-record 77 stolen bases in 1983. Rounding out the outfield was 24-year-old Harold Baines, who went from 25 homers, 105 RBIs, .271 in 1982 to 20, 99, .280 in 1983, while topping the AL in game-winning RBIs.

The infield's left side (Vance Law at third, Jerry Dybzinski and Scotty Fletcher at short) was nothing to write home about, but flashy second baseman Julio Cruz (acquired in June from Seattle for Tony Bernazard) tightened the defense and finished with 57 steals (24 after joining the White Sox). First base was manned by Tom Paciorek (.307) most of the time and rookie Greg Walker (.270) some of the time, and the DH was Greg Luzinski, who slugged 32 homers and drove in 95 runs.

The big surprise was Fisk, who after being very ordinary his first two years in a White Sox uniform, turned it around once manager Tony La Russa put him in the No. 2 spot in the order. Pudge finished at .289 with 26 homers and 86 RBIs.

Nor was the pitching ugly, at least in the second half, when the Sox got rolling after a 16–24 start and finished 99–63. Floyd Bannister, 1982 AL strikeout king and the top pitcher on the free-agent market, went 13–1 after starting out 3–9. Richard Dotson, who'd opened 8–5, won 14 of his next 16 decisions to finish 22–7. And Cy Young Award–winner LaMarr Hoyt won 15 of his last 17 and ended 24–10.

Winning ugly? If anything, the Sox, in the first two months, were losing ugly, a key reason why Kittle was the lone Sox

Harold Baines, Julio Cruz, and Rudy Law celebrate with champagne after defeating the Seattle Mariners to clinch the American League West. (Getty Images)

representative at the All-Star Game—and the game was played in Kittle's home park! After the break, the snub was soon forgotten when the Sox played 41 straight games against the stronger AL East and won 25 of them. They beat the Blue Jays three of four in Toronto when the Jays were leading the East. Then the Yankees, who had won 11 of their last 12, came to Chicago for a four-game series. Sox lefty Jerry Koosman beat Ron Guidry 7–2 on Friday night before 40,455 as Fisk and Luzinski homered; Dotson won 5–1 Saturday night before 46,219; and, after an 11-inning 12–6 setback Sunday before 40,778, Chicago won Monday night 4–1 (attendance: 44,812) behind Bannister's pitching and Luzinksi's slugging: two homers, one bouncing on the roof in left. The White

Sox, beginning to bludgeon opponents now, were on top of the AL West by four games.

Winning ugly?

Shortly after the Yankees left Chicago, the Sox went to New York for three games August 15–17. Britt Burns fired a three-hitter to outduel Dave Righetti 1–0 in the opener; Bannister and the bullpen held off the hosts 5–3 in the second contest, and the Sox completed the sweep with a 7–5 triumph as Mike Squires delivered a tie-breaking double in the 13th. Next stop was Texas, where the Sox swept a twi-nighter from Rader's Rangers on August 19 to stretch their lead to eight games.

September was more of the same, with the White Sox winning 18 of 20 in one stretch and finishing a then-record 20 games ahead of second-place Kansas City. Then came the ALCS with Baltimore, when people like Mike Boddicker, Mike Flanagan, Storm Davis, and Tito Landrum—*especially* Tito Landrum—ruined Sox hopes. And still we wonder, even now, what might have been had the Sox and not the Orioles won Game 4 (The Tito Landrum Game). LaMarr Hoyt vs. Scott McGregor at Comiskey Park for a trip to the World Series? Rest assured, the Orioles were glad there was no Game 5.

Movin' In—In Style

It hasn't been often that one has been able to say this about a Chicago pro sports franchise, but the White Sox did this one exactly right—"this one" being the move into their new ballpark in 1991. The timing could not have been any better.

The White Sox were picked to finish last or next to last in the AL West in 1990, the last year of old Comiskey Park. But manager Jeff Torborg, his staff, and his players had different ideas. The regular outfield (Ivan Calderon, Lance Johnson, and Sammy Sosa) covered ground and combined to steal 100 bases; the infield had a rookie (Robin Ventura) at third and, for the final two months, another rookie (Frank Thomas) at first. Up the middle, Ozzie Guillen, at 26 one of the captains, was at short with veteran Scottie Fletcher (32) at second, and 42-year-old but still formidable Carlton Fisk (the other captain) behind the plate, backed by cannon-armed Ron Karkovice.

There was defense and speed, young starting pitchers Jack McDowell, Greg Hibbard, Melido Perez, Alex Fernandez, and Eric King—all brought in by GM Larry Himes—and two relievers who were superb all year: setup man Barry Jones and closer Bobby Thigpen (then-record 57 saves).

By mid-June, when the world champion Oakland A's arrived for a four-game series, the White Sox were *the* story, and after they won the opener behind King, they were one game back. The A's won the next three, and doubters jumped off the bandwagon, only to get back on again after the Sox went to Oakland the next weekend and swept a three-game series. The Sox ran off 10 wins in 11 games, including the bizarre 4–0 triumph on July 1 over the Yankees and Andy Hawkins, who threw an eight-inning no-hitter but whose team saddled him with four unearned runs.

From July 20 through August 19 though, the team went 15–16, enabling Oakland to take a sizeable lead. (The Sox did defeat Texas' Nolan Ryan on August 10, when diminutive infielders Guillen and Craig Grebeck went deep on consecutive pitches from Ryan for their first homers of the year.) By the time the A's returned to Chicago on August 20, they led the Sox by 6½ games. That didn't stop the Sox from pounding lumps on Dave Stewart and winning the series opener 11–1 (three-hitter by McDowell and a Sosa homer that almost reached the roof) and taking the second game 4–1 (behind Hibbard). The lead was 4½, but the Sox could get no closer.

Still, a 90-plus-win team was going to open the new ballpark the next April. Himes' reward for putting the team together was a pink slip; his replacement was former Sox pitcher and pitching coach Ron Schueler. One of his first moves was to send Calderon and Barry Jones to Montreal for standout leadoff man, base-stealer supreme, and former NL batting champ Tim Raines. Other additions for 1991 were outfielder Cory Snyder and knuckleballer Charlie Hough. In spring training, Schueler caused a stir by signing Bo Jackson, who'd been released by Kansas City after a severe hip injury suffered that January while with the Oakland Raiders. Bo couldn't really contribute till 1993, after hip-replacement surgery, but he did provide some memorable moments.

This was the year Thomas and Ventura truly arrived and helped keep the 1991 Sox in contention. Thomas batted .318 (with a league-leading 138 walks and .453 on-base percentage) and led the Sox with 32 homers and 109 RBIs. Ventura hit .284 with 23 homers and 100 RBIs and absolutely owned July, when he hit .357 and blasted 12 of his homers and drove in 33 runs. He capped the month with a two-out walk-off grand slam to beat Texas 10–8. Said Detroit manager Sparky Anderson, "They're the best pair of hitters to come up with the same club since Jim Rice and Freddie Lynn."

The Sox spent most of the first three months of the 1991 season getting used to their new home. As of June 26, they were 35–34. But when rookie lefty Wilson Alvarez (another Himes find) completed his no-hitter August 11 at Baltimore in his first Sox appearance, Chicago had won 30 of its last 41 and was 65–45, one game behind the Twins. Then they dropped 14 of the next 17 (one a no-hitter by Kansas City's Bret Saberhagen) and faded to a second-place, 87–75 finish.

Schueler encouraged Torborg to look into the vacant Mets job, which he ended up getting, and the GM then brought in "Sleepy Gene" Lamont, who would have done better than 86–76 and third place had Schueler not traded for Steve Sax, an alleged second baseman, and erstwhile slugger George Bell, who came from the Cubs for Sammy Sosa, then 23 and still feeling his way. Lamont also had the misfortune of losing Guillen to season-ending knee surgery after only 13 games.

Everything came together, though, in 1993. Only lowlight was the sloppy release of Carlton Fisk, sent home a week after setting the record for most games caught. The outfield of Raines, Johnson, and free-agent signee Ellis Burks was in full flower. Guillen was back at short, with Ventura and Thomas at the corners, and Karkovice behind the plate. McDowell was 22–10, Fernandez 18–9, Alvarez 15–8, Jason Bere 12–5, and Roberto Hernandez saved 38 games and posted a 2.29 ERA. Thomas' first MVP year included 41 homers, 128 RBIs, a .317 batting average, and a .426 OBP—and only 54 strikeouts. Ventura totaled 22 homers and 94 RBIs, Raines batted .306 with 16 homers, Lance Johnson hit .311 with 35 steals, Burks added 17 homers and 74 RBIs, and Karkovice homered 20 times. And Bo Jaclson delivered the division-winning homer.

The key to the ALCS against world champion Toronto was McDowell's failure to pitch well in either of his two starts. The Sox lost all three at home and won two of three at Toronto.

The threat of a work stoppage hung over the 1994 season from the beginning, which put a damper on what could have been a glorious season. Thomas won his second MVP trophy for hitting .353 with 38 homers and 101 RBIs and a .729 slugging percentage in 113 games. One reason for the fantastic numbers was the new cleanup man, free agent Julio Franco, who batted .319 with 20 home runs and 98 RBIs himself. Not too long after play ended, the Sox were declared AL Central champs because their record was one victory better than Cleveland's.

It was an empty feeling, though. A chance for the original 1990 core group to win it all was ending all too soon. By Christmas, even Jack McDowell would be gone—to the Yankees. The team was no longer the team.

9 Wood Knuckles Down

Wilbur Wood had won acclaim earlier in his career with the White Sox as an extremely effective relief pitcher who, like his 1967–68 Chicago teammate, Hoyt Wilhelm, depended almost exclusively on his knuckleball. He did not become an almost-exclusive knuckle-baller, however, until Woodie first fell under Wilhelm's influence during spring training in 1967.

"Hoyt told me, 'If you're going to throw the knuckleball, you have to throw it 80 to 90 percent of the time. This is your 'out' pitch—this is what you're gonna get the hitters out with.' So I decided right then and there, the second day of spring training, 'I'm gonna do it, and let's see what happens.' It turned out pretty well for everyone."

After four years pitching out of the bullpen, Wood was approached during the final days of spring training in 1971 by new White Sox manager Chuck Tanner and new pitching coach Johnny Sain. They had an idea they wanted to run by him. Joe Horlen, one of the starting pitchers, had injured his knee in an exhibition game and likely would miss a few turns. How would Woodie like to be a starter?

"I was apprehensive about it," he admitted, "because if I didn't do the job as a starter, the job in the bullpen might not be waiting for me." A 19-year-old lefty smokeballer named Terry Forster was

Tanner's and Sain's choice as top bullpen lefty. "As it turned out," Wood remembered, "if I hadn't said yes, I wasn't gonna pitch that much. So I started a few ballgames and did well. After a few games, I really enjoyed it. I didn't want to go back to the pen."

His sentiment was perfectly understandable; that year, often pitching on two days' rest, he was 22–13 with a 1.91 ERA and seven shutouts. The next he went 24–17, 2.51, with eight shutouts. By the following May 24, after beating Nolan Ryan and the Angels that night, he was 11–3 and the 1973 White Sox were 24–13 and leading the AL West by 3½ games over the A's, Angels, and Twins. On May 28, the Sox and Cleveland had a scheduled Monday night game but first had to finish Saturday night's contest that had been suspended after 16 innings. Wood was supposed to pitch the regularly scheduled game, but Tanner asked him to finish up the suspended game and then worry about the regular one later.

One problem: The first one lasted into the 21st inning!

In the top half, an error by shortstop Eddie Leon led to ex-Sox favorite Walt Williams' RBI single, and Cleveland led 3–2. But Wood's teammate, Dick Allen, said not to worry.

"Dick was gonna bat [sixth] that inning," Wood said, "and he came over to me on the bench and said, 'If we get a couple guys on base this inning, I'll win this thing for you right now.'"

First, Leon made up for his error with a game-tying single that scored Tony Muser with one out. Next, Pat Kelly singled and then a young Cleveland reliever named Ed Farmer entered to face John Jeter, who forced Kelly at second. Sure enough, there were two on for Allen, who cracked a rising line drive that smashed against the seats in the lower deck in right-center for a three-run homer and 6–3 triumph. "I'll never forget that one," said Wood, who was now 12–3 and eager to get started on his next assignment. "That was funny," he said, "because when they went out with the lineups at the start of the suspended game, Cleveland wanted 20 minutes between games and Chuck wanted 10. They finally compromised, and it wound up [at] 15 minutes between games. So it was just like sitting through a long inning."

The only long inning in the second game was the home first, when Bill Melton doubled home Allen and Rick Reichardt drove in Melton with a single for a quick 2–0 lead over Dick Tidrow. That was all Wood needed as he blanked the Tribe 4–0 on four hits in just one hour and 57 minutes.

Now all the speculation was about when Wilbur would notch his 30th victory. After all, he was 13–3 through 40 games, which meant he was on pace to win 52. Within a month, though, Allen and standout center fielder Kenny Henderson were both out with season-ending injuries, Wood was on his way to a final record of 24–20, and the White Sox would end up 77–85.

10 Nellie Fox

For 14 usually eventful baseball seasons, Jacob Nelson Fox played second base for the White Sox. Played it pretty well, too. By the time he left the Sox—in a strange deal in December 1963 that brought in return two minor-leaguers—he had the following items on his resume:

- American League MVP, 1959
- Batted .375 in 1959 World Series
- Hit .300 or better six times
- Named to 12 All-Star teams
- Led AL in hits four times
- Stung by the stigma of striking out a whopping 18 times in 1953, he fanned 115 times over the next nine years (annual average 12.8)

- Played in 1,083 of a possible 1,086 games, 1953 through 1959
- Led AL second basemen in fielding percentage and assists six times
- Led AL second baseman in putouts 10 times
- Led AL second basemen in double plays five times
- Twenty-two years too late for him to enjoy it (Nellie had died of cancer in 1975), he finally was able to add one other notable item to the resume: inducted into Baseball Hall of Fame, 1997

Few people knew him better than his roommate of 11 years, Billy Pierce. "Nellie was always giving 1,000 percent. He was a ballplayer who you'd say, with his size and speed, had just average talent. But what he got out of it was All-Star talent. He never had the greatest arm in the world. He never had the greatest speed in the world. But he was still an All-Star."

After Little Nell hit just .247 for Chicago in 1950, new manager Paul Richards and his aides went to work on Fox in spring training of 1951. Coach Doc Cramer had him switch to a thick-handled "bottle bat," camp instructor Joe Gordon—the former Yankee All-Star second baseman—worked with him on turning the double play, and Richards spent hours teaching him the proper method of bunting. When the regular season rolled around, Fox was a different player. The little guy with the trademark chaw of tobacco in his left cheek batted .313 and collected 32 doubles, 12 triples, a flock of bunt singles, and an on-base percentage of .372. "The Mighty Mite" from south-central Pennsylvania was on his way.

He hit four home runs that season and reached a career-best of six in 1955, which he matched two seasons later. Teammates would rib him on occasion for his lack of power, but Fox knew hitting home runs was not his job. His job was starting innings or keeping them going with well-placed base hits.

"No one," he said, "had to tell me I was never going to be a home run hitter. I was hitting the same ball as the rest of the players, but when the big guys cracked one, it went out of the park. When I cracked one, it might get out of the infield."

There were those occasional moments, however, when Nellie would stun the big boys. He once hit two homers in one game, the nightcap of a weekday doubleheader in Cleveland in May 1955. First he victimized Mike Garcia with a leadoff home run in the seventh, then hit a two-out, three-run shot off lefty Don Mossi that tied the game in the eighth. Chicago lost that game, but the Sox won the 1959 opener in Detroit when Fox again homered off Mossi, then a Tiger, in the 14th inning for a 9–7 triumph. Generally, though, Fox home runs occurred even less often than Fox strikeouts.

"Nellie was the toughest guy in the league to face," one-time Yankee relief hero Ryne Duren once said. "Foul ball, foul ball, foul ball, foul ball, base hit, or walk."

Added one of Duren's New York teammates, Hall-of-Famer Whitey Ford, "He was always the toughest out for me. In 12 years, I struck him out only once, and I still think the umpire blew the call."

Another umpire's call angered Fox several years later, when he was with Houston and his old buddy, Pierce, was pitching for San Francisco, the only year they faced each other. "He bunted once and got thrown out on a pretty good bunt—it was a real close play—and oh, he griped." Pierce said, laughing. "Because he didn't like to bunt anyway unless he got a hit. Then he hit a line drive off me and a guy caught it. He wanted to get a hit off me so bad. So I always kidded him: 'You're 0-for-2 against me.'"

It stayed that way, because Billy retired after the 1964 season. Nellie played one more year, then went into instruction, eventually joining Ted Williams' staff, first in Washington and then in Texas. The two got to know each other very well. Then came Fox's losing battle with cancer. "The Splendid Splinter" was going to miss "the Mighty Mite."

"I just loved him," Williams said. "As a person, as an individual, you couldn't possibly not love him."

11 The Wizardry of Oz

The Yankees' Mel Hall swung mightily. The ball was popped up into "No Man's Land" in shallow left field, between left fielder Tim Raines and shortstop Ozzie Guillen.

Both went for the ball. Everyone feared what was coming next. They collided. Ozzie didn't get up. Raines called for trainer Herm Schneider and manager Gene Lamont. A few minutes later, Guillen was being helped off the field.

And a few minutes after that, doctors announced that the next day Ozzie would undergo complete reconstruction of the torn anterior cruciate and medial collateral ligaments in his right knee. He was out for the season.

This had been the Sox's 13th game of 1992. The division title would have to wait until next year. They certainly weren't going to win one without Ozzie, the live wire who kept everyone loose and had been one of the Sox captains since 1990 (the other was Carlton Fisk, 16 years older than Guillen).

"Hopefully, everyone can pull together," said Raines, before he pointed out the reality of the situation. "We're talking about a Gold Glove shortstop [1990] and a leader."

Many Sox fans were surprised to hear the word "leader" used in reference to the fun-loving Venezuelan, who had been a South Side favorite ever since his Rookie-of-the-Year season of 1985. But teammates and other baseball people know who the leaders are. They're the guys who, with their team down a run or tied in the eighth inning, figure out a way to get on and into scoring position. Ozzie, in any number of games during his days in Chicago, would lead off the eighth inning in a tie game with a single toward right-center but, knowing how important his run was, would continue on to second, just beating the throw with a head-first slide. Smart baseball, hustling baseball, winning baseball. That's what Ozzie Guillen was about.

"It's going to be different to look back and not see Oz," reliever Bobby Thigpen said the night of the injury. "The fact he's out there and what he does is going to be missed. Not everyone sees what he does, but we do."

Another reliever, Donn Pall, came right out and said Guillen was the one guy the team couldn't afford to lose. "That seems kind of strange when you think of all the good players we have on this team," Pall said, "but he's the guy we all look to."

Ozzie came back in 1993 at age 29, batted .280 and, though having lost some of his previous range, was again a welcome presence in the middle of the infield in the Sox's drive to the AL West title. He played well in the ALCS, too, playing errorless ball over the six games against Toronto and batting .273. The strike cost Guillen and the Sox another playoff trip in 1994, when Ozzie hit a career-best .288. He played three more years for the Sox, and when Ozzie walked off the field during the last game of the 1997 season, stopping to share a hug with third baseman Robin Ventura and then to wave to the crowd, most of the fans there likely figured they were saying goodbye for the last time. No. 13 had just finished season No. 13 in Chicago.

Guillen had different plans, however. He played three more years in the NL as a backup, then spent 2001 as third-base coach at Montreal and the next two years in the same role with the Florida Marlins. He interviewed for the Sox job, vacant in the wake of Jerry

Manuel's firing, and landed it, thus becoming the first Venezuelan to manage in the major leagues.

His first Sox team was 83–79 (he lost both Frank Thomas and Magglio Ordonez to injuries after mid-July), but that second team was something special. Understand that the 2005 White Sox had led from wire to wire, they had topped their league in victories and they had swept the World Series in four straight. Only one other team has ever done that: the 1927 Yankees.

Much of the credit had to go to Guillen. The Sox won with speed (Scott Podsednik stole 59 bases), power (200 homers, 40 by Paul Konerko), solid defense, and excellent pitching from starters and relievers alike. Ozzie got everyone involved, so that bench players like Pablo Ozuna, Willie Harris, and Geoff Blum were all able to contribute in the postseason.

As is too often the case, the party did not last, although the 2006 club won 90 games and the 2008 Sox reached the playoffs in dramatic style. The relationship between Ozzie and GM Kenny Williams worsened with each passing year until Guillen departed during the final week of the 2011 season to take over as manager of the Miami Marlins. It was in that position where Ozzie's penchant for saying some stunning stuff got him in the most trouble.

Here are some tamer—but still funny—quotes from the Chicago years:

"My mother [was] a high school principal. My brother is an engineer. One of my little sisters is a doctor. Another is a teacher. When you come from that kind of a family and you only get to eighth grade, it's kind of weird and awkward. But I make more money."

On Orioles manager Buck Showalter: "He never even smelled a jock in the big leagues. Mr. Baseball never even got a hit in Triple A. I was a better player than him, I have more money than him, and I'm better-looking than him."

And finally, his classic line about A.J. Pierzynski: "A.J. is the kind of guy, when he's on the other team, you hate him. When he's on your team, you hate him a little less."

12 Frank Thomas

On the evening of July 23, 2002, a man and his son were at U.S. Cellular Field, walking on the 100-level concourse in search of something to eat, when Frank Thomas stepped to the plate against Minnesota's Johan Santana with a runner on base and nobody out in the fourth inning. Frank, who'd missed all but 20 games the previous year with a triceps injury, was still adjusting to the 2001 strike-zone changes, which among other things called for umpires to now call the "high strike." As a consequence, he was struggling, hitting a very un-Big-Hurt-like .248.

The two had made their way to the left-field corner when the count reached 2-1 on Thomas. They stopped and watched Frank foul off a fastball. "Boy, Brad," the father said, not without a trace of melancholy, "if this had been two-three years ago, Frank would've hit that ball onto the concourse."

Seconds later, Santana let go with the 2-2 pitch, and Thomas did indeed hit the ball onto the concourse—in left-center, a shot measured at 495 feet. It was the longest at U.S. Cellular Field until a far less successful White Sox first-round draft pick, Joe Borchard, blasted a 504-footer in 2004.

"We've seen Frank Thomas do that before," Twins manager Ron Gardenhire said after Chicago's 8–7 victory. "He has always been capable of doing things like that. The ball was down in the zone. He went down and got it, and from where I was sitting, it looked like a golf ball, not a baseball."

"The Big Hurt"—the nickname was given him by Sox broadcaster Ken "Hawk" Harrelson—spent his first few seasons in Chicago making lots of baseballs look like golf balls. Thomas is the only player in history to have seven consecutive seasons with a .300 average and at least 100 walks, 100 runs scored, 100 runs batted in, and 20 home runs (1991 to 1997). The only other player to have more than five straight years accomplishing this feat was Ted Williams (six). The achievement is all the more remarkable considering The Greatest Hitter The White Sox Have Ever Had played only 113 games in 1994, due to the baseball strike.

His strike-zone knowledge was better than the umpires' and he was always hitting with 2-0 and 3-1 counts. He was a scary hitter, the kind who made the ballpark seem small and gave the impression that the pitcher was hopelessly overmatched. He was the third of Larry Himes' four terrific first-round picks: Jack McDowell and Robin Ventura preceded him and Alex Fernandez was selected a year later. Thomas provided, with Ventura, Julio Franco, Tim Raines, and Lance Johnson, much of the offense that enabled the Sox to win a division title in 1993 and helped Thomas win MVP awards in 1993 and 1994. Frank became the first White Sox since Luke Appling in 1943 to win a batting title when he followed up his .349 average of 1996 with a mark of .347 in 1997, when the man batting behind him was Albert Belle. In 1998, Belle stole the show numbers-wise and Thomas slipped to .265 with 29 homers and 109 RBIs.

He slipped even further in 1999, thanks to tendinitis, a bone spur on his right ankle, and a large corn on the same foot's little toe. He played through the hurt, but Thomas' power stroke was affected—he hit only 15 home runs in 1999. He was able to hit .305 but the slugging percentage—an incredible .729 in 1994—was

The Big Hurt drives another one into the seats.

down to .471. Thomas' decision to undergo surgery in September 1999 rather than wait till season's end angered his manager, Jerry Manuel, and some teammates, but the operation was necessary. The bone spur "was the biggest I have ever taken out," said Dr. Lowell Scott Weil, who also performed reconstructive surgery on Thomas' toe. "It was truly the size of a golf ball."

A healthy Frank Thomas, surrounded by talented young hitters like Magglio Ordonez, Paul Konerko, and Carlos Lee, led the 2000 White Sox to the AL Central title with "pre-1998 Frank" stats: .328 batting, .436 on-base, .625 slugging, plus a career-high 43 homers. After the wrecked 2001 season and a so-so 2002, he bounced back again in 2003 with 42 homers, 105 RBIs, and .267. A fractured ankle limited him the next two seasons and kept him off the Sox's World Series roster. So The Greatest Hitter The White Sox Have Ever Had finally made it to the World Series but couldn't play. Does this happen to other teams?

The Hurt spent 2006 with Oakland—he celebrated his return to Chicago in May by homering twice—and helped the A's win a division title with his 39 homers and 114 RBIs. With Toronto the next year, he hit his 500th career homer and a few more to finish tied with Ted Williams and Willie McCovey at 521. The Sox have since retired his No. 35 jersey and erected a statue in his likeness on the outfield concourse. Cooperstown will be welcoming him in July 2014. "I think my resume speaks for itself," he said in 2013. "The run I had was incredible, very historical. So, I think I've done enough to be a first-ballot Hall of Famer."

It turned out that more than 83 percent of the Hall electorate agreed with him. The announcement came on January 8, 2014; The Greatest Hitter the White Sox Have Ever Had can begin working on his Cooperstown speech.

13 Dick Allen

It's quite possible that Dick Allen was the greatest player to wear the White Sox uniform. He just didn't stick around long enough to prove it. During his stay in Chicago (1972–74), most Sox fans struggled with how they really felt about him. They loved him in 1972, when he won the American League MVP award and the White Sox almost stole the AL West title. They weren't sure just how badly injured he was in 1973, when he missed the second half with what was reported to be a broken leg. They weren't sure what to think about him in 1974 when, in September, he announced his retirement from baseball—particularly when he was back playing the next season with the Phillies, his original team. These days, people say, "Dick Allen could have owned Chicago." No one stops to consider that maybe he had absolutely no interest in owning Chicago.

Four decades have passed since Allen's days with the White Sox, enough time to hear the evidence. We've had time to read and hear what his White Sox teammates thought of him, and their responses, delivered in almost reverential tones, seem to leave no doubt that Allen was their team leader, the guy who taught the younger guys what it means to be a big-leaguer. His recent interviews, like the one he gave Bob Costas in 2012 on MLB Network, provided viewers a picture of Dick Allen very few had seen. And the picture is positive.

Of course, his exploits in Chicago were certain to get the rose-colored-glasses treatment from Chuck Tanner, who told author Tim Whitaker in the summer of 1987, "In all my years of baseball, I have never seen a season to compare to the one Dick Allen had in 1972. I mean, not even close. It wasn't that he did it all, which he did, it was the *way* he did it. He was on a rampage, a man on a mission. He could do anything he wanted. Dick Allen picked the White Sox up on his back and carried them all season. It was a powerful thing to watch."

Perhaps the most memorable of Allen's 1972 home runs came on Sunday, June 4, in Game 2 of a Chicago twin bill against the Yankees. The Sox had won the opener 6–1 behind Tom Bradley's pitching but trailed 4–2 in Game 2 with one out in the ninth. Then Bill Melton walked and Mike Andrews singled, and suddenly the crowd—almost half of the original Bat Day throng of 51,904 had long since departed after learning Allen was going to sit out the nightcap—halted its inexorable stroll toward the exits. Now, Yankee manager Ralph Houk called for his ace reliever, Sparky Lyle, the lefty with the killer slider who, through 15 games thus far in 1972, had allowed only 16 hits and three earned runs in 28⅓ innings (0.95 ERA).

But just then, from the White Sox dugout emerged Dick Allen. Tanner had decided he had rested long enough. As Dick approached the plate, the decibel level went up about 500 percent. In only two months, Sox fans had come to understand that the team for which they rooted had, at last, a slugger capable of breaking up ballgames in the late innings—even, they dared believe, the ninth. And indeed, Allen launched Lyle's third pitch deep into the lower deck in left-center for a 5–4 Chicago victory. Then-GM Roland Hemond will never forget it: "I still remember seeing Lyle walk off the mound the moment that ball was hit," Hemond told Whitaker, "and then seeing Dick put his fist up in the air as he was rounding first."

Then there was the blast off New York's Lindy McDaniel on a Wednesday afternoon in late August that seemed to zero in on broadcaster Harry Caray, who, as was his Wednesday custom those years, was calling the game from old Comiskey's center-field bleachers. The ball kept going and going and Harry, scrambling to get out of the way, knocked over his beer while beating a hasty retreat. Allen, with this 500-foot, two-run shot in the eighth, had increased Chicago's lead to 5–2—and that would be the final score. The Sox were a half-game ahead of AL West-leading Oakland.

Note the pitchers Allen had victimized: Lindy McDaniel and Sparky Lyle. Dick Allen didn't fatten up against second-line pitching. He hit *good* pitching and he did so in "game" situations. Unfortunately, he didn't do it long enough. After his MVP season of 1972 (37 homers, 113 RBIs, .308 batting average, 99 walks, 19 steals in 27 attempts), he broke his leg in a baseline collision with the Angels' Mike Epstein on June 28, 1973. Except for a three-game trial period (July 31–August 2) to see if he could go on the leg, he was lost for the season, having finished with 16 home runs, 41 RBIs, and a .316 average in 72 games at a time when the Sox trailed first-place Oakland by one game. Healthy again in 1974, Allen led the AL in homers with 32 and was hitting .301 when, with two weeks to go and the Sox one game below .500 and 10 out of first place, he suddenly announced his retirement—at age 32. It was an odd ending to the Sox-Allen saga, especially because he was back in action with his original club, the Phillies, by the following April.

It later came to light that Allen had become disenchanted with the lack of progress the Sox had shown and with the realization that time was running out on his career and his chances of getting to a World Series. The presence in the clubhouse of Ron Santo, acquired from the Cubs in December 1973, had not helped, either.

"Santo thought himself a Chicago institution because he had played all those years across town with the Cubs," Allen told Whitaker. "He thought he should be the team leader automatically. But you don't get to be a leader through longevity. I had become the White Sox team leader, not by choice, believe me. It just came my way by playing hard, leading by example. [Since 1972,] I'd been working a lot with a second baseman named Jorge Orta.

When Jorge came to us that year he was just a scared 21-year-old from Mexico. He was a sensitive kid—reminded me of myself. I worked on that boy's confidence, quietly, picking the right spots to build him up and the right time to let him know when he screwed up. Now here comes Santo, acting the grizzled veteran, barking at everyone and rattling everybody's cage.

"One day Jorge boots a grounder at second, and I overhear Santo yelling at him from third. I get hot. Between innings, I call Santo over. 'Hey, my man,' I say to him, 'how long you been in the big leagues?' 'Fourteen years,' he tells me. 'You ever screw up over those 14 years?' 'Yeah,' he says. I point to Orta. 'Well, that boy right there—this is his third season in the big leagues. He's still learning. But he's gonna be a good one. You got a lot to teach. Instead of yelling at Georgie, why don't you teach him a few things?' Santo doesn't say anything. He just sneers at me.

"After that, I had no time for Santo.... Santo was in his last big-league season. He was feeling washed up, and it showed. The tension between Santo and me began to spread to the other guys in the clubhouse. We stopped being a team. I was still hitting the ball, and hitting it good. But we weren't winning—and we weren't having fun."

With Allen gone, watching the Sox was not nearly as much fun. He had played less than 2½ seasons in Chicago, yet he had averaged .307 with 28 homers and 81 RBIs for that period. By extrapolating his 1972 figures, his full-season numbers for 1973 would have been 32/82/.316; for 1974, 35/96/.301. Remember that he played in old Comiskey Park, with its 352-foot foul lines and distant power alleys. It's safe to say that only Frank Thomas, of all the men who have worn the White Sox uniform, can be considered as having had as intimidating a presence at the plate as Dick Allen.

14 Luke Appling

We all know that the greatest fielding shortstop in White Sox history was Alan Bannister—only kidding. It was Luis Aparicio.

And the greatest hitting shortstop in White Sox history? No, it wasn't Willie Miranda. Greg Pryor? No. Swede Risberg? Jim Brideweser? Kevin Bell? Bee Bee Richard? Wrong.

It was Luke Appling, of course, the amazing batsman and funnyman from Atlanta who played his entire career (1930–1950) with the White Sox and captured two American League batting titles—he won with .388 in 1936 and with .328 in the war year of 1943. He hit the ball to all fields—and to all sections of the stands that were in foul territory. He said he did it to get his pitch. You can't repeat what opposing pitchers said.

Baseball Digest reported that in a 1940 game against New York, Appling fouled off 24 pitches in one trip to the plate, which served to befuddle right-hander Red Ruffing. The Sox were far behind, and Appling decided to have some fun.

"So I started fouling off his pitches," Appling said. "I took a pitch every now and then. Pretty soon, after 24 fouls, old Red could hardly lift his arm, and I drew a walk. That's when they took him out of the game and he cussed me all the way to the dugout."

Another time, facing Detroit right-hander Dizzy Trout, Appling fouled off 14 straight pitches. Angry now, Trout threw his glove instead of the ball. Said Luke, "I fouled that one off, too."

Luke was so well known for his hitting that many just assumed he was an average to below-average defensive shortstop. Not true. "The fans," he once said, "may be surprised to know that, during my freshman year in college, I waited on tables and never made an error, never dropped a tray, never broke a dish."

That school he attended was Oglethorpe College (now University) in Atlanta. The Atlanta Crackers of the Southern Association kept close tabs on this hometown star and had a scout at the dedication game for the school's new baseball stadium in nearby LaGrange, Georgia. All Appling did was hit four home runs to power Oglethorpe to a 7–5 triumph over Mercy University. He signed days later. "My advice," Luke said, "to any young man who hits four straight homers to win a close game for his college at a stadium dedication to keep his team undefeated is this: Sign with somebody before you have a chance to get into a slump."

The White Sox purchased him on August 19, 1930 from Atlanta, where in 104 games he had batted .326 with 19 doubles and 17 triples. After a couple seasons just feeling his way, he batted .322 in 1933 and .303 and .307 the next two seasons before piling up 204 hits and driving in 128 runs en route to that .388 average and the 1936 batting championship. An incredible closing push gave him the title. In the final month, he drove in 24 runs in 23 games and was 42-for-88 for a .477 batting average—and a .562 on-base percentage! Another batting title was almost his in 1940, but his .348 final average was four points behind Joe DiMaggio's .352.

What many people remember about Luke Appling was his nickname, "Ol' Aches and Pains." Seemingly, on those occasions when he complained about his health, it was a good sign; it meant he was hitting. If he was feeling fine, something had to be wrong. Early in the 1942 season, when he was really struggling, he said, "I can't understand it. My health has never been better than at any time in the last six years. I looked for pains everywhere. At night I would lie in bed real still, waiting for an excruciating twinge. But instead of misery in my torso, my health got better and better. The stronger I felt, the weaker my hitting got. After five games, I was 1-for-18, which, they say, figures out at .055."

He bounced back in 1943 with a .328 mark, good enough for the batting title. He spent 1944 and most of 1945 in the service, then closed it out from 1946 through 1949 by batting .309 at age 39, .306, .314, and .301. In 1950, Chico Carrasquel, a sensational Venezuelan acquired from the Dodgers' organization, took over at shortstop and Appling started only 28 games—15 at short and 13 at first base. It was time to retire, and he knew it. Now, more than 60 years later, he remains the club's all-time leader in games played, at-bats, and base hits; is second in doubles and triples; third in RBIs, total bases, and extra-base hits; fourth in on-base percentage; and seventh in career batting average (.310).

15 Billy Pierce

Without question, the greatest left-handed pitcher in White Sox history is Billy Pierce, whose No. 19 jersey has been retired by the ballclub, whose statue stands proudly on the center-field concourse at U.S. Cellular Field, and who is the best pitcher from the 1950s not in the Hall of Fame.

He holds the White Sox franchise record for career strikeouts (1,796), and his team totals of 186 wins, 2,931 innings, and 390 starts are records for a Sox left-hander. Overall, his career strikeout total is 1,999 and his career won-lost mark is 211–169 with a 3.27 earned-run average. So "Frantic Frank" Lane, whose first trade upon taking over the White Sox in November 1948 was getting Pierce from Detroit, apparently knew what he was doing.

When it came to All-Star Games, Billy was the pitcher you wanted to start if you were an American Leaguer. He started three Midsummer Classics and pretty much overwhelmed the National Leaguers. In three All-Star starts, covering nine innings, the

Nationals pounded Pierce for four hits and a run, not scoring on him till his third starting assignment (1956).

As long as we're on the subject, it's interesting to note that Pierce's won-lost record entering the 1955 All-Star Game was 5–6. His ERA, though, was 2.11. Also, the AL manager that year was Cleveland's Al Lopez, who had watched Pierce start against his Indians four times since May 24. In those four games, which the teams split, Billy worked 34 innings, allowed 24 hits, struck out 25, walked eight, and gave up a grand total of three runs (all earned) for an ERA of 0.79. Lopez made the right selection.

Pierce has always said that, for sheer consistency, 1955 was his best year. He won 10 of his last 14 decisions to finish 15–10 and led the AL with a 1.97 ERA. His won-lost record could have been better but for four 1–0 losses—to All-Star Bob Porterfield and Hall-of-Famers Bob Lemon, Early Wynn, and Whitey Ford. The White Sox led the league in team batting average in 1955 but didn't always bring the bats along when Billy was pitching.

Something else notable about Billy Pierce is his record in head-to-head competition with Ford, the Yankee great. The pair broke even (7–7) in regular-season games in which Pierce and Ford started against each other. In addition, in the April 27, 1955, game, Ford was KO'd in the first inning and was the loser; Pierce relieved starter Virgil Trucks in the third and got the win. On June 5 of the same year, Ford got a no-decision and Pierce a loss in a 3–2, 10-inning defeat. On April 30, 1959, Pierce was the winner as the Sox won 4–3 in 11, Ford getting the ND. In September of 1959, Pierce started a game in New York and won 4–3, while Ford, pitching a third of an inning in relief, was charged with the defeat.

The "tie-breaker" came in the 1962 World Series, after Pierce and Don Larsen had gone from the Sox to the Giants for a package of young players led by knuckleballer Eddie Fisher. With the Yankees leading the Giants three games to two, Pierce went up against Ford in Game 6 at Candlestick Park, where he was 12–0 that year. While Orlando Cepeda delivered the big hits (an RBI double in the fourth and run-scoring single in the fifth), Pierce fired a three-hitter to even the Series and defeat Whitey Ford.

"I left the Yankees behind," Billy said, "and I go over to the National League, and the first year I hit the Yankees in the World Series—and Whitey."

Pierce then made an admission, of sorts. "That was an exciting two to three weeks for me—probably the most exciting I had ever had," he said, referring to the thrilling 1962 race and then the best-of-three playoff with the Dodgers, followed by the World Series. He had proved to many people—especially those who didn't think him capable of pitching well in the 1959 World Series, when he was 32—that he could still win big ballgames at age 35.

"Through all the years with the White Sox, winning the pennant in 1959, pitching in seven All-Star Games—all that was exciting. But in 1962, we tied for the league lead, had a three-game playoff with the Dodgers, and then played a World Series that lasted seven games. And I was involved in everything. I won the first playoff game 8–0; then I relieved in the ninth inning of the last playoff game. I started two Series games, and when Willie McCovey lined to Bobby Richardson for the final out with Willie Mays on third in that seventh game, I was in the bullpen warming up to go in to relieve in case we had tied it up."

Two Octobers later he called it quits. He and his wife, Gloria (who'd been his high school sweetheart back in Detroit), then decided to call the Chicago area home. Those of us who know them are better for it.

16 Joe Jackson

What a shame it is that today, when you mention "Shoeless" Joe Jackson, most people immediately think of the 1919 Black Sox scandal or old ballplayers disappearing into an Iowa cornfield.

Joe Jackson was one of the game's greatest hitters; his .356 career batting average is third best all time, behind only Ty Cobb and Rogers Hornsby.

In three minor-league seasons, he batted .346 for his home-town's team (Class D Greenville, South Carolina), .358 at Savannah and .354 at New Orleans. A Greenville writer gave him the "Shoeless" nickname when Joe played in his stocking feet because his new baseball shoes weren't broken in. The Philadelphia A's, who signed him in 1908, included him in a deal with Cleveland late in 1910. Joe Jackson was about to take advantage of a major opportunity.

How's this for a rookie season? In 1911, Joe hit .408 with 45 doubles, 19 triples, 83 RBIs, a .468 on-base percentage, .590 slugging average, and OPS of 1.058. Jackson "slumped" to .395 in 1912 and .373 in 1913, when he topped the AL in hits, doubles, slugging, and OPS.

Jackson displayed his power on June 4, 1913, when he belted a fastball from the Yankees' Russ Ford off the right-field roof of the Polo Grounds and into the street beyond. The newspapers claimed that the blast traveled more than 500 feet.

He fell off to .338 in 1914 and was hitting .327 in August 1915 when Tribe owner Charles Somers, near bankruptcy, put Jackson on the market. The Washington Senators offered a package of players for Jackson, but Somers rejected the bid. White Sox owner

Charles Comiskey sent his aide, Harry Grabiner, to Cleveland with a blank check. "Go to Cleveland," Grabiner was told, "watch the bidding for Jackson and raise the highest one made by any club until they all drop out." It was a done deal on August 20. Somers signed Jackson to a three-year contract extension at his previous salary ($6,000 per year), then turned him over to the Sox for outfielders Braggo Roth and Larry Chappell, pitcher Ed Klepfer, and $31,500.

For Chicago, Jackson hit only .272 over the season's last 45 games, but he was the "Shoeless" Joe of old in 1916. He banged out 202 hits, including 40 doubles and a league-high 21 triples, collected 78 RBIs, and batted .341. Once again he was one of baseball's very best. The papers retold the stories of the young Joe, from Brandon Mills, South Carolina, whose family never had any money, who never went to school and who, at age six, went to work at a cotton mill. He was the player admired by up-and-coming Red Sox pitcher-slugger Babe Ruth, who a year later told sportswriter Grantland Rice, "I copied Jackson's style because I thought he was the greatest hitter I had ever seen, the greatest natural hitter I ever saw."

Ruth and the Red Sox beat out the White Sox (89-65) by two games for the AL pennant in 1916, but Chicago (100-54) turned the tables on Boston the following season and won the flag by nine games, despite a down season for Jackson, who was hampered by injuries all year yet missed only eight games and hit .301 with 75 runs driven in. In the four-games-to-two World Series triumph over the New York Giants, Jackson batted .304.

Then came 1918 and, with the U.S. having entered World War I, several Sox players joined the fight. Jackson, a married man, landed a deferment, but after hitting .354 in 17 games with the White Sox he was ordered to report for induction. Instead, he got a job in a Delaware shipyard, where he helped build battleships and played ball in a factory league. He was the first big-name major-leaguer to avoid the draft by taking a defense-related job, and he was hammered in the Chicago newspapers for doing so.

All was forgiven in 1919, though, when the Sox, at full strength (except for the second-half loss of Red Faber), won another pennant, Jackson leading the way with a .351 batting average and 96 runs batted in. But, like seven of his teammates, he conspired to throw the World Series to Cincinnati. His numbers (.375, six RBIs, and the Series' lone home run) would suggest he gave it his all, but he admitted he hadn't. The entire story came out the following year, which was one of his best (42 doubles, 20 triples, 121 RBIs, with .382 batting/.444 on-base/.589 slugging). It was also his last.

"Shoeless" Joe Jackson was promised $20,000 by the fixers; he received $5,000. Comiskey paid him the same $6,000 salary from 1916 through 1919, when he gave him a $2,000 raise for 1920. He surely wasn't one of the leaders of the fix, and he regretted what he had done. So, will the third-greatest hitter in history ever gain entrance to baseball's Hall of Fame? One who believed he should was Ted Williams, who stated, "Joe shouldn't have accepted the money…and he realized his error. He tried to give the money back. He tried to tell Comiskey…about the fix. But they wouldn't listen. Comiskey covered it up as much as Jackson did—maybe more. And there's Charles Albert Comiskey down the aisle from me at Cooperstown. And 'Shoeless' Joe still waits outside."

17 Luis Aparicio

It's difficult to tell someone why you believe a ballplayer belongs in the Hall of Fame.

There are no magical formulas. It is all subjective. So how do you know if someone belongs in Cooperstown's shrine?

You just know.

When baseball writers first had the opportunity to watch Luis Aparicio play shortstop at the major league level in 1956, they often were shocked by what they saw: a little guy, maybe 5'8" and 150 pounds, with a howitzer for an arm, gliding into the hole between short and third or ranging far to his left, on the right-field side of second base, gloving smoked groundballs and throwing missiles to first base to get the batter.

Remembered Sammy Esposito, a teammate at Memphis in 1955 and then for seven years in Chicago: "Best shortstop that ever played the game. Looie was unbelievable. He not only was flashy—he made the great plays—but he was also so steady. It's a combination you don't see that often."

Added Jim Landis, who played behind Aparicio in center field for a half-dozen seasons: "I haven't seen a shortstop yet who could top Aparicio. I don't care what anybody's gonna tell me. I've played behind him too long and I've seen what he has done. And I've watched others and I still watch others. But Aparicio was fabulous."

He also was fabulous on the basepaths, where almost single-handedly he brought back the stolen base as an offensive weapon. Beginning with his first year (1956), Aparicio led the American League in stolen bases nine straight seasons with these totals: 21, 28, 29, 56, 51, 53, 31, 40, and 57. In 1959, he was successful on 56 of his 69 attempts, so the stolen base actually was the main component of the pennant-winning White Sox's offense, such as it was.

When the 1962 season was drawing to a close, manager Al Lopez was concerned about his shortstop, who was now 28, had put on some weight, and had dropped off in stolen bases from 53 to 31 and in batting average from .272 to .241. Balls were getting through the left side that never had before. Then there was a contract dispute between Aparicio and Eddie Short. Things came to a head in January 1963.

The Sox traded Aparicio and Al Smith to Baltimore and received four players in return: the brilliant knuckleballer Hoyt Wilhelm, shortstop Ron Hansen (1960 AL Rookie of the Year), minor-league third baseman Pete Ward, and outfielder Dave Nicholson. The trade worked out well for both clubs, but at the time, Aparicio announced "The Looie Curse."

Aparicio sits upon the dugout roof at old Comiskey Park with a group of kids who got in free to watch the Sox practice for the 1959 World Series.

"It took the White Sox 40 years to win their last pennant," he said. "It will take them another 40 years to win their next." (He was close—it took 46.) Stung, the Sox assigned Aparicio's No. 11 jersey to Nicholson, the strikeout king.

Aparicio helped the Orioles win a World Series in 1966 before returning to do the same, it was hoped, for the White Sox in 1968. The Sox lost their first 10 that season and finished 67–95. Things got worse the next two years (68–94 and 56–106), and there was talk of Looie possibly being named the next White Sox manager. Instead, owner John Allyn brought in Stu Holcomb to revamp the operation. During the first week of September 1970, Holcomb canned Short and manager Don Gutteridge and brought in a pair of 41-year-olds from the California Angels' system—Chuck Tanner as manager and Roland Hemond as director of player personnel. Tanner and Hemond knew their most marketable players were Aparicio, 36 now but coming off a .313 season, and center fielder Ken Berry, who in 1970 had batted .276 and won a Gold Glove. By the end of November, Looie had been traded to the Boston Red Sox, with whom he would spend the final three years of his 18-season career.

He finished that career with 10 trips to the All-Star Game, nine Gold Gloves, and nine AL stolen-base titles. He had come a long way from the scared kid who was searching for his countryman and former Sox shortstop Chico Carrasquel before the Sox's 1956 season opener against Chico's new team, the Indians. "On my first trip back to Chicago, Luis was waiting for me. He told me, 'I want to go home.' 'Why?' 'Because Income Tax took all my money.' 'Speak to the White Sox. I know they're going to help you.' 'No, no, no. I want to go home tomorrow.' 'Luis, you can't go home. You've proved to everybody that you can play in the big leagues. And it's because of you I now play in Cleveland. So you better stay here.' So that's when Aparicio started to collect his salary without being taxed. The White Sox paid his tax in order to keep him in America."

The way they'd gotten him to America in the first place represents one of former GM Frank Lane's finest hours. Aparicio, whose father, Luis Sr., had been one of the greatest shortstops in Venezuelan history, had replaced his dad on the Gavilanes team in 1953 and began showing off skills never seen before, according to Cleveland scout Cy Slapnicka, who was practically living with the Aparicios. Lane learned of Cleveland's red-hot interest in Aparicio and hoped it wasn't too late. He did learn that the Aparicio family wanted $10,000 for their gifted son to sign. That, Lane realized, could be a problem. At that time, anyone receiving more than $4,000 to sign was considered a bonus player and required to be with the big-league club two years before he could go to the minors to hone his skills.

While Indians GM Hank Greenberg was trying to figure out a way to sign Looie without having to keep him at Cleveland for two years, Lane struck. "Acting as vice president of our Waterloo [Iowa] farm club," Lane said, "I signed him to a contract worth $4,000. Then I gave him a bonus of $6,000 for reporting to Waterloo. See, it was just another way to skin a cat."

And this cat wound up in Cooperstown.

18 Harold Baines

No doubt there are those who think that the oft-told tale of Bill Veeck having first spotted the baseball skills of Harold Baines when the latter was a 12-year-old Little Leaguer in St. Michael's, Maryland, is apocryphal—or, at the very least, a story containing a goodly amount of exaggeration.

In any event, Veeck, like the Baines family, (A) lived on Maryland's Eastern Shore from the early '60s through the mid-'70s, (B) watched and had his scouts watch Harold play high school ball several times and (C) made Baines the top pick in the 1977 amateur draft, ahead of better-known first-rounders such as pitcher Bill Gullickson, catcher Terry Kennedy, and shortstop Paul Molitor.

Two years later, when Baines was struggling in June at Triple-A Iowa, Veeck, like a protective father, was assuring a Bards Room visitor at old Comiskey Park that the then-20-year-old outfielder was merely biding his time. "He was hitting in the .180s last July at [Double-A] Knoxville," Veeck said, "and he finished at .275. He's going to be just fine." The interviewer wanted Veeck to compare him to the defensive right fielder of choice during those years, Montreal's Ellis Valentine, who had a great arm and excellent speed. Surely the Baines kid didn't have those kinds of tools, did he? "He's not as fast," Bill conceded, "but he's quick—very quick." And the throwing arm? Said Veeck, "It's not as strong as Valentine's. But it is more accurate."

It was time to go. As the visitor headed for the elevator, Veeck called after him, "Remember, don't worry about his hitting." And indeed, Baines finished the 1979 season at Iowa with a .298 batting average to go with 22 home runs and 87 RBIs. Up to the White Sox he went for the 1980 season, and Veeck watched with tremendous pride over the next few years the development of the raw rookie into an outstanding All-Star-caliber major leaguer. In three years he went from a .255-hitting rookie with 13 homers to a star who totaled 25 home runs and drove in 105 runs in 1982. So Veeck had known whereof he spoke. So too did Paul Richards, whom Veeck had brought in to run the Chicago farm system.

"Harold Baines?" Richards had said. "He's on his way to Cooperstown. He's just stopping by Comiskey Park to play right field the next 20 years or so."

Knee injuries prevented Baines from playing much more than seven seasons in the outfield, though, so he became a designated hitter the final two-thirds of his 22-year career and continued to put up the usual Baines numbers: 25 homers, 90 runs batted in, a .290 batting average. And he would do so quietly, without fanfare, just as he did everything, it seemed. If ever there was a man of few words, it was Harold. His best friend in baseball, Ozzie Guillen, told the following story to Alan Solomon, a former colleague of the author's.

"Once," Ozzie said, "we drove back from a series in Milwaukee. All the way back, he said one word." Guillen, as he tells the story, was his usual chattering self. He drove out of the County Stadium parking lot talking. Baines said nothing. They drove past Racine. Past Kenosha. Guillen said he talked about baseball, about the things grown men talk about. Baines said nothing. This went on for more than an hour. Then Guillen pulled off the road to buy gas, looked at Baines, and asked a question.

"Want a Coke?"

Baines turned, looked at him and said the only word he would say during a two-hour drive.

"Diet."

Speaking of silence, the early ballyhoo over Baines had quieted down considerably as the 1982 season approached the halfway mark. The smooth, lefty-swinging 23-year-old who looked so good just wasn't producing the way the No. 1 pick in the country should have been producing. This, after all, was his third season in the majors. Yet, here it was July 7, and he was batting just .253 with six home runs. If he was headed to Cooperstown, as Paul Richards had said, wasn't it time for Baines to do something spectacular?

Indeed it was. That night, at old Comiskey Park, Baines came to bat in the fifth inning against Detroit's Jerry Ujdur, who had not yet allowed a hit. Baines changed that by lining a shot into the first row of seats in right feld. It was still 1–0 and Ujdur had a two-hitter when the pair faced off in the seventh. This time Baines crushed one into the seats in deepest right-center for a 2–0 lead. Finally, in the eighth, facing reliever Elias Sosa, Baines lined a grand slam over the fence in center. One game, three straight home runs, six runs batted in. Harold Baines had done something spectacular.

When he finally retired in 2001, he could look back on a career that included the retirement by the White Sox of his No. 3 jersey, six All-Star Games, and these rankings among the club's all-time leaders: third in home runs, fourth in RBIs and extra-base hits, fifth in doubles, sixth in hits, and a tie for seventh (with Eddie Collins) in games played.

It appears that Bill Veeck was right all along about Harold Baines.

19 Carlton Fisk

The Carlton Fisk story, if it ever gets written, will have so many almost-unbelievable chapters that libraries may demand the book be placed in the fiction section. There would have to be a chapter that includes the Boston Red Sox's 7–6 1975 World Series Game 6 triumph over the Cincinnati Reds, the game that ended with Fisk waving fair his drive toward the left-field foul pole.

There would be chapters on the New York–Boston rivalry, one of which surely would discuss the relationship between the two great catchers, Fisk and the Yankees' Thurman Munson. But among the best sections would be the one that covers the off-season of 1980–81, when the Red Sox front office's clerical error left Fisk a free agent. New owners in Chicago, Jerry Reinsdorf and Eddie Einhorn, were convinced by holdover GM Roland Hemond that it would be well worth their while to visit with Fisk and his agents to determine if the All-Star catcher might have interest in changing the color of his socks.

Indeed he was, and suddenly the White Sox, who less than two weeks later acquired Greg Luzinski from the Phillies, were serious contenders in the AL West. As it happened, the Sox were to open the season at Boston's Fenway Park, Fisk's summer home since 1972. The sellout crowd both booed and cheered their fellow New Englander, especially in the top of the eighth. Boston led 2–0 when Bobby Molinaro walked and Ron LeFlore singled off starter Dennis Eckersley. Bob Stanley took over on the mound, and Mike Squires bunted the runners over. Fisk then swung at the first pitch and drove it over the Green Monster in left, and the Pale Hose led 3–2 and went on to win 5–3.

"You always fantasize that the game might turn out the way it turned out," Fisk said, "but you never think it's going to."

The home opener was four days later, before a record Opening Day crowd of 51,560. Sox lefty Ross Baumgarten was opposed by Brewers ace Pete Vuckovich, once a top Sox prospect. The Sox already led 3–0 when Fisk came up with the bases loaded and two out in the fourth and cracked a line drive into the first row of the lower deck in left for a grand slam. Sox fans kept roaring until Fisk responded to the curtain call. "That's the first time I've ever done that," he said. "I've never been called back by the crowd before."

Alas, what might have been a fine season was ruined by an eight-week strike, and Fisk finished the year at .263 and, in 1982, hit .267 wth 14 home runs. When Pudge started off slowly in 1983 (he was batting .168 on May 28), people started wondering aloud if perhaps he was done at age 35. But Fisk soon went on a tear that mirrored that of the White Sox's. The old bat speed returned, the hits kept coming, and by July 20 he was up to .265. Then, in two big four-game series against AL East powers Milwaukee and

Toronto, he went 14-for-28 and drove in 11 runs. He was now at .288 and on a roll, just like the ballclub—and just like the Sox pitchers whose improvement he was overseeing.

Those who had counted him out remembered again the old saw: Never count out the great ones. No one counted out Carlton Fisk again—not till he was 45 years old. His last big year was the first year of the Sox's new ballpark, 1991. At age 43, he batted .241 that summer in 134 games, hit 18 homers, and drove in 74 runs.

Now all that was left was Cooperstown's call. That came in 2000.

20 Ted Lyons

The best pitcher to wear a White Sox uniform also wore the green and gold of Baylor University in Waco, Texas. Who was he? No, Kip Wells is not the correct answer, nor is Scott Ruffcorn. Or Ken Patterson. Matt Batts? He was a catcher.

No, the No. 1 No. 1 was Ted Lyons, who went directly from the Baylor campus to the White Sox and pitched a 1-2-3 eighth inning in their game at St. Louis that very first day, July 2, 1923. He went on to pitch 21 years, all of them on the South Side—it would have been 24 had he not enlisted in the Marines at age 41 in September 1942. As it was, even missing those three seasons, he won 260 games for the Sox against 230 losses and had a 3.67 career ERA. Three times the right-hander from Lake Charles, Louisiana, was a 20-game winner, remarkable when one considers how awful some of his White Sox teams were: 69–85 in 1923, 66–87 in 1924, 59–93 in 1929, 62–92 in 1930, 56–97 in 1931, 49–102 in 1932, 67–83 in 1933, and 53–99 in 1934.

Unfortunately, as the Sox began improving—thanks to Luke Appling, Zeke Bonura, Mike Kreevich, Rip Radcliffe, and others—Lyons was approaching 40. Manager Jimmy Dykes proposed that Teddy pitch once a week. In 1938, the year Appling missed half a season with a broken leg, he was 9–11 with a 3.70 ERA in 23 starts. The next season, he became, at age 38, the Sox's "Sunday pitcher," going 14–6 with a 2.76 ERA (second in the AL to Lefty Grove), completing 16 of his 21 starts and walking only 26 in 173 innings.

There was more of the same the next three seasons. Lyons went 12–8 with a 3.24 ERA in 22 starts in 1940, 12–10 and 3.70 in 1941, and then 14–6 in 20 starts (all complete games) and a league-best 2.10 ERA in 1942. Then came his military service, which of course included baseball. In one contest, held at the U.S. base on Guam, Lyons gave up a home run to Joe DiMaggio in an Army-Navy game. Said Ted, "I left the country to get away from DiMaggio, and here he is!"

The conversation would sometimes turn to Lyons' former batterymate, Moe Berg, the erudite backstop who was serving in the top-secret O.S.S. at the time and decades later was the subject of the book, *The Catcher Was a Spy.* "He could speak in eight languages," Lyons said, smiling, "but he couldn't hit in any of them."

When the war ended, Lyons—now 45—returned for one final shot. After five starts and a 1–4 record in 1946, he retired and replaced Jimmy Dykes as manager. The Sox were 30 games out of first in 1946 and 27 back in 1947. They were so far behind in 1948 a search party couldn't have found them. Ted paid for the 51–101 finish with his job but remained in the organization.

He was a top White Sox scout for 20-plus years—Gold Glove center fielder Ken Berry and standout right-hander Joe Horlen were among his finds—and finally got a taste of a championship in 1955. Jack Cassini, player/manager of the Sox's Memphis affiliate in the Southern Association, was seriously beaned with about six weeks left in the season. The Sox sent Lyons down to Memphis to manage the team the rest of the way,

"We were down seven or eight games with three weeks to go to Birmingham, the Yankees' farm," recalled Sammy Esposito, who played third base for Memphis with Luis Aparicio at shortstop. "We had a nine-game series with them, won all nine games and won the pennant with about three games to go.

"And Ted was a Hall of Famer, a great pitcher for many, many years, but had never been on a winner. He'd win 20, 22 games every year and the White Sox would finish last. And then he ended up managing us to a championship."

Yet to those who know him best, he'd always been a champion.

Said Charles A. Comiskey II, grandson of "The Old Roman," "He raised me. He was like a father to me. He was a very moral and high-class man."

Luke Appling, the famous Georgian, summed it up. "He had a heart as big as Stone Mountain. What a grand person he was. I am certainly glad I was there to know him."

21 Bill Veeck

If there was one truth Bill Veeck wanted everyone to know about baseball, it was this: It's supposed to be fun.

That explains having a little person, Eddie Gaedel, bat during a game. It explains fireworks displays after games and an exploding scoreboard for home runs. It explains Bat Day, S&H Green Stamp Day, Lucky Seat Nights, Music Night, Belly Dancers Night, Beer Case Stacking Night, and between-games circuses and cow-milking

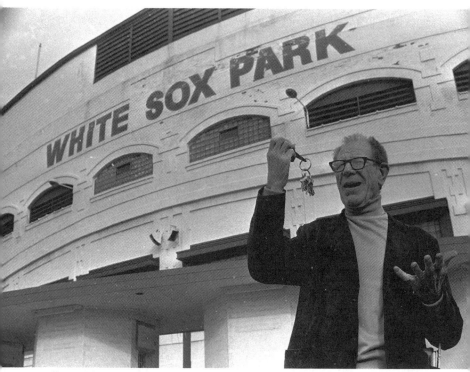

Bill Veeck holds the keys to Comiskey Park after once again becoming owner of the White Sox in 1975.

contests. It explains the shower built in the center-field bleachers at old Comiskey Park.

Some would go a bit further and add that getting a chance to spend an hour or so with Bill Veeck in the Bards Room at old Comiskey Park must have been fun as well. And it was. He would answer his own phone and talk to the caller as if he were speaking to his visitor. One caller hoped to secure Veeck's services as a speaker. Said Veeck, "I'm booked solid through January. It's not, you must understand, because I'm good. It's because I'm cheap."

He was not cheap when it came to payroll, though, or providing the proper amenities when his teams were World Series hosts.

In 1959, for instance, when the nation's sportswriters descended upon Chicago, their first question was generally, "Where's the hospitality room?" The LaSalle Hotel was the answer, and Veeck had spared no expense in making sure plenty of food and drink would be available at all hours. When the Series moved to Los Angeles, however, there was much grumbling from the writers, who complained that Dodgers owner Walter O'Malley had shut down his hospitality room at 10:00 PM. Before the Series returned to Illinois for Game 6, Veeck announced, "When we get back to Chicago, gentlemen, our hospitality room will be open 24 hours a day. You are welcome to have Scotch with breakfast or *for* breakfast."

One lucky fan had cupcakes for breakfast most of that year, thanks to one of Veeck's Lucky Seats promotions. The season's first was April 30, when the Sox edged the Yankees 4–3. In addition to the woman who wound up with 1,000 cupcakes, winnings included 1,000 kosher hot dogs and 1,000 cigars. Veeck played it again for the Memorial Day twin bill against Detroit. This time, the lucky fans could look forward to delivery people showing up at their homes during the next week with 22,000 fig bars, 50,000 assorted screws, 1,000 cans of chow mein noodles, 1,000 cartons of orange juice, or 10,000 Hostess cupcakes.

The season's first cow-milking contest, in early June, saw the Sox lose badly to Boston. A problem was that Nellie Fox's cow kicked over Nellie's pail three times. A suddenly worried Veeck watched. "The cow kept kicking and Nellie kept trying, and I started writing mental headlines: FOX IN HOSPITAL IN CRITICAL CONDITION AS RESULT OF VEECK GAG." Nellie, thankfully, survived.

His first trade as Sox owner came on May 1, when he landed veteran National League long-ball hitter Del Ennis from Cincinnati for outfielder Lou Skizas and lefty Don Rudolph, whose wife was what in former days was called an exotic dancer. "Alas," Veeck said, "the wrong Rudolph had the right curves." Later that month he purchased from Detroit the man he had signed in 1947 as the AL's first black player: outfielder Larry Doby.

In July 1961, his doctors at the Mayo Clinic suggested he "get his affairs in order," even though it was 1984 before he had surgery to remove a malignant lung tumor. So he sold his White Sox holdings and moved with his family to Easton, Maryland. There he remained until 1975, when good friend Andrew McKenna, a Sox board member, advised him to "come home"—American League owners were planning to transfer the White Sox franchise to Seattle. Veeck quickly put together a purchase group that halted the move.

He did not have many friends among AL owners, who didn't care for Veeck because he so thoroughly outworked them, wooden leg and all. In fact, they found another way to annoy him by putting together a 1977 schedule that had the Sox opening in Toronto, one of the two new expansion teams. He told famed author Roger Kahn, "How's that for a natural rivalry? The White Sox, a charter American League club, at Toronto? But we have a chance to win, if we can get there. If necessary, I intend to lease dog sleds."

The team Veeck had taken control of in December 1975 had gone 64–97 in 1976, but Veeck's "South Side Hit Men" led the AL West in mid-August 1977 before finishing third at 90–72 and setting a club attendance record of 1,657,135. There would be few thrills at 35th and Shields the next three seasons, however. Veeck sold the club—including future stars such as Harold Baines, Richard Dotson, Britt Burns, and LaMarr Hoyt—to a group headed by Jerry Reinsdorf. Bill Veeck, believe it or not, was going to take it easy.

Thomas Boswell, the noted Washington-based baseball columnist, tried to put into words that spring the essence of Bill Veeck:

"His cause of death should read: Life."

Bill Veeck was born and raised in Hinsdale, Illinois, a western suburb of Chicago. He was a month away from his 72nd birthday when he passed away in January 1986. He entered the Hall of Fame in 1991.

22 Four Hall of Famers You Should Know About

Eddie Collins

Few of us ever saw him play, but the records certainly indicate that Eddie Collins, who went into the Hall of Fame in 1939, was the greatest second baseman in White Sox history. He was the first "modern-era" player to steal 80 bases in a season, and his career batting average was .333, a figure he topped six times in his 12 seasons on the South Side. He graduated from Columbia University during a period when very few ballplayers were collegians.

He helped the Philadelphia A's win four AL pennants in five years (1910–1914) before owner/manager Connie Mack feared losing a fight with the new Federal League for talent. So he sold Collins to the White Sox after the 1914 season for $50,000, at that time the highest figure paid to obtain a player. Charles A. Comiskey paid him $15,000 for 1915, making Collins baseball's third highest-paid player, behind Ty Cobb and Tris Speaker.

In Chicago, Collins helped the Sox win pennants in 1917 and 1919. He hit just .226 in the 1919 Series but was never accused of being involved in the fix. He later managed the Sox for two years (1925–26).

Red Faber

The noted spitballer from Iowa—a 1964 Hall of Fame selection who was signed by the White Sox at the end of the 1913 season—caught his break when he was asked to be a last-minute replacement for Christy Mathewson of the New York Giants for the World Tour the Sox and Giants organized during the 1913–14 off-season. He pitched extremely well during the tour, and Giants manager

John McGraw kept trying to get him from Comiskey, but the Old Roman held firm. Faber debuted with the Sox early in 1914 and immediately became a staff mainstay.

He was at his best in the 1917 World Series against McGraw and the Giants. He threw a complete-game 7–2 victory in Game 2 and lost when the Sox were shut out 5–0 in Game 4. Faber relieved on just one day's rest in Game 5, threw two scoreless innings, and was credited with the 8–5 triumph. He topped it off by pitching a series-clinching complete-game 4–2 victory in Game 6, again on a day's rest. Spanish flu, which killed millions, caused him to miss the 1919 Series.

Faber rebounded in 1920, when he was 23–13 with a 2.99 ERA. He then posted 25–15 and 21–17 marks the next two years while leading the AL in ERA both seasons. His 254 wins are second only to Ted Lyons' 260 on the club's all-time list.

Ray Schalk

Schalk's 1955 induction at Cooperstown was a victory for defense over offense. The catcher on the great White Sox teams of 1916–1920 was a take-charge guy despite his size: 5'9", 160. He led the league's catchers in fielding percentage eight times and putouts nine and was the first to catch four no-hitters. "Cracker" was also among the fastest catchers in history, stealing 30 bases in 1916, a record that stood for 66 years until Kansas City's John Wathan stole 36 in 1982. Not a powerful hitter by any means, he had a career batting average of .253, lowest for any Hall member.

He broke in with the Sox in 1912, played a dozen full seasons with them and also managed them two years. A graduate of Litchfield (IL) High School, Schalk worked well with fastball, spitball, and knuckleball pitchers alike, filling the role of pitching coach before there were pitching coaches.

Schalk played a big role in the 1917 World Series victory over the Giants, catching every inning and batting .263. In 1919, he was one of the "clean Sox" and hit .304 in the Series. He aided the Sox again in 1923 when he saw a young Ted Lyons pitching for Baylor and convinced Comiskey to sign him.

Ed Walsh

They called him "Big" Ed Walsh because he was taller than the batters he faced. But actually, the 1946 Hall of Fame inductee from Plains, Pennsylvania, stood just 6'1". He used a dominating spitball to average 24 victories per season over a seven-year span (1906–1912). The right-hander, who twice threw more than 400 innings in a season, is remembered best for his 1908 campaign, when he finished 40–15 and had 42 complete games in 49 starts, 464 innings pitched and 269 strikeouts. Big Ed finished his career with a 195–126 record and also coached, managed, and umpired. He also has the lowest career ERA in history: 1.82.

He did his best work in the 1906 World Series against the mighty (even then) Cubs, beating them twice in two starts, giving up one earned run in 15 innings and striking out 17. In 1907 he was 24–18 with a 1.60 ERA; then, in a remarkable flag race with Cleveland and Detroit, he won those 40 games in 1908 with a 1.42 ERA and an AL record-breaking 11 shutouts. One of his 15 defeats was on October 2, when Cleveland's Addie Joss threw a perfect game against the Sox. In the end, Detroit finished a half game ahead of Cleveland and 1½ in front of Chicago.

23 The White Sox? 29 Runs?

Okay, the wind was blowing out pretty hard. We'll give you that.

But this was a White Sox team that could hit the ball on occasion. The 1955 Sox would go on to lead the American League in team batting average and set a team record for home runs with 116.

Also, they were facing a Kansas City A's pitching staff this day—Saturday, April 23, 1955—that would finish the season with a 5.35 earned-run average, worst in the league by quite a bit.

Maybe it was just the Sox hitters' turn to have one of those days. In any event, they had one.

Final score: White Sox 29, Athletics 6. Believe it or not.

A's lefty Bobby Shantz, a former MVP coming back from arm trouble, was the unfortunate starter for the home team. Another lefty, Jack Harshman, started for Chicago. "I was fortunate to be pitching on the day we scored a lot of runs," Harshman said decades later. "And I was fortunate they didn't get that many balls up in the air."

The wind was blowing at 25–30 miles per hour, with some strong gusts to left field, where the fence was 312 feet from the plate and the power alley about 382. "It was just one of those real windy spring days," Harshman recalled. "I'll tell you how windy it was. The flag poles on top of the fence and on the roof were almost snapping off. You'd get the ball up in the air, and it would just keep going and going."

The Sox hit a total of seven homers that afternoon: Bob Nieman and Sherm Lollar each hit two and Minnie Minoso, Walt Dropo, and Harshman (a dangerous hitter for a pitcher) each belted one.

"I remember," said Harshman, "we had to laugh. One of our guys—I think it was Lollar—nearly fell down while swinging, but he got it up in that wind and it went out."

Harshman gave up a three-run homer to Bill Renna in the first, so the Sox's quick 4–0 lead was almost gone—with the wind. But then came a seven-run second inning, a three-run third, a two-run fourth, a six-run sixth and a three-run seventh, and it was 25–6 Chicago heading to the eighth. Now it was Harshman's turn. He drove a two-run homer, his third hit, over the fence in deepest right-center to make it 27–6.

"What I remember clearly about that day is that of all the home runs hit in that game [nine], mine was the only one hit by a left-handed hitter," he said. "All the others were by right-handed hitters, and they all went to left field."

Another oddity about this one: A's left fielder Gus Zernial, an ex-Chicago slugger who was AL home run champion in 1951, had hit 42 homers in 1953 and would hit 30 this season, went homerless—in fact, hitless.

Said Zernial, decades later, "Jack threw the screwball, which broke down and away from right-handed hitters [such as Gus], and he had a real good sinker, too. He obviously didn't let me get any up in the air."

An RBI single by Minoso and a sacrifice fly by reserve infielder Stan Jok made it 29–6 in the eighth, but the home team went down in order in the ninth, meaning they would share the (modern, post-1900) 29-run record with the Red Sox, who had pummeled the dear departed St. Louis Browns 29–4 in 1950. The Sox, Red and White, ended up sharing the mark until the Texas Rangers hammered the Baltimore Orioles (formerly the St. Louis Browns) by a 30–3 score in 2007.

Thus, the White Sox had a piece of the record for 52 years.

"We won that game with 29 runs and 29 hits," Harshman remembered, correctly. "And the next day, [A's lefty] Alex Kellner shut us out on five hits."

And the game after that, the Yankees' Bob Turley shut them out on one.

24 The Longest Day —and Night

The 2013 season was over rather early on the South Side. Most of the second half, in fact, was spent reading scouting reports on prospects the White Sox either had landed or hoped to land by trading off a veteran here and a veteran there. Later in the year came the race for the major leagues' worst won-lost record and, with it, the awarding of the top pick in next June's amateur draft.

Now that they have tasted a World Series championship, many White Sox fans really have only one request of their team: meaningful games in September. This year, they ran out of meaningful games in May. Sure, some fans held out hope for an eventual turnaround, but they had to be dreaming. And once the Cleveland Indians, for most of the last 60 years patsies for the White Sox, came to town the weekend of June 28–30 and swept four straight and made the home team look absolutely awful, even those dreamers had to come to the realization that 2013 was to be a season that belonged in a straitjacket.

The "fun" started Friday with the makeup of an early-season rainout. The early start guaranteed a slim turnout, and indeed there were a few hundred folks in the stands when the first game began at 5:10 PM. Hector Santiago, young Sox lefty, set the pace for the day with a lengthy opening half-inning, walking two but striking out three. In the bottom half, the Sox KO'd Cleveland starter Trevor Bauer en route to a five-run inning, highlighted by Adam Dunn's two-run homer, Jeff Keppinger's solo shot, and Gordon Beckham's two-out RBI double.

When given a 5–0 lead after one inning, you want to shut down your opponent in the second. Santiago, sadly, gave up a five-spot, Drew Stubbs delivering a two-run two-out single, Jason Kipnis a two-run double, and Nick Swisher a game-tying single to left.

It got worse in the fourth. Ryan Raburn, one of those guys who hits .225 against everybody else and .425 against the Sox, broke the tie with a bases-loaded single that scored two. Lonnie Chisenhall followed with a double to right that made it 8–5, Mike Aviles (see Ryan Raburn, above) singled to center for two more runs and Stubbs tripled him home. Now it was 11–5, and that soon became 14–5.

The Sox got four of the runs back in their half of the fifth, three on Tyler Flowers' drive over the center-field wall, and Keppinger singled in a run in the sixth. Chicago had crawled to within 14–10—already an embarrassing score—but Raburn drilled a two-run homer in the Cleveland seventh to put the game away. Not totally satisfied, the Tribe scored three in the eighth for a final score of 19–10. It had been an afternoon rough on ERAs, especially those of Sox relievers Brian Omogrosso (up to 9.37) and Ramon Troncoso (7.27). The highlight of the game was watching outfielder Casper Wells come in to pitch a hitless, scoreless ninth.

Then, after the normal break between games and the unexpected 25-minute rain delay just as Game 2 was getting underway, the Tribe picked up where it had left off. The Indians scored four runs off the Sox's fine young lefty, Jose Quintana, cobbling together three hits, two walks, and the obligatory 2013 run-scoring passed ball.

This time, though, the Sox fought back, scoring four in the sixth and two insurance runs in the eighth, the big hits coming from Alexei Ramirez (RBI double) and Keppinger (RBI triple). So, with an 8–5 lead to protect, in came closer Addison Reed to nail it down. The Indians had other ideas. That man Raburn led off again and singled to center, then went to third on Asdrubal Cabrera's single to right. Michael Bourn then singled a run home, Cabrera racing to third. Ancient Jason Giambi then pinch hit, and Reed uncorked a wild pitch, a run scoring, and it was 8–7. After Giambi's flyball to center sent Bourn to third with one out, Kipnis' sacrifice fly tied the game.

It didn't stay tied for long. Up stepped Swisher, who had come to the Sox in a 2008 deal that sent two top farmhands, lefty Gio Gonzalez and outfielder Ryan Sweeney, to Oakland. (Swisher hit .219 for the Sox and fanned 135 times; Gonzalez won 21 games for Washington in 2012; Sweeney has hit in the .290s twice.) This night, Swisher swung at a pitch from Reed and lost it in the seats in right. The Tribe led 9–8. That was the final score.

It was *the* low point in a season loaded with low points. An alleged 28,628 had shown up for 7 hours 53 minutes of baseball— the longest doubleheader in major league history in which neither game went extra innings.

And then the final crusher: Because the games had lasted so long, it was now too late for the postgame fireworks display.

You almost had to cry.

In This Corner...
Art "The Great"

If you thought that self-absorbed professional athletes didn't happen upon the scene until the arrival in the '60s of Joe Namath and his ilk, you've never heard of Art "The Great" Shires. The White Sox's rookie "find" of the '20s had to be among the most boastful, outrageous players ever to wear a major league uniform.

The Shires saga began when the Sox, on July 31, 1928, purchased him from Waco of the Texas League, where he was batting .317. Two days later, he ripped the purchase price and said the Cleveland Indians had made a better offer—which would've meant more money for him. He refused to report to the Sox and signed with a Texas semi-pro team. But, by mid-August, Shires, a high school teammate of Paul Richards in Waxahachie, Texas, ended his "holdout" and joined the Sox in Boston. Facing Red Ruffing, he tripled to deep center his first at-bat and added three singles for a 4-for-5 day. "So this is the great American League I've heard so much about? I'll hit .400!"

As it turned out, he hit .341 in 33 games and, in his mind, was well on the way to stardom. He was not above stopping folks and asking if they were on their way to the ballpark to see that great first baseman—meaning himself, of course.

At spring training the next March, manager Lena Blackburne named Shires, an unlikely candidate if there ever was one, to the team captaincy. One night, he arrived at the team's hotel long after curfew and quite drunk. He walked out into the courtyard and began howling at the moon. Blackburne right there stripped Shires of his captaincy and told him that more immaturity might mean suspension without pay and a $100 fine.

That came on May 15, before a game with Boston at Comiskey Park. During batting practice, Blackburne tore into Shires, who was wearing a red felt hat, for not taking his job as a big-leaguer seriously. Shires responded with a profanity-laced attack upon the manager and his ability. Blackburne, as promised, suspended him on the spot and fined him $100. Art The Great left the park but was back later to confront his manager. Words were exchanged, as were punches, each man landing a shot to the face before players and coaches could separate them.

Blackburne said he was finished with Shires and that it was up to owner Charles A. Comiskey to figure out what to do with

This Fight's Big Winner Didn't Throw a Punch

The White Sox were about to sweep a doubleheader from their hosts, the lowly St. Louis Browns, on Sunday, May 1, 1949. They led 14–3 with the dependable lefty Bob Kuzava on the mound.

Then, with one out and one man on base, it started.

Double, double, single, force-out, single, single, double, walk, triple. Suddenly, the score was 14–11. But Randy Gumpert saved matters by striking out future teammate Al Zarilla to end it.

For Sox manager Jack Onslow, though, it was not a happy ending. He sarcastically second-guessed his catcher, a second-stringer named Joe Tipton, for his pitch-calling during the ninth inning. Tipton could take only so much before he threw his shin guards to the floor and went after Onslow, both men getting in a couple of punches before they were separated.

Onslow went to GM Frank Lane and said Tipton had to go. For once, the two agreed on something. However, it took until October 19 for Lane to find a taker. It turned out to be A's owner/manager Connie Mack, who sent Lane a 21-year-old backup second baseman named Nellie Fox as payment for Tipton.

Sometimes it takes a little luck.

him. Shires said he was through with baseball and was going back to school to get a law degree. What actually happened: Shires, after apologizing, was reinstated by May 30 and back in the starting lineup by June 4. Soon he was sounding like a guy from the "Chicks Dig the Longball" '90s.

"No [sense in] a great hitter like me getting a flock of skimpy singles. You never get your name in the headlines with singles. It's distance the public wants. From now on I'm aiming for the next county. I'm going out for home runs. Come on out and razz me; you'll go away cheering me when I slam them against the bleachers. I sure can hit that ball, and I'm not so bad around first base either."

He finished the 1929 season with only three homers but batted .312, led the Sox with a .370 on-base percentage and slugged a career-best .433. But he couldn't stay out of trouble.

He was suspended again in mid-September after another fight with Blackburne in a Philadelphia hotel room. When Blackburne accused Shires of being drunk again, "the Great" knocked the skipper down and repeatedly pounded Blackburne's head on the floor. He also went after traveling secretary Lou Barbour, who had tried to intervene. Police took Shires into custody, but, for some reason Blackburne and Barbour refused to press charges.

Shires was suspended for the rest of the season, then held out for a salary of $25,000. He was, after all, he said, as big a drawing card as there was in the AL besides Babe Ruth. He signed for $7,500, then looked around that off-season for potential boxing opponents. He KO'd "Dangerous Dan" Daly in 21 seconds in front of the biggest fight crowd in the history of White City amusement park in Chicago (Daly was actually Jim Gerry, a friend of Blackburne's from Ohio). Then came a bout with Bears center George Trafton, who beat him up badly.

Shires had hoped for a fight with Cubs slugger Hack Wilson, another who had the reputation for settling disagreements with fists. That's when Commissioner Landis stepped in with this ultimatum: "Quit the prize ring or quit baseball." The edict affected more than Shires, however. "Hereafter," Landis said, "any person connected with any club in this organization who engages in professional boxing will be regarded by this office as having permanently retired from baseball. The two activities do not mix."

Nor did Shires and the White Sox, who finally traded him to Washington in June 1930.

26 The Babe on the South Side?

Think about this for a moment or two: a 1919 White Sox outfield with Shoeless Joe Jackson in left and Babe Ruth in right.

That's right, Shoeless Joe and the Babe in the same outfield. It could have happened. Before we tell why it did not, some stats:

In 1919, a season that should have ended with a Sox world championship but instead ended with rumors—which turned out to be true—that Chicago had lost the World Series on purpose, Jackson posted a batting average of .351 with 31 doubles, 14 triples, 7 homers, and 96 RBIs for the American League champions. Ruth, the former Red Sox pitching star in his first season as a full-time outfielder in Boston, hit .322 and added 34 doubles, 12 triples, and league highs in homers (29) and runs batted in (114).

Now check the 1920 season, the first featuring a new, livelier ball, the first for Ruth with the New York Yankees and the last for Jackson in organized baseball. (That's because, with a week left on the 1920 schedule, baseball's crusty new commissioner, Judge Kenesaw Mountain Landis, suspended for life Shoeless Joe and seven of his teammates for their roles in the 1919 fix.) In 1920, Ruth batted .376, laced 36 doubles, 9 triples, and an unheard-of 54 home runs while totaling a league-best 137 runs batted across. Jackson was no slouch, either. He finished at .382 with 42 doubles, an AL-high 20 triples, plus career-bests in homers (12) and RBIs (121). And he struck out only 14 times all year.

Those numbers, as one would expect, dwarfed those of the men—Shano Collins and Nemo Leibold—who essentially shared the Sox right-field assignment during that 1917–1920 period. Collins, for example, hit four home runs in the four years, Leibold

Sox Almost Had *Him*, Too

Buzzy Bavasi, at the time general manager at Brooklyn, had no comment when asked about it years later. Marty Marion, at the time the White Sox's manager, had no recollection whatsoever. Frank Lane, however, the White Sox GM back in 1955, swore it was true.

The White Sox came "this close" to bringing Jackie Robinson, the aging Dodger great, to the South Side of Chicago in the summer of 1955—the summer the Sox, Yankees, Indians and, for a time, the Red Sox waged a terrific race for the American League pennant.

Lane knew Robinson and second-year Brooklyn manager Walter Alston were having difficulty getting along. Alston was using youngsters Don Hoak at third and Sandy Amoros in left field and leaving Jackie on the bench, where the latter was seething. He ended up getting into just 11 games in July, going 5-for-23 (a .217 batting average). On the field, the Dodgers were running away with the National League pennant. In the AL, New York led at the All-Star break by five games over Cleveland and six over Chicago. By month's end, that trio would be bunched at the top, within a couple games of each other.

Lane, nearly 25 years later, recalled having pieced a deal together with the Dodgers during the July waiver period. First he had to make sure the Dodgers could waive Robinson out of the NL. Then would come the job of getting him through the AL, by reverse order of the standings. The Sox at that moment were behind only Cleveland and the Yankees. Lane figured none among Washington, Kansas City, Baltimore, Detroit, or Boston would claim Jackie, whose age (36) and large salary made him unattractive to most non-contending clubs.

In the end, certain movers and shakers woke up just in time to make sure this National League icon did not play his next game in a White Sox uniform. Lane's belief was that, at the final moment, league president Warren Giles, former boss at Cincinnati, put a call through to Gabe Paul, the Reds' GM, and all but demanded the Reds put in a claim for Robinson, thus blocking his departure.

"He'd have fit right in with us." said Lane. Among Jackie's new teammates would have been Minnie Minoso, the Sox's first black player, and his former Kansas City Monarchs teammate, pitcher Connie Johnson. "Jackie could have backed up George Kell at third and Walt Dropo at first," Lane said, "and we could've used him in the outfield and to pinch hit. And of course there is no question he would have helped us at the gate."

one. Neither, however, would have played much at all had Charles A. Comiskey, "the Old Roman," taken advantage of a 1914 offer that only recently came to light, thanks to Robert Edward Auctions. The firm earlier this year came into possession of a scrapbook that contained letters and telegrams from Comiskey to his top scout in the East, a New England sleuth named George Mills, from 1909 through 1914. It was Mills' granddaughter who provided the auction firm with the scrapbook. Among the album's contents were 41 letters signed by Comiskey—including three that indicate the White Sox had the first chance to buy Babe Ruth from the minor-league Baltimore Orioles and their owner, Jack Dunn.

The three messages are 1914 Western Union telegrams from Comiskey to Mills, then staying at a Baltimore hotel. The first message, sent on June 9, 1914, said, "Follow Baltimore Club and advise of best players there." The next, dated June 17, told Mills to "Secure best price on men mentioned in your wire, and when Dunn will deliver advise me at once." The names had been written in pencil in the margin of the telegram: "Cree, Daniels, Twombly, Midkiff, Derrick, Ruth." A June 27 telegram from Comiskey indicates he didn't like the price. "Do not need pitchers bad[ly] enough to go that high—get prices on other men and stay in Baltimore until further advice." A note from Orioles owner Dunn is written on that telegram: "Will sell Ruth to Chicago club for $16,000. Dunn." That, apparently, was the end of Comiskey's communications with the Baltimore club regarding Ruth. There is in the album another telegram from Comiskey to Mills, dated June 30: "After you have secured price on other men of Baltimore club, it is satisfactory to me for you to proceed north to look over the New England League and the others that you mention."

Within a week, Baltimore's Dunn offered Ruth (and others) to Cincinnati and the Philadelphia A's, but neither club was interested. Finally, on July 9, Dunn found a taker—the Red Sox. Boston, for the amount of $25,000, landed pitchers Ruth and Ernie Shore and catcher Ben Egan. Just 5½ years later, the Red Sox sold Ruth to the Yankees. And the rest, as has been said so often, is history.

And it could have been White Sox history.

27 Disco Demolition (What Went Wrong?)

The goofiness started early.

The TV went on about 7:00 PM, so the first game of that evening's twi-nighter with Detroit was about three innings old. The ballpark looked almost packed. It was great to see the old place jammed like that, and to hear the crowd chanting, "Let's Go Sox! Let's Go Sox!" Soon enough, though, one came to the realization that they were chanting something else: "Disco Sucks! Disco Sucks!"

That's right, this was supposed to be Disco Demolition Night, with a special between-games destruction by fireworks of any and all disco 45s within reach. Emcee of the affair was rock-station WLUP-FM's Steve Dahl, years later a Sox season-ticket holder. Here was the plan: Anyone bringing along a disco disc could get in for 98 cents. Thousands of records would be blown to kingdom come by the fireworks crew, and the proceedings, it was anticipated, would be cheered by Dahl's army of followers—maybe 30,000 at most—in the stands. And then the grounds crew would clean up Dahl's "launching pad" and, soon thereafter, Game 2 would get underway.

Things did not exactly turn out as planned. During Game 1, kids kept pouring into the ballpark. By the late innings of the opener, "regular" fans, fearing the worst, started to depart, leaving seats for the anti-disco types who were still coming in. Kids began

People storm the field on Disco Demolition Night, July 12, 1979.

sailing their disco records like frisbees around the stands. Signs hanging from the railings carried the apparent motto of the night: "Disco Sucks!"

When the game ended, the Sox having lost 4–1, a huge pile of disco records began forming behind second base. Then came the fireworks, and the pile went sky-high and the crowd went nuts. Kids from everywhere began running onto the field, security having no chance to stop them, and there they stayed. Soon came word that the umpires had declared Detroit winner of Game 2 by forfeit. The field, they said, was unplayable.

It was not Bill Veeck's finest hour.

"Disco Demolition was a disaster," he said a year later. "And the strange part about it, it was a disaster because I had done insufficient investigation. It had never occurred to me that anything like that could have happened."

Surely he never figured 47,795 people (the wildly low attendance figure eventually given out by the Sox) would come to see disco records getting blown up. Although admittedly it might be a tad more exciting than watching Claudell Washington bat.

"The most [Dahl] had drawn anywhere before that was 4,500," Veeck noted. "He drew that night, in total, at least 100,000 people. Because there were more people outside the park than there were inside. It took six squads to close the gates so no more people could get in, although we hadn't sold the place out. And cars were backed up on the Dan Ryan [Expressway] all the way to north of Fullerton [that's 2400 North; the ballpark was at 3500 South]. This was after the first game was over. They were still backed up.

"But it was remarkable what a good promotion it was. The promotion was too good. It was a disaster only because if we'd had any idea what was going to happen, we could've controlled it. But they just kept coming and coming."

And then they refused to leave. Veeck himself hobbled onto the field, took the P.A. mike and pleaded with the kids to clear the field so the second game could start.

"I couldn't get anybody to leave, which was a pretty humbling experience." Bill said. "I stood on that field for 45 minutes. I couldn't get anybody off. But I didn't want to cause a real riot by bringing in the police."

His son, Mike Veeck—who had a rock band, hated disco, and had done much of the planning—had made the same errors as his dad. "My mistake," he recalled, "was thinking that we'd get about 35,000 for the promotion. It turned out there were 60,000 inside the park and another 30,000 to 40,000 on the streets around the park. Who had any idea that that many kids would come out?

"The other thing that happened was that we moved some of the police off the field. We had an adequate security force for 35,000 fans but not for 60,000. Outside of the park there were some temporary ticket booths staffed by older people. The kids were starting to get out of hand and started rocking those booths. We moved some of the police off the field outside to help. What happened next was…the crowd began thinking as one and they realized there were only 35 to 40 police on the field.…They said, 'Let's go on the field!'"

For Mike Veeck, Disco Demolition was a statement against disco music, particularly the group KC and the Sunshine Band. That's because Veeck believed that disco had ruined his band's hope for success. In addition, he was so linked to that night that it took years for him to get a job in baseball. He was with Tampa Bay and then moved on to the then-Florida Marlins in 2001. A colleague there reminded him that July 12—Disco Demolition's anniversary—was near, that the Marlins were home that night and that K.C. (Harry Wayne Casey) lived in the area.

"'You ought to apologize to him,'" Veeck recalls the Marlins employee saying. "I said, 'Not on your life.' But the litmus test with all these ideas is: Are they funny? And I laughed and realized it was a great gag."

So Veeck forgot past resentment and, standing at home plate, delivered a 90-second, tongue-in-cheek "apology" to K.C. He closed it with, "I'm sorry—from the bottom of my leisure suit."

28 "Exciting White Sox Baseball, Brought to You By..."

We knew the commercials by heart, but they surely weren't targeted for us. Certainly neither Jack Brickhouse on TV nor Bob Elson on radio wanted to turn all of us 10- and 12-year-olds into lushes so early in life. But we had most of the ads down perfectly.

There was Hamm's, the beer refreshing, from the land of sky blue waters, with those clever raccoons always making the Hamm's Bear look like a sap. Budweiser was the beverage that Elson peddled on WCFL and later WMAQ. "Keep plenty of cold, golden Budweiser on hand...chilling and ready...for yourself...your family...and your friends. That's world-famous Budweiser—St. Louis, Newark, Los Angeles, and Tampa...that Bud...that's beer."

Bob would also want us to have a White Owl cigar to go with the Bud. He would list the cigars of the White Owl line: the Invincible, the Panatella, the Perfecto Special, the New Yorker, and the Ranger—Texas tall and slim as a branding iron. And every 1950s and '60s White Sox player who accomplished that rarest of feats—i.e., hitting a home run—knew what awaited him at game's end: "There was a White Owl wallop...and a box of White Owl cigars...for Walt Dropo...and the Sox now lead Cleveland 4–0."

Sometimes the home run was a different kind of "wallop"—with a product we could all relate to. "There was a grand slam...a Coca-Cola wallop...and a case of Coca-Cola...for Orestes Minoso, and the White Sox have a 5–0 lead in Washington."

Both Brickhouse and Elson tried to convince us to take out loans through either Household Finance (Brickhouse) or General Finance (Elson). Eventually we would realize we wouldn't have gotten very far in the loan application process—not at age 11. But we watched *The Tenth Inning* on good ol' Channel 9 faithfully, and Brick always had that HFC sign by his side, with this musical advice for us from the HFC Singers, or whoever they were:

"Never borrow money needlessly;
But when you must,
Borrow from the oldest company,
From folks you trust;
Borrow con-fi-dent-ly
From H…F…C."

Elson, as with everything he said, took his time while reading the General Finance ads.

"…So remember that *who*-ever you are and *where*-ever you are, if you have a money problem, large or small, help is just as close as your telephone. Just call Friendly Bob Adams at AN-dover three… two-oh…two-oh. Tell Friendly Bob *how* much you need and *when* you expect to stop by…and then, whenever you do, at any one of our *fifty* General Finance offices in Chicagoland, your money will be ready…and waiting [voice almost inaudible]. Remember, that loan-by-phone number: AN-dover three…two-oh…two…oh [again, barely audible]."

When the White Sox picked up Cincinnati's Bobby Adams for infield help in the summer of 1955, the question in the neighborhood was: Which of the two Bob Adamses is the friendliest? No one had the answer.

In later years came new sponsors and Harry Caray as a new pitchman. The beer of choice, if only briefly, was Falstaff, "because we're all in this together," the slogan said. Falstaff ran commercials that starred two cowboys, Gabe and Walker. Walker was played by a then-little-known actor named Sam Elliott.

Harry also did Falstaff ads: "Boy oh boy, what I wouldn't do right now for a nice plate of *bore*-becue rib…and an ice-cold Falstaff." But he branched out occasionally, doing Chicken Unlimited spots right from the booth. "Crisp on the outside…" (he'd take a big bite) "moist on the inside…" (showing the chicken leg with the bite mark) "marinated from an old family recipe. Need I tell you, it tastes delicious? Chicken Unlimited! Tell 'em Harry sent you."

Time to get something to eat.

29 Old Comiskey's Greatest Weekend

It was a series for the ages.

"Friday night, Saturday afternoon, and a *big* Sunday double-header," Bob Elson said. "This place ought to be mobbed."

And it was.

A crowd of 48,346 was on hand for Friday night's thriller that, three decades later, a *Chicago Tribune* panel selected as the greatest game ever played at the old South Side ball yard.

A shade under 30,000 came out Saturday, and 47,225 showed up for a Sunday doubleheader that had more fun moments than any paying customer had a right to expect.

It was White Sox vs. Yankees, June 22–24, 1956.

Said manager Marty Marion, "The greatest series that was ever played in Marty Marion's life was when we beat the Yankees four straight at Comiskey Park in 1956."

Said Larry Doby, whose bat powered Sunday's sweep, "One of my greatest days in baseball, and my greatest day with the White Sox, without a doubt."

A little background: The Yankees had played 60 games and Mickey Mantle already had 27 homers—putting him on pace to break Babe Ruth's record. In addition, New York catcher Yogi Berra had hit 17 home runs; as a team, the Yanks had 88. The

White Sox had hit 33. Still, they had won seven of their last eight games. The Yankees (40–20) came to town with a seven-game winning streak and a five-game lead. One other note: The Sox (32–22) were without their best player, Minnie Minoso, sidelined by a broken toe, courtesy of wild Baltimore lefty Don Ferrarese.

FRIDAY NIGHT: This one had everything. Through seven, Dick Donovan had a no-hitter and a 2–0 lead, thanks to Dave Philley's RBI single and Doby's home run. Billy Martin's run-scoring single in the eighth broke up the no-no, and Mantle singled in the tying run in the ninth. Joe Collins' two-out single with the bags loaded put New York up 4–2 in the 11th, but with runners at second and third and two out in their half, the Sox tied it on rookie Sammy Esposito's pinch line-drive double to right. They left the bases loaded that inning, but in the 12th—with two out and the bases jammed—Esposito, South Side resident and graduate of Fenger High School, blooped a single over shortstop Phil Rizzuto's head to win the game 5–4.

SATURDAY: The day centered around the two men—pitcher Jim Wilson and outfielder-first baseman Dave Philley—acquired in May from Baltimore in a rather unpopular six-player deal that cost Chicago George Kell, Bob Nieman, and pitchers Connie Johnson and Mike Fornieles. In the sixth, Philley, unhappy at being thrown at by New York's Bob Grim, charged the mound. No effective punches were thrown, and peace was soon restored, but the brief bout served as a spark for the Sox. Sherm Lollar followed with a run-scoring double, and rookie Luis Aparicio added an RBI single, giving Wilson a 2–0 lead. That's how it ended. Wilson (10–3) finished with a four-hitter before 29,832.

SUNDAY: Billy Pierce was matched up against Whitey Ford in Game 1 and gave up a first-inning run, but Ford ran into far more trouble than that. Esposito singled to center to start things and went to second on Nellie Fox's infield out and to third on a wild pitch. Minoso, wearing a shoe cut out at the toe, was hit by a pitch, and Philley singled to tie the score and send Minnie to third. Doby then stepped up and drove one into the center-field bullpen, where the fence was 415 feet from the plate. The 4–1 lead became 8–2 after three innings, Lollar contributing a two-run homer, and 11–2 after four, Lollar contributing a two-run double. The Sox kept pouring it on until Pierce, with a 14–2 lead, retired Martin on a pop-up to end it.

Marion started his old St. Louis Cardinal teammate Gerry Staley in Game 2, and Staley went five shutout innings before having any trouble. His opponent, lefty Mickey McDermott, had trouble from the get-go. Esposito walked to open the first, Fox singled off McDermott's glove and Minoso walked to load the bases. Philley's sacrifice fly to Mantle in center scored Esposito, and then Doby launched another three-run homer, even farther than his Game 1 blast. It was 4–0 and the place was rocking. By the seventh inning, the first of some 200 on-field celebrants, more than one a bit inebriated, were running around on the outfield grass, most hoping to shake hands with Doby or Mantle. When Aparicio threw out Hank Bauer to end the 6–3 victory and complete the sweep, it was hard to tell who were more joyous, the Sox or their fans. After all, Chicago was just a game back.

Esposito, years later, still remembered the weekend clearly. "That Friday night game, to have played a part in beating the Yankees—especially as a rookie—was a great feeling for me. But what made me feel just as good was the fact that I played darn well in the other games [5-for-11 for the series]. It was a nice weekend for me. We had tremendous crowds. Those were exciting days."

30 The Pennants That Never Were

Older White Sox fans remember the 1959 World Series and the heroics of Ted Kluszewski, Jim Rivera, and the rest. Younger ones can still see the Sox celebrating on the field at Minute Maid Park in Houston seconds after Juan Uribe fired to Paul Konerko for the final out of the 2005 Series.

Why only two World Series trips in 50-plus years? You should know some of the reasons.

1955: The Sox showed all season they were the equal of the AL's best—they finished 11–11 vs. the Yankees and 10–12 vs. defending AL champion Cleveland. After splitting a pair with the Yankees before 50,990 on August 28 at Comiskey Park, the Sox swept two from fourth-place Boston and set off on a 19-game trip. Chicago held a half-game lead over the Indians and Yankees and was five ahead of Boston. The journey began well, with an 8–1 rout of the Tribe, but on Saturday, Nellie Fox, George Kell, and Minnie Minoso reached to open the first inning. With a grand chance to jump on Indians starter Early Wynn, the Sox let him off the hook: Rivera grounded into a double play, a run scoring, and Bob Kennedy bounced out to third. The Sox lost that one 6–1 and two the next day. Just like that, they were in third, 1½ games out. They never got closer.

In the final two months, they were always missing that one other top pitcher to go with Billy Pierce. Jack Harshman, Connie Johnson, and Virgil Trucks had their moments, but Dick Donovan's appendectomy on July 30—when the big right-hander was 13–4—was too much to withstand. "Tricky Dick," attempting to come back too soon, wasn't the same pitcher: He was 2–5 with a 5.17 ERA after the operation.

1960: This team often is portrayed as the one Bill Veeck was stuck with after he traded one top prospect after another in the off-season for Minnie Minoso, Roy Sievers, and Gene Freese. Actually, the 1960 team fielded better than the 1959 Sox, turned far more double plays, stole more bases, and had a team batting average of .270 (tops in the AL) compared to 1959's .250. But the 1959 bullpen heroes, Gerry Staley and Turk Lown, betrayed them, and their record in one-run games dropped from 35–15 to 22–23. Still, with two weeks to go, they were only two games out. That's when New York went on a 15-game winning streak to close out the season.

Black Wednesday

Sonny Siebert and the Cleveland Indians had blanked Boston 6–0 that afternoon, September 27, 1967, at Fenway Park. "We thought it was over," "Hawk" Harrelson, then with the Red Sox, remembered. "We all figured the White Sox had it wrapped up."

Entering Wednesday's twi-nighter between the White Sox and 10th-place A's in Kansas City, Minnesota led the wild AL race by a half-game over Chicago with Boston and Detroit one game out of first. If the Sox swept, they'd be a game ahead with three to go—at home against eighth-place Washington. And they'd won nine of their last 11.

"We really felt we would do it," said Pete Ward. "Then we were rained out Tuesday night so we had to double up Wednesday. And we walked out there onto the field, and the A's, when they were supposed to be taking batting practice, were running football plays in the outfield."

At least the Sox were taking this seriously. They had Gary Peters and Joe Horlen, their best, going against the last-place team. The A's went with two kids, Catfish Hunter and Chuck Dobson, with a gathering of 5,325 on hand.

In Game 1, Peters struck out 10 but was KO'd in the sixth. Dobson had a two-hit shutout entering the 9th and won 5–2. The A's scored four in the sixth inning of Game 2 and won 4–0. The Sox had seven hits all night.

Everyone knew it was over.

1964: Explaining how this team failed to win the pennant despite a 98–64 record is rather simple: The Yankees won 99. Also, the Sox had this little problem: They could not beat the Yankees during the season's first half. New York won the clubs' first 10 meetings—these were the scores of the games in Chicago: 1–0 (in 11 innings), 2–0, 3–0, 2–1 (in 17) and 6–5.

After the mid-July acquisition of ex-Yankee Bill "Moose" Skowron, things changed. The Sox split a four-game series in August at Yankee Stadium; a week later, in Chicago, the Sox swept the Yanks four straight to move into first place on August 20 by a half-game over Baltimore and 4½ over New York. The Yankees then lost two more to run their skid to six games. Then, led by a rejuvenated Roger Maris, they went 30–11 the rest of the way.

1967: Their problem was not that they couldn't hit New York. They couldn't hit anybody. Yet they won. Said Tommy McCraw: "We'd score five runs in a three-game series and sweep it. You know, 2–1, 2–1, 1–0, that's it, see ya later."

The pitching was sensational all season. The offense got a bit of a boost with the late-season additions of Ken Boyer and Rocky Colavito. The Sox would have been worthy champs because, in their final series with the other three contenders, they won three of four at Boston, split four at home with Detroit (including Joe Horlen's September 10 no-hitter) and swept three at home from Minnesota. They came into the final week having won nine of the last 11 and were in third place, one game out of first. Five games remained on the schedule: two at 10th-place Kansas City, then three at home vs. eighth-place Washington. They lost all five.

1972: This was the year Dick Allen performed all sorts of miracles, Carlos May got in the fun with walk-off homers, Wilbur Wood and Tom Bradley pitched brilliantly, and Terry Forster, the 20-year-old closer, blew away hitter after hitter. It was also the year Bill Melton, the AL home run champion who had hit 33 long ones each of the previous two years, was sidelined from June 24 till season's end with back injuries. Ed Spiezio, of Morris, Illinois, was brought in from the Padres' organization to play third. Though he came through with some big hits and won a huge game at Oakland in August with an extra-inning homer, he was no Melton. With "Beltin' Bill" out, the Oakland A's could breathe easier. They went on to win their second straight AL West title and the first of three straight World Series trophies. But Melton is confident it would have been the White Sox and not the A's in the World Series had he been available. "Without a doubt," he said, "we'd have made it happen."

31 Breaking In with Style

The 1964 pennant race was heating up. Baltimore was back on top, a game and a half ahead of New York and two up on the White Sox, who had just lost two in a row at Cleveland. The Sox needed a lift, something to get them going again as they prepared for a two-game set September 15–16 at Detroit.

Then came word that the Sox had landed pinch-hitter supreme Smoky Burgess from the Pittsburgh Pirates. "Old Smokehouse," out of rural North Carolina, was the kind of guy the Yankees always used to have and the White Sox didn't—someone who could come off the bench in the late innings and get the big hit.

He didn't look like a hitter, certainly: He stood just 5'8" and was listed, politely, at 187 pounds—which might have been his weight when he signed his first pro contract with the Cubs back in the '40s. By now, he had zoomed up past the 220 mark, which, with his height, created some spectacle. But no one laughed when Smoky swung a bat—other than authors Brendan C. Boyd and Fred C. Harris:

"The sight of him standing in the batter's box, his voluminous *avoirdupois* impinging on a full 45 percent of the natural strike zone, his stubby arms flailing out in that curiously hitched and compacted swing that made him look for all the world like a spastic rhinoceros beating a rug…is one that those who have been gifted to witness it are not likely to forget."

In successive seasons, starting in 1952, he had hit .292, .296, .368 and .301. From 1959 through 1962, his batting averages were .297, .294, .303 and .328. As recently as 1962, he had posted a .500 slugging percentage. Now, at 37, he still had several big hits left in his bat.

Manager Al Lopez put him right to work in Detroit on the night of September 15. The Sox trailed the Tigers and right-hander Dave Wickersham 2–1 in the top of the eighth when Lopez sent up Burgess, hitting for Joe Horlen, to lead off the inning. First, Smoky drilled a liner into the right-field corner, just foul. Then he swung again and the ball went higher and deeper this time, and well off the right-field line, landing way up in the upper deck. The game was tied.

The contest moved to the 10th. J.C. Martin led with a single, took second on Hoyt Wilhelm's sacrifice and third on Bill Freehan's passed ball. Jim Landis was batting, but Lopez worried about Jim's penchant for striking out. So he called on 22-year-old Marv Staehle, former baseball and basketball star at Oak Park–River Forest High School in Chicago's near west suburbs and just up that day from Indianapolis. Staehle (pronounced STAY-lee) had grown up in south Oak Park as a big Sox fan and even bigger Nellie Fox fan. This definitely was a dream come true. But it almost became a nightmare.

Staehle, inheriting Landis' 0-1 count, took a ball to even the count at 1-1. Then he asked for time to visit with third-base coach Tony Cuccinello. "I asked him, 'Was the squeeze on?' He said, 'Yeah, but it's too late now.'" So Staehle went back to the plate.

"I got a pitch on the outer half, at the knee, and I poked it to left for a base hit." Martin scored the go-ahead run, Wilhelm stopped Detroit in the bottom half, and the Sox—with aid from welcome additions Burgess and Staehle—were back in second place, one game behind the Orioles.

"The nice thing about it," Staehle remembered, "was that when I got back to the dugout, Joe Horlen was waiting on the top step. He shook my hand and said, 'Where the hell have you been all year?' Made me feel pretty good." Five days later, at Comiskey Park, Staehle again drove in the winning run with a pinch RBI single to left to beat Washington 4–3. The Sox dropped the next game—in Los Angeles, 1–0—then won the remaining nine dates on the schedule.

They finished one game out.

32 Up Went the White Flag

Still controversial these many years later, a discussion of the so-called "White Flag Trade" of July 30, 1997, can bring a good helping of vitriol into the conversation.

A review is necessary.

The White Sox had signed Mr. Warmth, slugger Albert Belle, away from AL Central champ Cleveland during the off-season for a then-gigantic five-year, $55 million contract. But during spring training, third baseman Robin Ventura ripped up his ankle on a play at the plate and was to be lost to the club until mid-August, doctors estimated. Ventura was coming off a 1996 season in which he had batted .287 with 34 homers and 105 RBIs. The hope was that the Sox could just hang close to .500 and to Cleveland, and that perhaps Robin could get back sooner than expected. The season might not yet be a lost one.

And that's what happened. On July 30, the Sox were 52–53, Ventura had rehabbed like a madman and had returned the previous Thursday to drive in the winning run against Texas. And despite their mediocre record, the Sox were just 3½ games back of the Indians, who were just completing a 4–10 homestand.

So did the Sox pull off a deal at the July 31 trading deadline to strengthen their bullpen or their catching? No, GM Ron Schueler and owner Jerry Reinsdorf decided that four losses in the last six games—all at home—proved the Sox weren't good enough to catch Cleveland—even though the teams still had seven meetings remaining in September and Ventura would be in the lineup for each.

Said Reinsdorf, "Anybody who thinks this White Sox team can catch Cleveland is crazy."

And with that, Schueler, who had already sent DH Harold Baines (hitting .305 and on pace for 20 homers and 84 RBIs) to Baltimore for a Double-A middle infielder of no consequence, put together a nine-player head-scratcher with the Giants. To the Bay went Wilson Alvarez, the Sox's best starting pitcher; another free-agent-to-be, Roberto Hernandez, their top reliever; and swing man Danny Darwin. In return the Sox received Keith Foulke, who was to become one of the game's best relievers; Bobby Howry, another reliever who enjoyed big-league success; shortstop prospect Mike Caruso, who played two seasons in Chicago but seldom showed why; pitching prospect Lorenzo Barcelo, who soon developed arm trouble; and two others (pitcher Ken Vining and outfielder Brian Manning) who never made it.

Ventura's reaction came quickly and directly. "I didn't know the season ended the last week in July."

There was this from Akron columnist Terry Pluto: "Why would you spend $55 million on Albert Belle and then give up six months later? This [the Tribe] is no juggernaut here. They've underachieved all year."

Elias Sports Bureau's John Lambombardo was asked how many times a team had come back from 3½ back on July 31 to win. "That would be a major research project. I mean, it's probably happened so many times. I couldn't give you a number. When I first heard that...I thought, 'Are we talking Cubs here or White Sox?' The Cubs are in last place, so they might want to do something like that. But you'd think the White Sox would be saying, 'We just got Robin back: Let's add to that.'"

In the end, the Sox lost five of those seven September matchups with Cleveland and finished 80–81, six games behind the 86–75 Indians, who led Game 7 of the World Series 2–0 before falling in extra innings to the Florida Marlins. Alvarez and Hernandez helped the Giants win a division title, then fled via free agency to Tampa Bay.

The Reinsdorf-Schueler camp in later years would boast that the "White Flag" trade won the Sox a division title in 2000. Only Foulke and Howry were regulars on that club, so to place such value on the 1997 trade takes away from the contributions of the likes of Magglio Ordonez, Paul Konerko, Carlos Lee, Ray Durham, Chris Singleton, and Jose Valentin (Caruso's badly needed replacement)—plus the MVP-type season enjoyed by Frank Thomas.

There is this, also, to consider: Maybe the Sox would've been much better than 52–53 that July 30 had someone other than Terry Bevington—the Reinsdorf-Schueler choice—been managing the ballclub.

33 Those '30s Weren't *That* Bad

The Great Depression was a difficult time for just about everyone, and, in the earlier years of the financial crisis, it was especially depressing for White Sox fans.

The decade of the 1930s began with the White Sox finishing seventh (of eight teams) with a 62–92 record.

And then it got worse.

They were 56–97 in 1931, shortstop Luke Appling's rookie season, and finished last. They bolted from the cellar in 1932 and leaped to seventh, but their record of 49–102 was rather embarrassing. After the 1932 season, owner J. Lou Comiskey—son of "the Old Roman"—met with Connie Mack, who apparently was intent upon making life miserable for A's fans by again breaking up his ballclub and getting cash, lots of it, in return—just as he had in 1914–15. Here was the deal: outfielders Al Simmons and Mule Haas and third baseman Jimmy Dykes to the Sox for $150,000. Sox fans took notice: The Comiskeys were spending money, and this trio was worth it.

Simmons and Dykes were voted in as American League starters in the first All-Star Game, played as part of the Century of Progress World's Fair in Chicago. Not even Simmons' nice season (.331 with 14 homers and 119 RBIs) could prevent a sixth-place finish and 67–83 record. And in 1934, despite big years by Simmons (.344, 18, 104) and the slow-moving rookie first baseman Zeke Bonura (.302, 27, 110), Chicago fell back to last place at 53–99.

Things began getting more interesting in 1935, when the Sox moved up to fifth place and a 74–78 record. Again, Bonura was a top contributor (.295, 21, 92), but Dykes was frustrated by Zeke's problems with signs. He recalled that one game got him so flustered that he yelled out, "Bunt, you meathead! Bunt! Bunt! B-U-N-T." That didn't work, either.

Bonura was dealt to Washington in 1938, but Dykes didn't bother to change the signs because, he claimed, Bonura couldn't remember them anyway. But he did, in a way. Zeke made it to third base in a Sox-Senators game, and he saw Dykes in the dugout swatting at a mosquito. "Swat means a steal," Bonura suddenly remembered. He took off for home, kicked the ball away from the catcher and scored. Said Zeke afterward, "I saw Dykes give the sign to steal, but I forgot I wasn't on his team anymore."

Bonura still was on Dykes' team in 1936, though, when the Sox (81–70, third place) finally finished better than .500 for the first time since 1926. On a club that hit .292 as a team, the big guns were Appling, who drove in 128 runs and hit .388 to win his first batting championship; Bonura, who batted .330 and collected 138 RBIs; left fielder Rip Radcliff (.335, 120 runs scored and 82 RBIs) and rookie center fielder Mike Kreevich (.307 with 99 runs scored). Vern Kennedy won 21 games (he lost nine) to lead the pitching staff, and Sugar Cain (14), John Whitehead (13), and Ted Lyons (10) all won in double figures.

It got better in 1937, when the White Sox, with their 86–68 record, finished a solid third with an offense powered by Bonura (.345, 19 homers, 100 RBIs), Appling (.317), and this high-octane outfield: Rip Radcliff (.325, 38 doubles, 10 triples), Mike Kreevich (.302, 29 doubles, 16 triples, 12 homers), and right fielder Dixie Walker (.302, 28 doubles, 16 triples, 95 RBIs). Top performers on an improved pitching staff were Monty Stratton (15–5, 2.40), Kennedy (14–13), Thornton Lee (12–10), Lyons (12–7), and Whitehead (11–8). And for the first time, Dykes generally used one pitcher, Clint Brown, to finish games and keep the opponent from scoring late. Brown was 7–7 with a 3.42 ERA in 100 innings and posted a league-best total of 18 saves.

In fairness, the Sox's 1938 season (65–83) shouldn't be counted: Appling broke his ankle in spring training and played in only 81 games; Bonura, holding out, was shipped out—to Washington for first baseman Joe Kuhel; Dixie Walker went to the Tigers in a winter deal; and second baseman Jackie Hayes and pitchers Stratton (15–9), Brown, and Bill Dietrich all went down with assorted ailments during the summer.

People began worrying about the 1939 season in November 1938, when word came from Texas that Stratton, just 26, had shot and wounded himself in his leg and would need an amputation. This Chicago club, however, was strong enough (89–65) to overcome the tragedy. Thornton Lee and Johnny Rigney each won 15, Ted Lyons went 14–6, and Jack Knott 11–6. Clint Brown, healthy again, appeared in 61 games and saved 18. Joe Kuhel hit .300 and drilled 15 homers, Mike Kreevich batted .323 with 85 runs scored and 23 steals, and Gee Walker—Dixie's replacement in the outfield—batted .291 with 111 RBIs.

What had started out as a decade of defeat for the White Sox ended with unanticipated success—the best kind.

34 A Homestand to Remember

Al Lopez admitted he had been a bit worried.

His 1961 White Sox were wallowing in the muck of last place, trailing even the new expansion team, Washington.

"We were in last place and we were playing at Baltimore," Al remembered. "I figured we were in trouble: 'If we lose three in a row, we'll really be in bad shape.' So I called a meeting. I had kind of a talk with the fellows. I went around asking, 'Is

Minoso was a big part of the historic 1961 homestand.

everyone all right. Everyone healthy?' 'Yeah.' 'Well, it's early. Let's get going. This is a much better club.' I wanted to pump them up, make them believe they were better than what we were showing—which they were. And then we went out and got shellacked real bad."

Frank Baumann, the 1960 ERA champion, was tagged for 10 hits and eight runs in Game 1 of a Sunday doubleheader, and the Sox got three hits and committed three errors and lost 8–2.

"So I was burned up," Lopez recalled. "I came back into the clubhouse and I went through there and said, 'Fellas, I want to apologize. I thought I knew something about baseball. I thought that this was a good club. But I can tell you the way you played today that this is not a good club. This is a horseshit club.' And I just kept on walking. Nobody said a word. After that, we went on a streak and got back into contention."

The streak was 19 victories in 20 games and included a homestand during which the home team won 15 of 16 games. The surge began with Billy Pierce's 7–1 triumph in Baltimore over Steve Barber in Game 2 of the twin bill. Besides Pierce, the Game 2 hero was Roy Sievers, the 34-year-old slugging first baseman who was 4-for-5 and drove in three runs. Next night, Sievers and Al Smith each had three hits—including two home runs by Sievers—as the Sox held on to win 9–8.

Now it was back home to Chicago and five games with the expansion Los Angeles Angels. The Sox swept the Tuesday, June 13, twi-nighter, Cal McLish outdueling Ryne Duren 2–1 in the opener, and 24-year-old Juan Pizarro striking out 10 in 7⅔ innings and winning his second Sox start 10–2. Another twi-nighter was set for Wednesday, and Ray Herbert—acquired in the big deal June 10 with Kansas City—stopped the Angels 4–1 in the first game. In Game 2, the Sox hit L.A. with a 7-spot in the first inning and held on to win 9–8. The series' fifth and final game was Thursday afternoon, when ex-Yankee Eli Grba took a 2–0 lead into the eighth before the Sox scored three, the key hit a bases-loaded single to center by Al Pilarcik, to win 3–2.

With the Sox streak at seven, next to try their luck were the Minnesota Twins, the former Washington Senators. Lefty Danny McDevitt walked three and hit two batters and was gone after one inning. In came Pedro Ramos, who allowed just four hits to get the 6–1 win.

A new streak began Saturday, when Pizarro beat the Twins 5–1 with offensive support from newly acquired third baseman Andy Carey, who had three hits and three RBIs. In Sunday's first game,

Sievers' Biggest Night

The White Sox were leading Cleveland 4–3 going into the last of the fourth inning in Game 1 of the June 21, 1961, twi-night doubleheader at Comiskey Park.

Here's what happened:

Andy Carey singled and took third on Sherm Lollar's hit to right. Don Larsen, on in relief of starter Frank Baumann, reached on an error, Carey scoring. Luis Aparicio reached on another error, filling the bases. Nellie Fox singled, Lollar scoring, Larsen reaching third, and Aparicio second. Jim Landis hit into a force at second, Larsen scoring, Aparicio taking third. Minnie Minoso singled, scoring Aparicio, Landis stopping at second. At this point, Indians manager Jimmy Dykes, the old South Side favorite, brought in lefty Johnny Antonelli to replace Tribe starter Gary Bell. Antonelli, the former Giants hero, hit Al Smith with a pitch to fill the bases. Sox manager Al Lopez here sent up Roy Sievers—scheduled to sit out Game 1—to bat for rookie J.C. Martin, and Sievers drove a grand slam off the foul pole in left, 352 feet away, and it was 12–3.

Two innings later, Minoso walked, Smith singled, and Sievers—again facing Antonelli—crushed another home run, this one into the left-field upper deck, and now it was 15–3. The seven RBIs in one game were a career high for Sievers, who added another home run in the nightcap.

Twins rookie Bert Cueto led 3–1 in the ninth before some strange things occurred. With Carey on first and one out, pinch-hitter Billy Goodman, of all people, hit a home run to tie the game at 3–3. And then, after Luis Aparicio flied to right, for the second out, Nellie Fox—again, of all people—hit a home run too, and the Sox had won 4–3. Then Smith homered and Carey added two doubles and two RBIs as the Sox built a 9–2 lead and won the second game 10–7.

The Cleveland Indians, coming to town in second place—a game behind first-place Detroit and a half-game ahead of the Yankees—started Jim "Mudcat" Grant in Tuesday night's series opener. Grant entered with a 7–0 record and a 2.87 ERA, but the Sox made short work of him—Fox and Smith singled in runs and rookie J.C. Martin, playing first base to give Sievers a little time off, belted the ball into the right-field seats to cap a five-run first that enabled Chicago to win 5–3.

The next evening, 45,125 fans (37,558 paid, 7,567 free guests) saw the climax of the homestand. In Game 1 of a twi-nighter, the Sox led 4–3 in the fourth—and then came the bombardment. When the inning was over, the Sox led 12–3, thanks in part to Roy Sievers' pinch grand slam off Johnny Antonelli (see sidebar). After this 15–3 win, the Sox mistreated Cleveland pitchers Wynn Hawkins and Barry Latman and won 11–1 as Juan Pizarro won his third straight start. Al Smith hit a pair of two-run homers and Sievers added a solo home run.

A weekend series with Washington remained on the homestand, and though the Sox won Friday night 4–3 behind Herbert's pitching, Sievers injured a shoulder diving for a grounder and had to leave the game. He did not play the rest of the series. Minoso and Smith homers led a 17-hit attack in Saturday's 12–6 romp, and in Sunday's first game, Pierce went the distance and struck out 10 to beat old friend Dick Donovan 7–3. Martin homered and Floyd Robinson went 4-for-4 in Early Wynn's 6–3 Game 2 victory.

The White Sox had just wrapped up a 15–1 homestand, had won 17 of 18, and now headed for a Tuesday twi-nighter in Detroit, where the first-place Tigers and a crowd of 57,271 awaited them.

Quick note: The Sox won both games, 6–5 and then 11–1, Pizarro winning again by that score and going 3-for-4 with the bat. The 19-of-20 stretch was the high point of the 1961 White Sox, who finished fourth, 23 games out of first.

35 Roadkill No More

Just to give you an idea:

In 1950, the White Sox were 25–52 on the road, owning a winning record only in St. Louis, where they were 6–5 against the dreadful Browns. They were 4–7 at Philadelphia, New York, and Washington, 3–8 at Cleveland, and 2–9 at Boston and Detroit.

The 1951 season—and a new manager in Paul Richards—changed everything. For several reasons (mainly, better players), the White Sox were quite a bit more competitive on the road (42–35) in 1951 than they had been in 1950. The remarkable change began in mid-May, when the Sox left Chicago on their first Eastern trip—this time with a 12–9 record and in third place, just 2½ games out of first.

The initial stop was Boston on Tuesday, May 15. Ted Williams hit his 300th career home run in the fourth for a 5–3 Red Sox lead, but in the ninth, Nellie Fox doubled home a run to put Chicago's Sox on top 7–6. At the start of the Red Sox half, Richards moved right-handed reliever Harry Dorish to third base and brought in lefty Billy Pierce to face Williams—who popped out. Dorish went

...And Don't Forget 2000

The 2000 White Sox, surprise AL Central champs, put together a terrific little run to all but clinch the division title in June. Chicago was two games ahead of perennial Central champ Cleveland, which is where the Sox were headed that June 12. Before successive crowds of 43,200-plus, the Sox swept the Tribe three straight, but not without some frightening moments.

The Sox built an 8–3 lead for Cal Eldred in the opener, but it was 8–7 in the ninth, and the bases were loaded with one out. Keith Foulke got Sandy Alomar Jr. to rap into a 6–4–3 double play to end the thrills—for one night.

The Indians tied Tuesday night's contest 3–3 on Brook Fordyce's passed ball in the eighth, but Ray Durham's 11th home run gave the Sox a 4–3 lead in the 10th. Bobby Howry got the save when, again with two on and one out, Russell Branyan hit into a 4-6-3 twin killing. In the finale, the Sox led 10–4 after two and coasted to an 11–4 win as reserves Jeff Abbott and Tony Graffanino each had three hits and combined for five RBIs. The Tribe was five games back.

It was on to Yankee Stadium, where the 2000 White Sox this weekend would avenge some of the horrible defeats and general evil treatment the Yankees had inflicted upon the Sox and their fans for too many years.

Magglio Ordonez homered and Paul Konerko delivered a two-run double as the Sox rolled 12–3 Thursday night. Friday night, before 41,910, James Baldwin (10–1) outdueled David Cone 3–1. The streak was at five.

The Sox led 8–0 in the third inning on Saturday and then held off the Yankees 10–9 as 54,053 looked on. Bernie Williams' two homers and seven RBIs weren't quite enough. On Sunday, 52,856 saw the upstarts from Chicago complete the sweep of the world champs by scoring nine runs in the first, three in the second, and four in the fifth to go up 16–0. Jose Valentin capped the huge first wth a grand slam off "El Duque," starter Orlando Hernandez. Konerko and Carlos Lee each had three hits in the 17–4 romp.

The White Sox had gone 7–0 on the trip, they led Cleveland by 7½ games and 43,062 turned out the next night at The Cell to give the runaway AL Central leaders a thoroughly appropriate standing ovation.

back to the mound and was tagged with the tying run, but in the 11th, Eddie Stewart walked and Fox hit his *first* career homer for a 9–7 lead. That was the final score.

Before the next day's 9–5 Chicago triumph, keyed by the pitching of ex-Red Sox Joe Dobson and ex-Red Sox Al Zarilla's two-run double in a five-run first, White Sox GM Frank Lane announced the purchase of former AL All-Star third baseman Bob Dillinger from Pittsburgh. The day before he had announced the trade of left-hander Bob Cain to Detroit for right-hander Saul Rogovin, who would go on to lead the league in earned-run average.

Next stop was New York, where rain reduced the series to a Friday night game, which Pierce and the Sox won 7–4 with a solo homer by Fox and Stewart's grand slam in the eighth. Then came three straight victories in Washington by scores of 5–4, 5–3 and 9–8, Fox breaking a 6–6 tie with a two-run inside-the-park home run in the third meeting. Only one game was played in Philadelphia, the Sox's Randy Gumpert going nine to win it 5–2 with thanks to Eddie Robinson, who cracked a double and a homer.

The streak was at seven, but the Sox, as their train headed for Cleveland, knew the real test was right ahead of them. The Indians had the pitching to shut down any offense and the longball threats to worry any pitcher. So what happened? Pierce beat Bob Lemon 6–4 Friday night, Ken Holcombe blanked the Tribe 6–0 Saturday, and, on Sunday, Dobson topped Early Wynn 5–2 and Zarilla homered, doubled, and singled for four RBIs in Game 2 to help Howie Judson win 6–4. Also, Minnie Minoso had hit .412 (7-for-17) in his first big series against his former teammates.

These 11 straight triumphs on the road left the Sox 23–9 and in second place, one game behind the Yankees. They had chased the Korean War off the front page. While winning three more from the Browns at home, they passed the Yankees and stretched the overall winning streak to 14 before the A's ended it on June 2.

The Sox went on to finish fourth in an eight-team league, but a new era had begun. As it turned out, 1951 was the first of 17 straight winning seasons for the White Sox.

36 Would the Hawk Walk?

This book's author, for one, would be disappointed if Ken "Hawk" Harrelson, the White Sox TV play-by-play man from 1982 through 1985 and then again from 1990 to the present, were to leave the job after next season, which would be his 30th year with the White Sox.

Here's why: He's the only sportscaster in town who talks about "the glory days"—the 1960s.

Many years ago, a trio of would-be sportscasters from Chicago's west suburbs would go to old Comiskey Park, sit in the first row of the left-field upper deck (in 1968 through 1970, they'd have plenty of room), and do play-by-play and tape it. Then, either on the way home or later, they'd critique their work. Two of them thought the introduction of the Cleveland Indians' defensive alignment that August night in 1969 might have been unnecessarily harsh.

It went something like this:

"The Indians have taken the field....In the outfield they'll have rookie Frank Baker in left..."

One of our crew shouted at Frank Baker below us, "Baker! That's what you'll be in two years!"

After the laughter subsided, it was back to the defense. "Cardenal in center and 'the Hawk,' Ken Harrelson in right... Klimchock at third, Eddie Leon at short, Vern Fuller at second, and Tony Horton—he's the only major leaguer on the team—he'll be at first....Duke Sims is the catcher, and on the mound..."

With Hawk at the Helm

A list of the key deals and moves made by Ken "Hawk" Harrelson in his one and only year as White Sox GM:

November 25, 1985: Traded infielder Scott Fletcher, pitcher Edwin Correa, and ML infielder Jose Mota to Texas for pitcher Dave Schmidt and infielder Wayne Tolleson.

December 10, 1985: Selected outfielder-infielder Bobby Bonilla from the Pittsburgh organization in the minor-league draft.

December 12, 1985: Traded pitcher Britt Burns, ML infielder Mike Soper, and ML outfielder Glen Braxton to New York (A) for catcher Ron Hassey and pitcher Joe Cowley.

February 13, 1986: Traded catcher Ron Hassey and three minor leaguers to New York (A) for pitcher Neil Allen, catcher Scott Bradley, and ML outfielder Glen Braxton.

June 2, 1986: Selected left-handed pitcher Grady Hall of Northwestern as club's No. 1 pick in amateur draft. Also drafted lefty Scott Radinsky in third round.

June 5, 1986: Fired assistant GM Dave Dombrowski.

June 20, 1986: Fired manager Tony La Russa and replaced him with Jim Fregosi.

June 26, 1986: Traded catcher Scott Bradley to Seattle for outfielder Ivan Calderon.

June 29, 1986: Traded pitcher Tom Seaver to Boston for infielder-outfielder Steve Lyons.

July 23, 1986: Traded outfielder-infielder Bobby Bonilla to Pittsburgh for pitcher Jose DeLeon.

July 29, 1986: Traded outfielder Ron Kittle, catcher Joel Skinner, and infielder Wayne Tolleson to New York (A) for ML infielder Carlos Martinez and catchers Ron Hassey and Bill Lindsey.

August 12, 1986: Signed pitcher Steve Carlton as free agent.

August 14, 1986: Signed outfielder George Foster as a free agent.

September 26, 1986: Resigned as GM.

NOTE: (ML) signifies minor-league player.

It's difficult to believe, but the young "broadcaster" was unwilling to bestow upon Harrelson major-league status. He would tell you today that Hawk has been a far better broadcaster than he was a ballplayer, and it's likely Harrelson would agree, but he did have that one big year for Boston in 1968 (.275, 35 homers, 109 RBIs). That helped his celebrity to grow considerably, as did the *Sports Illustrated* cover story with the photos of the "mod" slugger in Nehru jackets and turtlenecks. He was also well known for his switch to pro golf and that he was good enough to qualify for the 1972 British Open.

His baseball career ended, for all intents and purposes, when he broke his leg sliding into second base in a 1970 exhibition game. He tried pro golf until 1975, when the Red Sox hired him as part of their broadcast team. He remained there until 1982, when he changed to the White Sox. He and Don Drysdale did the telecasts through the 1985 season, after which it was announced that Roland Hemond was out as Sox GM and the Hawk was in.

Harrelson departed after one rather unfortunate season and returned to broadcasting—with the Yankees. He returned to the South Side as the TV voice for 1990 and has remained in that spot ever since, providing great nicknames (among them "the Big Hurt," "Black Jack," "the Panther," "One Dog," and "El Caballo" for, respectively, Frank Thomas, Jack McDowell, Sammy Sosa, Lance Johnson, and Carlos Lee) and much more.

From his opening "So sit back, relax, and strap it down," to "When that ball comes down this game will be...*ovah!*" very few baseball telecasts are anything like one by the Hawk. His "homer" style is the one so many Chicagoans grew up with when Harry Caray, Jack Brickhouse, Lloyd Pettit, and others owned the airwaves. His down-home touches, as well as his periods of seething silence, make him unique.

For instance:

A Sox pitcher strikes out the side with high heat: "Gas! Mercy! Grab some bench!"

A different way to deliver a stat: "Frank is 5-for-16 against him, and all but three of those hits have left the premises."

Fearing that a Bobby Thigpen or a Bobby Jenks is about to walk the first batter in the ninth: "C'mon, Bobby—no walks." And then silence from Hawk as the batter heads for first with that "dreaded leadoff walk."

You can't help but smile when he says, "Conor [Gillaspie] has one of the five quickest left-hand bats in the American League," or "I haven't seen the National League, but Tank [Dayan Viciedo] has one of the three liveliest bats to come into our league in years."

The "homerism" has landed him in trouble, however, in a few cases, one of them in 2012 in Cleveland, when plate umpire Mark Wegner tossed Sox rookie Jose Quintana for throwing behind a hittter. Hawk: "That is absolutely brutal! That is totally absurd! Send him back to school and teach him what this game is all about! … Here's an umpire in the American League who knows nothing about the game of baseball!" Hawk got a phone call and a tongue-lashing the next day from Commissioner Bud Selig. And yet you get the feeling that even Selig might have been smiling on the other end.

37 Around the World —with Giants

One could be cynical and point out that had "the Old Roman," Charles A. Comiskey, not put together his grandiose world tour with John McGraw's New York Giants in the winter of 1913–14, there would have been money aplenty in the bank to buy young Babe Ruth from the Triple-A Baltimore Orioles when they gave the White Sox first crack at "The Babe" the following summer.

But why spoil the legend, the concept of Comiskey doing something to make baseball not just the nation's game, but the world's game as well? That's how he sold it to McGraw, who finally accepted the idea after his Giants lost the 1913 World Series to the Philadelphia A's.

The players who made the journey were not all Giants and White Sox. A half dozen, perhaps, from each of those clubs were joined by other major leaguers: The White Sox, for example, wound up with Tris Speaker of the Boston Red Sox and Sam Crawford of the Detroit Tigers.

The grand tour lasted almost five months, covered five continents and an estimated 38,000 miles, and attracted such spectators as King George of England, a khedive (ruler) of Egypt and, in Ceylon (now Sri Lanka), the billionaire tea magnate Sir Thomas Lipton. The trip also provided side visits to the Pyramids and the Sphinx and, in Rome, an audience with Pope Pius X.

The actual itinerary called for departure from Vancouver, British Columbia, on November 19, after a string of post–World Series exhibitions across the country. First stop would be Yokohama, Japan, where the teams were to play each other as well as a Japanese all-star team. After all, baseball had been played in that country for 60 years. Then it was on to Shanghai, Hong Kong, Manila, and Australia, where the travelers would spend nine welcome days—in cities like Brisbane, Sydney, Melbourne, and Adelaide. White Sox rookie pitcher Red Faber, borrowed by the Giants for the trip, later told his son "that his favorite place was Australia. They could speak English there."

Some could do so in Ceylon, where Lipton, himself a sportsman and renowned yachtist, held forth. Each guest received a gift of 10 pounds of boxed tea. Next stop was Egypt (Cairo and Alexandria), where games were played at the base of the Pyramids. Italy was next, featuring Naples, Rome, Florence, and Milan. Then on to the French Riviera—Monte Carlo, Nice, and Marseilles—before three days in Paris. A visit to Berlin would be followed by one to Amsterdam, and then the party headed to London.

The tour ended with a game played before 30,000 fans, including King George V, at the Chelsea Football Grounds in London. The 11-inning game—won by the White Sox, 5–4—caused the king to ask some polite questions about baseball. But the British press was less than impressed. Baseball was dismissed as a game of "glorified rounders," and, despite the spirited level of play, "it was all Greek to the crowd," one reporter wrote.

Dublin and Queenstown were the final stops, the travelers sailing to New York in early March 1914 aboard the *Lusitania*, which, 14 months later, was sunk by a German U-boat, an action that helped put the U.S. on the road to war.

A final note: Depending on whose report you wish to believe, Red Faber, the Sox pitcher loaned to McGraw for the tour, either impressed or did not impress the Giants' manager. One report said McGraw didn't think much of him; another claimed McGraw made four or five different offers for him. In any event, when the Sox beat the Giants four games to two in the 1917 World Series, Faber won three games for Chicago.

38 Portrait of the Artist as a Young Outfielder

They were heady days for Brian McCall, those final days of the 1962 baseball season. Here he was, just 19, getting to travel with the White Sox for the final week and a half after spending the year with three minor-league clubs, the latest being Class B Tri-Cities, where he had batted .303.

The left-handed-hitting outfielder from southern California had been to bat twice thus far, each time as a pinch-hitter. He had failed his first two tries but then, on Saturday, September 29, he batted for Luis Aparicio and singled to right off the Yankees' Tex Clevenger.

Now, on the final day of the regular season, McCall had checked the lineup card and learned that manager Al Lopez not only had him starting in center, he was going to bat leadoff against 14-game winner Bill Stafford, getting his final World Series tuneup. First time up, Brian grounded out to first baseman Bill Skowron, but the next time, with pitcher Ray Herbert on first, he smoked a Stafford fastball into the Yankee Stadium seats in right for a homer that put Herbert a run ahead in his quest for his 20th victory.

In the seventh, McCall, now facing 23-game winner Ralph Terry, hit a line drive into the right-field lower deck and Chicago led 7–4. The Sox went on to win 8–4, and people started asking about Brian McCall. The next year, at Double-A Lynchburg, he hit .253 with just seven homers and was 0-for-7 with the Sox in September. He never played in the major leagues thereafter. He kicked around the minors for three more seasons but, by the third, his arm was hurting so badly he retired—at age 23.

Now he had to choose another career.

"My body was sore, and baseball wasn't fun any longer," he told an interviewer. "I dreamed the future, trying to see myself in different roles, and the only one that made sense to me was 'artist.' I sent a portfolio of drawings to California College of Arts and Crafts. Got accepted and drove to Oakland to begin a new life and career.

"I could always draw. If I needed an 'A' in a class, the surest way was to draw a great report cover. Embellishment works. I don't think there's a great connection with baseball and art. I'm very goal-oriented. When I start a drawing, I see it as a goal just like beating a pitcher who is trying to fool you with a curveball. The best part of being an artist is I can work into my 90s, and I don't have to listen to a manager."

In 1986, he and his wife bought, as their new house, an old church in her hometown of Greensburg, Pennsylvania, and the downstairs level serves as Brian's studio. He does some sketching and has worked mostly as an illustrator and animator. Lately he has worked in polystyrene foam, which allows him to do more sculpture work. His three-dimensional store signs dot the area. A 40-pound papier mache train he created appears in King Street Blues in Alexandria, Virginia, replacing the train McCall made for the restaurant years ago. Another of his works, a 110-foot historical mural, can be viewed at the Hyatt Regency in Baltimore's Inner Harbor.

But he never goes to watch the Orioles—or any teams, for that matter—and has never sketched at a sporting event.

"I basically hate professional sports," McCall said. "It opens doors when I need to go through—great party conversation—but I do not hold professional athletes in very high regard. The fact they have mastered a skill is laudable, and I admit to a little jealousy over all the money they are paid to hit or throw a good curveball. But, as people, they are generally arrogant, stilted, uncouth young men who have a very high opinion of their place in the world, and it is too bad that society feeds that view. I guess the same could be said for actors or any individuals in the limelight. Fame itself, and our need for heroes, should be scrutinized. I just want some more worthwhile heroes."

There is something cool, though, about his baseball career that occasionally puts him in the limelight: He was the first teenager to hit two home runs in one game. There are only two others: Bryce Harper and Ken Griffey Jr.

39 The Mastery of Larry Himes

All White Sox fans should take a few moments at least once every few months and thank the baseball gods for allowing Larry Himes to spend four years as the team's general manager.

Himes received a blistering review from Jerry Reinsdorf when the Sox chairman fired him after the 1990 season for supposedly being difficult to get along with and not being capable of taking the Sox from Point B to Point C, which apparently meant "Championship." Reinsdorf conceded that Himes had been able to get the Sox from Point A (the "A" perhaps meant "Amusing," which is what the club was under "Hawk" Harrelson in 1986) to Point B. Maybe "B" was for "Better, much better," which is what the Sox were in 1990, when they finished 94–68 and runners-up to mighty Oakland in the AL West.

Overlooked was what Himes, a USC alum and onetime minor-league catcher from Riverside, California, had done for the South Side franchise since taking over for Harrelson in 1987. There were trades, some of which did not seem critical but turned out to be. Richard Dotson went to the Yankees for left-handed power possibility Dan Pasqua; Floyd Bannister went to Kansas City for four minor-league pitchers, two of whom (Melido Perez and Greg Hibbard) became key contributors; Jose DeLeon to the Cardinals for lefty Ricky Horton and a center-field prospect named Lance Johnson; minor-league outfielder Mark Davis to the Angels' system for reliever Roberto Hernandez; and Himes' very best, Harold Baines (and Fred Manrique) to Texas for Scottie Fletcher and two kids—19-year-old lefty Wilson Alvarez and 20-year-old outfielder Sammy Sosa.

The amazing thing Himes and top aide Al Goldis were able to do, though, was outwork and outproject everyone else for four straight years to come up with superb picks in the first round of the June amateur draft. The four taken by Himes and his staff were thoroughbreds, and all had marvelous careers. None was taken with the first, second, or third selection, either.

1987: Jack McDowell, Stanford pitcher, fifth player selected.

1988: Robin Ventura, Oklahoma State third baseman, 10th player selected.

1989: Frank Thomas, Auburn first baseman, seventh player selected.

1990: Alex Fernandez, Miami Dade South CC pitcher, fourth player selected.

That foursome helped form the backbone of the 1991 club that opened their new ballpark in style and the 1993 team that won a division title, as well as the 1994 team that was leading the division at the time of the players' strike.

Here's a quick look at Himes' Harvest:

McDowell overcame some early trouble (an arthritic hip kept him in the minors for all of 1989, when he made changes in his mechanics and was 5–6, 6.13 ERA at Triple-A Vancouver). Fit and ready to go in 1990, "Black Jack" went 14–9, tied Hibbard for most wins on the staff and started and won the final game at old Comiskey Park 2–1. He then ran off successive seasons of 17–10, 20–10 and 22–10, winning the Cy Young Award in 1993. He annoyed Reinsdorf and Himes' successor, Ron Schueler, by going to arbitration every year—and winning. So they traded him to the Yankees for two minor leaguers before the 1995 season.

Ventura, after just one year in the minors—at Double-A Birmingham, where his manager was former Sox Gold Glove outfielder Ken Berry—survived an early-season 0-for-41 slump in 1990 as if it were nothing. He developed a penchant for winning

Frank Thomas congratulates fellow Larry Himes draft pick Robin Ventura as Ventura crosses the plate for the winning run in a 1996 game.

Gold Gloves (six) and hitting grand slams (18, fifth all time). He still holds the NCAA record for longest hitting steak, 58 games, which was snapped by McDowell.

Other teams had doubts about Thomas, but Himes liked everything about him. After seeing how he was destroying Southern Association pitching in early 1990, fans began clamoring for him to be brought up to Chicago. Himes' plan was to give him a full season of Double-A ball, but he came up August 2 and held his own (.330 in 60 games).

117

Fernandez also came up August 2, 1990, and did well, although his real success came after a few seasons. In fact, he even spent a few weeks of the 1992 season at Vancouver, working on his craft. The next year he was 18–9 to help the Sox win the AL West title. Then came years of 11–7, 12–8, and 16–10 before he went to Florida via free agency and won 17 for the world-champion Marlins.

As for Himes, he took the Cubs' GM job in 1992 and almost immediately stole Sammy Sosa from the Sox for erstwhile slugger George Bell. Sammy took the Cubs to Point C—with "C" this time meaning "cork."

40 Home Run Derby in Detroit

This would have been unthinkable back in the day, back when Minnie Minoso would lead the White Sox with 15 home runs or when Jim Rivera would do so with 14.

But there it is, in black and white. The record for most home runs combined in a single game by both teams is 12, set by the Tigers and White Sox in 1995 and equaled in 2002—again by the same two clubs.

"I don't think that's a record to be cherished," Tigers manager Sparky Anderson said after the 1995 foolishness. "It was ridiculous. It's silly to give up runs like that. It looked silly after about the second inning."

The May 28, 1995, game was played in one of the great bandboxes in the game's history—Tiger Stadium in Detroit. It was, very much so, a place for struggling pitchers to avoid. And this day, balls were flying out of the place like they used to fly out of Los Angeles' Wrigley Field on the old "Home Run Derby" show.

The Sox failed to score in the first inning against David Wells, but rookie right-hander James Baldwin of Chicago was not as fortunate. Chad Curtis led off with a home run, Lou Whitaker walked, Alan Trammell singled, and Cecil Fielder crushed one 463 feet, and it was 4–0.

The visitors scored in the second before the Tigers started all over again, Curtis homered, Whitaker singled, and Fielder homered again. It was 7–1 and Baldwin was led to safety. But this was Tiger Stadium, and the wind was blowing out.

"It was the jet stream today," said Whitaker. "Or something out there was streaming. Actually, it was more like screaming."

Chicago scored three runs in the third without a homer, but rookie Ray Durham, Ron Karkovice, and Craig Grebeck went back-to-back-to-back in the fourth and it was 8–7 Detroit. When Frank Thomas blasted one to open the sixth, it was 10–10, but Kirk Gibson's second homer of the day made it 11–10 after six. Then it was time for Karkovice's second of the afternoon, and the game again was tied.

The Sox broke the 11–11 tie in their eighth without a home run. Rather, they scored on a fielder's choice and Durham's two-out double, which sent across John Kruk and Mike Devereaux. Now it was 14–11. Whitaker's shot in the home eighth ended the scoring. Detroit lost 14–12 but won the "derby" 7–5.

The July 2, 2002, game was nowhere near as competitive, although Detroit did take a 3–0 lead in the first inning against Todd Ritchie (4–10 going in) as Dmitri Young homered, Randall Simon—the enemy of racing sausages everywhere—drew a walk, and Robert Fick hit one out, his 11th. The hosts cut the lead to 3–2 in their half on homers by Kenny Lofton and Magglio Ordonez. Maggs, annoyed to be passed over for the All-Star team earlier that day, would be heard from again.

Jose Valentin's long one tied the contest at 3–3, and the Sox answered Detroit's single run in the third with a four-run fourth, highlighted by Durham's two-run double and a solo shot by Sandy Alomar Jr. Alomar connected his next at-bat, too, and it was 8–4 before Detroit's George Lombard hit one to make it 8–5 in the seventh. Then the Sox scored twice for a 10–5 lead through seven.

There was more fun in the home eighth. Jose Paniagua, who would wear a Sox uniform for less than a week in September 2003, allowed singles by Alomar, Royce Clayton, and Lofton to load the bases with no outs. Durham walked to force in a run, and after Thomas struck out, Ordonez sent Paniagua to the showers with a grand slam. The score was 15–5, and more runs were coming, but most fans were leaving. Detroit's final two homers came in the ninth off the bats of Wendell Magee and Damian Easley. Final score: 17–9. "Derby" score: 6–6.

41 The White Sox's "Moonlight" Graham

When "the Voice" tells Ray Kinsella to go to Chisholm, Minnesota, to find an old ballplayer in the wonderful movie *Field of Dreams*, he learns that the former player, "Moonlight" Graham, has been dead for years. He also learns he was actually Dr. Graham, a medical doctor known and beloved by just about everyone in town.

As the story unfolds, we learn that "Moonlight" Graham had been an outfielder in the minor leagues who was brought up to the New York Giants in 1922 for a September look-see. He played one inning, that in the season finale, as a defensive replacement but never had the opportunity to bat in the big leagues. The season ended and he decided to quit baseball and go to medical school.

He became a doctor and never regretted his decision, the ghostly Graham tells Ray, but he adds that he wishes he had had at least one at-bat in the majors.

The White Sox had a player with a similar story—minus the ghost. That was Bob Powell, Michigan State outfielder signed by the Sox to a $36,000 bonus in June 1955. As his 1956 Topps baseball card shows, he did appear in one game with the Sox in 1955, but had zero at-bats. He had entered as a runner for the portly pinch-hitting specialist Ron Northey one September night in Kansas City and was erased at second base on a double play.

That off-season, he completed work at Michigan State on his engineering degree and, having been a member of the ROTC program at East Lansing, he did six months of active duty in the Army in 1956. When he arrived at the Sox's spring-training camp in March 1957, he learned from new manager Al Lopez and pitching coach Ray Berres that they would like to have him try pitching.

"I didn't want to try pitching," Bob said decades later, from his Las Vegas home, "unless I found out I couldn't be the player they had envisioned when they signed me. I wanted to be convinced I couldn't make it as an outfielder."

He did break camp with the White Sox and again got into a game as a pinch-runner (April 20 at Comiskey Park) and this time scored. But out of the game he came. That was his last game in the big leagues. By late May, he was pitching and playing the outfield for the Sox's affiliate at Colorado Springs. He hit .307 with eight homers as an outfielder and, on the mound, was 6–5 with a 4.86 ERA.

During that summer at Colorado Springs, a local sportscaster introduced Powell to a superintendent from Robert E. McKee General Contractor, a firm doing construction at the new Air Force Academy campus nearby.

"He said, 'Bob, I can put you to work right now,'" Powell recalled.

The offer stuck in his mind. At season's end, he learned from farm director Glen C. Miller that the Sox's plans for 1958 were to send him out again, possibly to Indianapolis but more likely back to Colorado Springs. "I wasn't going down again," Powell remembered thinking. "I said to them, 'I don't have to play ball to make a living.' They didn't like that."

He got in touch with the McKee people, was hired immediately, and ended up working there for 35 years. He did field engineering work on the Air Force Academy chapel, the cadets' quarters, and some of the athletic buildings on campus.

Later he was the chief field engineer on the construction of the terminal buildings and underground parking garages at Los Angeles International Airport. Thanks to McKee, he was also a survey chief for an electrical and engineering firm at a Nevada nuclear test site.

As it turned out, Powell was right: He didn't need to play ball to make a living. But every once in a while, that old yearning to bat in the big leagues returns.

"I look back now, and, yes, I do wish that I'd gotten that chance," he said. "But I have a lot of memories, most of them good."

42 Songs of the Sox

The old 1960s rock standby "Na Na Hey Hey Kiss Him Goodbye" has been a staple at White Sox games since Nancy Faust helped make it a staple over an early July weekend in 1977. It has been and remains perfect for serenading luckless and perturbed departing pitchers on their slow, pitiful walk from the mound to the dugout.

It was perfect because the younger fans in the stands had sung the same song in the closing seconds of their schools' basketball games just a few years back.

But few there are who know the glorious lyrics of two other fine, fine White Sox songs. Or, if they did know them, would be willing enough (foolish enough?) to sing them out for all at the ballpark to hear.

To provide help, we present here the words to those two tunes. First is "White Sox Theme Song," written way back in 1962 by Marvin Frank of the W.B. Doner Co., the Sox's ad agency at the time. Okay Nancy!

The White Sox are playing a game today,
Come on and get out in the air;
You'll forget your troubles watching singles and doubles,
As the Sox hit the ball to everywhere;
And it's a wonderful way to get away from it all
When the umpire yells: 'Play Ball!'
There's plenty of action—the crowd is tense;
There goes a long one over the fence!
So go go go go—go, you White Sox!
Let's have another win today!
They're all game at the ballgame;
Come out and watch your White Sox play!"

Then, of course, there's the song that was first written, sung, and recorded back in 1959 and then was resurrected in the glory year of 2005. The title is "Let's Go! Go-Go White Sox!" and the song belongs to Captain Stubby and the Buccaneers. The ditty is still played during those occasional Sox rallies at The Cell—so when you hear the music, be not ashamed: Join in and sing. There's a good chance you've already made a fool of yourself in other ways, so why let a song stop you?

Without further ado, we bring you the classic lyrics of "Let's Go! Go-Go White Sox!":

"Let's Go! Go-Go White Sox!
"We're with you all the way;
"You're always in there fighting and you do your best;
"We're glad to have you out here in the Middle West.
"We're gonna root root root for the White Sox,
"And cheer you on to victory!
"When we're in the stands,
"You'll hear those rafters ring;
"All through the season you will hear us sing:
"Let's Go! Go-Go White Sox!
"Chicago's proud of you!"

Now you are totally prepared for your next trip to the ballpark on 35th Street.

43 Desecrating Fenway

There are no baseball fans anywhere who take their favorite team more seriously than those of the Boston Red Sox. These creatures come from all over New England and claim to be members of something called Red Sox Nation. They fancy themselves as "scholars" of the sport who know far more baseball than rubes from such out-of-the-way locales as Chicago or St. Louis. They wax poetic about beautiful, unique Fenway Park and become somewhat overbearing when discussing what a marvelous baseball town Boston continues to be.

Forgotten is that Boston used to be a two-team town like Chicago and that, apparently, it didn't have enough great baseball fans to keep the Braves from pulling up stakes in 1953. Or that while major league baseball has seen, in the last half-century, new ballparks built by the dozens, Fenway, despite all the moves to modernize, still reminds one of dear departed Tiger Stadium or old Comiskey Park—where, after so many, many years, a former colleague used to say, you "could not cover up the unmistakable odor of urine and a hint of decades-old vomit."

As for those "scholars," one wonders how much baseball they truly do know, because the game the Red Sox played, until quite fairly recently, was not real baseball but rather a team collecting right-handed sluggers trying to hit flyballs against and over the close-in "Green Monster" in left field (310 down the line).

All this is meant to be fun preparation for a brief description of Fenway Park' s "Dedication Day" on May 17, 1912. Rain had put quite a damper on the Red Sox's plans for the inaugural of the new Back Bay ballpark. The opener against New York had been rained out three straight days before Boston finally won 7–6 on April 20, as Tris Speaker singled in the winning run in the 11th before 24,000 fans. Now the official "Dedication Game," scheduled for May 16, had been rained out as well. Finally skies cleared, and the Pale Hose and Carmine Hose were ready to go. So was Boston's mayor, John "Honey Fitz" Fitzgerald, who threw out the ceremonial first ball. In years to come, "Honey Fitz" would enjoy bringing his grandsons—Joe, Robert, Ted, and John Fitzgerald Kennedy—to games at Fenway.

One sportswriter, T.H. Murnane of *The Sporting News*, anticipated that the formal dedication ceremonies would draw "25,000 or 30,000 red-blooded fans, from the finest baseball fan army in the country." Maybe that's where the "Red Sox Nation" concept began.

The crowd wasn't quite that big, but it was a great event nonetheless. The grandstands were draped in bunting, potted plants lined the walkways and a band played throughout the afternoon. Before the contest, Red Sox and White Sox players marched to the flagpole and raised Old Glory as the fans sang "The Star-Spangled Banner."

The Red Sox touched up Ed Walsh for two runs in the first inning but, from then on, "Big Ed" allowed only two more hits and a walk. The White Sox managed only one run off Larry Pape, however, so Boston took a 2–1 lead into the ninth. The festive crowd grew more so when Jack Fournier grounded out and Walt Kuhn struck out. The pitcher was due up for the Sox, and because it was Walsh (a .243 hitter in 1912), he batted for himself and singled to center. Then Morrie Rath doubled, Walsh advancing to third. The Red Sox decided to walk Harry Lord intentionally to fill the bases with still two outs and Boston up 2–1. Frank Lange, hitting in the spot earlier occupied by ejected Chicago player-manager Jimmy Callahan, took a pitch in the back, forcing Walsh to come home with the tying run.

Then Ping Bodie rapped a grounder to second baseman Clyde Engle, who booted it for an error that broke the 2–2 tie. Shano Collins then singled to center, scoring Lord and Lange for a 5–2 lead. Walsh shut down the Red Sox 1-2-3 in the home ninth, and Chicago officially had wrecked "Dedication Day" and Boston's festive mood.

44 The Wizard of Waxahachie

The man with the No. 22 on the back of his White Sox uniform was at it again, the boy noticed as he passed by the television set. "Is Paul Richards gonna get thrown out of the game again, Dad?"

Before his father could answer the boy's question, the umpire gave the heave-ho sign, and yes, Richards had been tossed. Again.

The totals are remarkable: Richards, in his four years (1951–54) as manager of the White Sox, had 29 ejections. In contrast, his successor, Marty Marion, was ejected four times in two years, and Marion's successor, Al Lopez, was tossed 15 times in nine seasons. In 1952, a season in which Paul had 10 ejections, umpires began referring to him again as "Ol' Rant and Rave," his nickname when he managed at Triple-A Buffalo in the late '40s.

Said Charlie Silvera, former Yankees backup catcher and later a longtime scout: "Ol' Richards, he could cuss more in 30 seconds than some guys could in a lifetime. Once he left the dugout and came out to argue, he was gone. He knew it, everybody knew it. But Richards was a hell of a manager."

Richards, who hailed from Waxahachie, Texas, and also was one of baseball's greatest golfers, knew pitching and defense were the most important elements in baseball. Among his credoes: "Defense, particularly pitching, is the key to success. Most games are given away rather than actually won by the opposition." A willing student was his fellow Texan, Eddie Robinson, who played for Richards in Chicago and Baltimore and worked for him in the Houston, Atlanta, and Texas front offices. "I always felt," Robinson said, "and I still feel I know a lot of baseball other people may not know simply because I had the privilege of being associated with him."

Certainly no other manager of his time was more innovative than Richards when it came to strategy. In addition to his switch of pitcher Harry Dorish to third base at Fenway Park in 1951 (See "Roadkill No More"), he moved Billy Pierce, who in a June 1953 game at Yankee Stadium had a 4–2 lead in the ninth, to first base and brought in the right-hander Dorish to face Hank Bauer. Yankees manager Casey Stengel sent up lefty-swinging Don Bollweg to hit for Bauer, and Bollweg beat out a drag bunt toward

Pierce at first—although Richards thought he was out and ended up with one of his seven 1953 ejections. Bollweg moved up on Gil McDougald's chopper to third, and Pierce then returned to the mound and Sam Mele replaced him at first base, thus becoming the record fifth Sox player used at the position that day. Pierce, after walking Gene Woodling, got Johnny Mize—like Woodling a left-handed hitter—on a force-out and then struck out Bill Renna to end it.

He managed the White Sox till mid-September 1954, when the Baltimore club offered him the chance to be both their field manager and general manager. Unable to get a contract extension from the Sox, he took the Baltimore offer and set about building a franchise that became a perennial contender starting in 1960.

Richards also was in on the development of the Houston organization, was GM at Atlanta for six years before returning to Chicago to serve as manager of Bill Veeck's White Sox in 1976. The team was dreadful, but when he discussed that club a few years later, he did so with a smile.

"Had one fella," he said, "who always dressed pretty and wore an earring. Coggins. Rich Coggins was his name. Never quite could play, but he sure did have some nice clothes."

One other note about those 1976 White Sox: The manager, Paul Richards, was not ejected even once.

He passed away in Waxahachie—during a round of golf—in May 1986.

45 The Sox Owed Kenny

There was always the feeling among some White Sox watchers that the Sox were always going to do what they could to make sure Kenny Williams was taken care of. After all, it was the least the franchise could do for him after the way it messed up his playing career.

The Sox had selected him in the third round of the 1982 amateur draft out of Mt. Pleasant High School in East San Jose, California. He played football at Stanford for one season (1983) before concentrating on baseball. Williams, an outfielder with excellent speed and a strong throwing arm, made stops at Appleton (1983–84), Glens Falls (1984–85), Birmingham (1986), and Buffalo (1986). Almost everywhere he went, he'd steal 20-plus bases and hit double figures in home runs and strike out four to five times as often as he'd walk. Sox minor-league personnel figured Kenny eventually would become a bit more selective at the plate, but he never did.

Nonetheless, he received a summons to the Sox to join the ballclub in Milwaukee on May 19, 1987, from Triple-A Hawaii, where he had been batting .269 with just a .310 on-base percentage. Williams, 1-for-4 against Brewers ace Teddy Higuera in that night's 5–1 Chicago triumph, grabbed the center fielder's job and held onto it, ending up in 116 games with 18 doubles, 11 homers, 50 RBIs, 21 steals, and a .281 batting average (.314 on-base). Kenny, it seemed, was on his way.

Then came the development that changed everything. GM Larry Himes worked all off-season trying to deal for a third baseman but was unable to get the job done. He discussed with manager Jim Fregosi the possibility of making a third baseman out of Kenny Williams. They presented the idea to Williams, who, having just finished his first season in the big leagues, was in no position to turn down his bosses.

We'll never know what might have happened had Himes been able to acquire an every-day major-league third baseman. What we do know is that Kenny was the star of the 1988 opener at old Comiskey Park, hitting a two-run homer to put the Sox ahead of Mike Witt and the Angels 3–2 in the fifth inning and then delivering a game-tying double, a key blow in a five-run seventh that helped the Sox to an 8–5 triumph. He also committed an error, but who was paying attention?

Well, after he'd made 14 errors in 32 games at third (.860 fielding percentage), lots of people were paying attention. The glove problems affected his hitting as well: He was down to .158 by the end of April, .165 by the end of May. The experiment wasn't working. Himes, hoping to give Williams a fresh start, traded him to Detroit for pitcher Eric King before the 1989 season. He drifted on to Toronto and finally Montreal in 1991 before rejoining the Sox as a scout, and then began his slow, steady climb up the organization's ladder, finally culminating with his being named general manager after the 2000 AL Central championship campaign.

As Sox GM, he was like a latter-day Frank Lane, not as prolific as "Frantic Frank" but always making things interesting and, most important, making the White Sox interesting. Williams was always looking for ways to improve the ballclub. He'd come up with a key player to help down the stretch and you'd wonder how he had done it. Not all worked out, but among acquisitions added for pennant drives were solid veterans like Robbie Alomar and Carl Everett in 2003, Freddy Garcia in 2004, Geoff Blum in 2005, Ken Griffey Jr. in 2008, Alex Rios in 2009, Manny Ramirez in 2010, and, in his final season on the job (2012), Orlando Hudson, Brett Myers, Francisco Liriano, and Kevin Youkilis—all at extremely attractive costs.

Kenny's steals became so remarkable you could say to someone, "I heard the Sox are about to get Robinson Cano from the Yankees for two minor-leaguers," and have the guy half believe it.

Maybe that's the best way to sum up Kenny Williams' dozen memorable years as Sox GM: anything was possible.

Even a World Series title.

46 The Strange Case of Albert Belle

A guy from Chicago kept calling the sports desk that November 1997 night from Las Vegas, long after the sport section's replate had been, as they say, "put to bed." The man was giving an almost-breathless account of how Jerry Reinsdorf and Albert Belle and two or three other men had been making the rounds in Sin City. "Albert Belle's gonna sign with the White Sox," the alleged Chicagoan said.

All the desk could do, considering the hour and the very real possibility that the caller was inebriated and/or not on the level, was get in touch with the paper's baseball writers and see what they could find out. By early morning they had lent credence to the Vegas caller: Arn Tellem, Belle's agent, was in Las Vegas. So was Albert Belle. So was Jerry Reinsdorf. The day after that, Belle was being introduced to the Chicago media as the new White Sox left fielder and owner of a five-year, $55 million contract.

Eveyone smiled and said the right things, but not everyone was comfortable. In Belle, the Sox had added one of baseball's problem children. In his days as a Cleveland Indians slugger, he had (A) thrown a baseball at a taunting fan and nailed him in the chest, (B) charged the mound twice to put worried thoughts in the minds of Royals pitchers Neal Heaton and Hipolito Pichardo, (C) ripped

Albert Belle's short stay with the Sox resulted in historic numbers but not many wins.

into sportscaster Hannah Storm in 1995 for having the silly notion that he might agree to an interview, (D) was caught using a corked bat against the Sox in 1994 and ended up serving a seven-day suspension, and (E) he had chased down some teenaged trick-or-treaters who had thrown eggs at his house.

But now he'd be starting over again with the White Sox, batting fourth behind Frank Thomas, his buddy from the SEC (Belle was from LSU, Frank from Auburn). Behind Belle was No. 5 hitter Robin Ventura, third baseman supreme. However, things that look great on paper seldom work out as planned. Yes, Thomas won the batting title with his .347, but Ventura broke his ankle in spring training and missed four months, and slow-starting Albert was hitting .206 on May 3 and the Sox were 8–17 and in the AL Central cellar. People forgot about the team—until July 30 and the "White Flag Trade." And then, soon after, they were forgotten again. As for Belle, he finished at .274 with 30 homers and 116 RBIs.

The next year was a remarkable one for Belle but not for the Sox, who were 29–44 by mid-June and way back on the burner, what with Sammy Sosa tearing it up on the North Side. Yet Belle, who was hitting just .244 on May 25, woke up in June and then had a terrific July, hitting 16 home runs, driving in 32 runs and raising his average on July 1 from .275 to .307 by month's end. He kept hitting and hitting until he closed the season at .328 with club records in homers (49), RBIs (152), doubles (48), and total bases (399). He didn't do much for the gate, though: The Sox drew 1,391,146 in 1998 compared to 1,865,222 in 1997. Reinsdorf couldn't keep Belle's contract on the books, so he invoked a clause in Belle's contract that said if Albert's salary was no longer one of the top three in the game, he would become a free agent for 30 days. If there were no higher bidders, Belle could return to the Sox.

"Arn Tellem sold me on the clause by explaining it would be good for me too," Reinsdorf said of Belle's agent. "It gave me an escape plan if Albert didn't work out." Despite the numbers, Belle didn't. "Two years later," Reinsdorf said, "he was very unpopular with our fans."

Belle did get a better offer: five years for $65 million, from the Orioles. When he retired two years later with a bad hip, the O's still owed Belle $39 million.

Today, he lives quietly with his family in Scottsdale, Arizona. Trick-or-treaters need not fear him.

"I'm 46 now, compared to when I was 26, so I'm pretty mild-mannered," he told Comcast SportsNet Chicago's Chuck Garfien. "I've got a wife and kids and stuff. It's a different personality now.

"My career was cut short, but it was a great run. I certainly would have liked to have done it for a few more years, but it didn't work out that way. I don't have any regrets. I enjoyed everything."

47 Quick Quiz

This was back in the Dark Ages—the late '80s—when Jim Fregosi was the White Sox manager, people like Jose Segura and worse populated the bullpen and when Don Drysdale and Frank Messer were doing the Sox telecasts.

"Double D" and Messer, trying their absolute best to fill dead air while describing the activities of a dead ballclub, somehow began discussing names on the back of athletes' jerseys. Which team, they wondered aloud, was the first to do it?

"Fine," several viewers thought, "they're going to tell a few Bill Veeck stories and maybe remember the 'Z' in Ted Kluszewski's name being sewn on backward back in 1960."

No such good fortune. No, the two of them finally decided it must have been the Oakland A's, thanks to their colorful, innovative owner, Charlie Finley, who first came up with the idea of putting names on uniforms. "C'mon, you guys! Think! A hint: What team do you cover?" But they never did correct themselves, and people watching and thinking of calling the station must have figured, "What's the point?"

The answer, of course, is the 1960 White Sox, whose names were placed on the backs of their visiting uniforms. Veeck, then in his first stint as Sox president, believed there was no reason to force fans to buy a scorecard when you could simply have the players' names sewn onto the jersey. The other owners were outraged, alarmed that Veeck's shocking innovation might cut deeply into their scorecard sales. So they banded together and forced Veeck, in 1961, to put the names on the back of the Sox home jerseys as well.

Another time, thought was given to the subject of "curtain calls" after home runs. Both Dan and Frank had worked the 1977 World Series more than a decade earlier, so they were sure about this one. "Had to be those Yankee fans, Don," Messer said, "after Reggie Jackson's third homer in Game 6 of the 1977 Series."

Well, they had the right year. The correct team, of course, is the White Sox. Just ask former Royals star Hal McRae. He's the guy who could not stand the "curtain-call" concept. He could not understand it, either. It all started—like several things, such as the singing of "Na Na Hey Hey Kiss Him Goodbye"—on the first weekend of July, when the Sox knocked the Twins out of first place with a four-game sweep at Comiskey Park. During Sunday's doubleheader, the fans wouldn't stop cheering until the Chicago home run hitter stepped out of the dugout and acknowledged the crowd of 33,898 with a tip of the cap.

The defending AL West–champion Royals came to town the last weekend of July and lost Friday night, Saturday afternoon and Sunday's first game. Kansas City finally salvaged the finale, during which McRae hit a solo homer and, as he closed in quite slowly on home plate, took off his cap and waved it to the 50,412 people.

"I just wanted the White Sox to know what it looks like from the other side," McRae said, "It's bush, what they do. It's a disgrace to baseball. It makes the game a sideshow, and those fans are just making clowns of their players with all that jazz.

"They stand at the plate when they hit a home run, they run the bases real slow, they tip the hat, they come out of the dugout and tip their hat again. It's bush. It's a joke."

Final question, and it's no joke. Which team's fans began the tradition of standing and cheering with two outs in the ninth and the home team ahead? Drysdale and Messer decided quickly on an answer: "The Yankees."

Wrong again. If you've seen a pattern developing, you have this one correct. That's right: White Sox. Yes, Sox fans had a lot of fun in 1977, and don't think Bill Veeck didn't notice.

"I have never seen anywhere," he said, "the kind of enthusiasm that was engendered in this ballpark in 1977."

Too bad Don Drysdale and Frank Messer couldn't have been there.

48 The Chamber of Horrors

Most Sox fans were rather confident after the opening game of the 1983 American League Championship Series in Baltimore. LaMarr Hoyt had beaten the Orioles' Scott McGregor 2–1, meaning the Sox actually had won a game in that evil place, Memorial Stadium, where they'd had so much trouble since the ugly-looking structure had opened for baseball in 1954.

At least the Sox were not going to have to come back and play another game in what the late Bob Elson, even way back in the '50s when the Orioles were pretty bad, used to call "The Chamber of Horrors."

The strangest things happened to the White Sox in that stadium. Maybe the strangest one was "The Paul LaPalme Game," played on Preakness Saturday in 1957. It was Catholic Charities Night at the park, and the O's had shown some to the Sox, who had to catch a train to Boston for the next day's game. The managers, Al Lopez and Baltimore's Paul Richards, had agreed with the umpires that the gane would end at exactly 10:20 p.m, regardless. It is not clear to this day if all the players knew about the coming curfew, which now was just minutes away.

The Sox had scored four in the seventh to lead 4–3. It was still 4–3 in the ninth as Dick Williams strolled to the plate to face lefty knuckleballer Paul LaPalme. Remembered Williams: "George Kell, as I left the dugout, said, 'Better be swinging at anything.' I said, 'Why?' 'This is going to be the last pitch. Get a good cut.' I thought that no inning could *start* after 10:20.'"

LaPalme received no such reminder. "All the guys in our bullpen," he said, "were former National Leaguers—me, Gerry Staley, Dixie Howell. We figured it'd be played like the normal rain-delayed game, and I had to get three outs." He didn't even need three strikes. He could've held the ball for a few more seconds or called the catcher out for a brief confab, etc. But he did not. He threw and Williams swung, and the ball sailed into the seats in left, the game was tied 4–4 and the Sox hustled through their showers to catch their train.

Afterward, Bob Maisel of the *Baltimore Sun* walked into the Sox clubhouse to find Lopez still seething.

"Al was in shock," Maisel said. "His mouth was hanging open. He couldn't believe it. I saw him at the Hall of Fame ceremony when Chuck Thompson went in a few years ago and needled him about it. Lopez said, 'I'm still in shock.'"

Incidentally, the game was replayed in its entirety later that season. The O's won.

Then there was the time in May 1959 when Billy Pierce, in the second inning of a scoreless game, facing Billy O'Dell, gave up a pop fly headed for the right-field foul line, which was made of wood. O'Dell's ball hit the line in such a way that the ball bounded over the head of an oncharging Al Smith and rolled around in the corner while the first two runs of the game scored in a 2–1 Sox loss.

"When I was traded to San Francisco," Pierce said, "O'Dell was already there with the Giants. And he kidded me in the clubhouse: 'Oh, yeah, I remember the night I ripped that home run off of Billy.' Made it sound like he'd really belted it."

A year later, on a late-August Sunday afternoon, Milt Pappas led the Sox 3–1 with two out and two on in the eighth. Lopez sent up Ted Kluszewski to bat for Minnie Minoso, and "Big Klu" laid into one and drove it over the high wall in right for a three-run homer that put the Sox up 4–3.

But wait.

Third-base umpire Ed Hurley, just as Pappas delivered the pitch, had called time to tell Sox reserves Earl Torgeson and Floyd Robinson they should be warming up in a different location than the one they were using. A huge argument ensued, but, in the end, "Klu" lost his homer and the Sox lost the game. They were now three games back of New York; the O's trailed by two.

Remembered Klu: "I didn't know what had happened until (pinch-runner Jim) Rivera started back toward me and said, 'He called time.' I said, 'Called time? For what?' It was a real strange situation."

Almost as strange as Bill Melton camping under a pop fly near third base in 1970, then losing it in the lights and ending up with a broken nose—and a new position, right field. Which is almost as strange as Richard Dotson in 1983 taking a no-hitter into the eighth inning but giving up one hit—a slicing drive over the 309-foot sign by Dan Ford, the only hit the Orioles had in their 1–0 victory.

A final word: The Sox, in 38 years, were 116–163 at Memorial Stadium, a percentage of .416.

49 Biggest Homer in Sox History?

Fortunately for those who seek to ponder possible reactions to the question raised by the chapter title, the White Sox, up until the last 20 years or so, never hit many home runs. That makes this subject a bit easier to research.

The guess here is that the most popular answers would be those two huge homers in Game 2 of the 2005 World Series between the Sox and the Houston Astros.

The tendency would be to put Paul Konerko's grand slam in that thrilling second game ahead of Scott Podsednik's game-winner, because if Paulie doesn't hit the slam, Houston still leads that game 4–2 with only two innings to go. Podsednik, if his drive is caught on the track instead of by a fan, is not a failure: He merely has sent the game to extra innings.

Another choice that surely makes sense would be Geoff Blum's pinch homer in the 14th inning of Game 3 of the Series, because it was the blast that told the world that the White Sox were world champions, even though a fourth triumph was still formally required.

Think back to some of the big home runs in Sox history. Some come to mind almost immediately.

Minnie Minoso's 1951 shot against the Yankees in his first at-bat in a Sox uniform, an event fraught with significance for sports as well as society.

Carlton Fisk's game-winner on Opening Day 1981 at Boston and his grand slam at his first White Sox home opener a few days later.

The back-to-back homers by Al Smith and Jim Rivera in the pennant-clincher at Cleveland in 1959.

Frank Thomas' 30th homer of 1993, the two-out two-run blast in the eighth inning that beat the Royals in Chicago, 5–4, and kept the lead from being cut to 1½ games.

And there are so many others.

Yet it makes sense that one would think that the biggest home run in a team's history would be one hit in a World Series. The World Series, after all, is the place where champions are crowned, and the name of the game is striving for a championship.

So, without further ado, the home run judged here to be the biggest in White Sox history is…(drum roll).

Joe Crede's 10th-inning leadoff shot halfway up in the left-field seats on September 20, 2005, to give the sagging Sox a 7–6 victory over second-place Cleveland and move their lead up to 3½ games— when a defeat would've left the Tribe 1½ games back with 12 to go.

The reasoning here is that had Crede not stepped up when he did, there quite possibly might not have been a World Series stage on which Konerko and "Scottie Pods" could perform. Remember that the Tribe won the next night 8–0 at the Cell, and that the Sox lost at home the night after that to the Twins in 11 innings. The very real possibility was that the Sox, had it not been for Crede's heroics, could have been out of the AL Central lead by that weekend.

Though he greatly downplayed it, Joe had an idea the home run, his second of the night and 19th of the season, carried with it some importance.

"I've had other walk-off home runs," he said that night, "but they were either really early in the season or we were already out of it. But with the fact that we're in first place and we're in the last week and a half of the season and we're battling back and forth here, I think it is one of the biggest hits of my career."

Judging by the way he shouted out Crede's name, it sounded that night like Hawk Harrelson agreed with him.

50 The Longest Homer in Sox History

If you don't think May 6, 1964, was a night of "fun at the old ballpark," just check out these items:

It was the night that Minnie Minoso, 38 years young, hit his last major league home run, a pinch line drive into the lower deck in left with two teammates aboard in the seventh inning of Game 2 that provided the final score: White Sox 11, Kansas City A's 4.

Dave Nicholson, the powerful, 6'2", 215-pound Chicago left fielder, also hit a home run in Game 2, this a two-run shot into the upper deck in left off Aurelio Monteagudo to give the hosts a 5–3 first-inning lead.

Nicholson also belted a two-run homer into the left-field upper deck off Game 1 starter Moe Drabowsky, as part of a game-clinching four-run rally.

The blast of the night, Nicholson's leadoff missile in the fifth inning of the opener, was a rising line drive to left-center that was still going upward when it reached the upper-deck facade. If one was seated in the lower deck in right, the view was perfect: The ball could not possibly have done anything but clear the roof.

Up On the Roof: Other Sox Who Reached the Top of Old Comiskey

A look first at those White Sox hitters besides Dave Nicholson who hit balls over or on top of the roof at old Comiskey Park:

Eddie Robinson: First baseman hit career-best 29 homers in 1951, one a two-run shot off the Browns' Al Widmar on April 25 that landed on the roof in right. Sox won 8–6.

Minnie Minoso: On night of September 21, 1960, broke a scoreless tie in fourth against Kansas City's Bud Daley with two-run homer onto the roof in left, his 19th long one of the season. Sox and Herb Score won 7–2.

Buddy Bradford: Entered April 25, 1969 game with Twins hitting .405 and took the very tough Tom Hall deep for his 4th homer. Sox went on to win 6–5.

Tom Egan: Big backup catcher put one on the roof in left off future Sox pitching coach Jackie Brown during Game 2 of twin bill with Washington July 25, 1971. Egan went 3-for-4 in 9–6 Sox victory.

Dick Allen: Baltimore standout lefty Mike Cuellar gave up two Allen homers this night (May 1, 1973), the first one—in the first inning—bouncing on the roof in left. Sox won 6–5.

Richie Zisk: Zisk's 15th homer of the year was a shot up on the roof in left off Yankees lefty Don Gullett on June 4, 1977. Yankees had 7–0 lead in second, held on to win 8–6.

List of Sox who hit roof shots (and how many) after home plate was moved out 8 feet for 1983 season:

Ron Kittle (7), Greg Luzinski (4), Carlton Fisk (2), Harold Baines (1), and Dan Pasqua (1).

In any event, the Sox won that game 6–4, and between games it was announced that the roof-clearing blast had traveled 573 feet. Sox representatives who immediately had left to try and find the ball had found a group of youngsters who had been playing ball in Armour Square Park, just north of the ballpark, at the time of the massive blast. The kids had the ball—it was eventually handed over to "Big Nick"—and walked over and pointed to where they found it. The Sox math whizzes took in the height of the left-field roof in doing their calculations and eventually came up with the 573 figure—8 feet more than Mickey Mantle's 565-foot homer in Washington in 1953.

Some 22,550 people (14,707 paid) had been in on some interesting baseball history.

"I think at least 300,000 people have told me they were there," Nicholson said, smiling.

After June 14, he hit only four home runs the rest of the 1964 season and ended with 13. And, over the final two months of the campaign, he played in only 17 games out of a possible 61. The next season he played even less, and he was gone to Houston by 1966, leaving behind memories of gigantic home runs and whopping strikeout totals. His club-record 175 K's in 1963 was busted with plenty to spare by Adam Dunn in 2011 (177), 2012 (222), and 2013 (189). But "Big Nick" enjoyed his time with the White Sox, strikeouts or not.

"Oh, it was fun. We were pretty close to winning the pennant every year. We had a good ballclub. Real good pitching, adequate hitting, a good defensive club. We didn't lose too many games by throwing the ball around. We just didn't hit enough to win it."

51 Yes, Virginia, There Was a Smead Jolley

Smead Jolley hit line drives to all fields in every league and in every ballpark in which he played. He stood 6'3", weighed 210 pounds, and knew he had the power to hit lots more home runs than he did. But hitting well over .300 was more enjoyable to him than hitting the ball out of the park, because he liked to see the other teams' outfielders chasing down triples and doubles and making the same kinds of mistakes he had always made.

The defensive side of baseball, though, never really interested him. Like Al Lopez said years later about a young Carlos May, "You could tell the way he stood up there that he had confidence that he could hit. Now, in the outfield, I don't think he cared if he caught the ball or not. But he could hit."

Jolley played in the minors for 16 years and with the White Sox and Boston two seasons each, and he hit everywhere he played. But he had the knack of also providing the spectators with something to remember him by—in a comedic way. So if the designated-hitter rule had been in vogue in the '30s, Smead Jolley might well have been one of that decade's biggest stars.

From his dad's farm near Three Creeks, Arkansas, eventually he made it to the Pacific Coast League with the San Francisco Seals, for whom he hit .346, .397, .404, and .387 with 138 homers in a four-year period (1926 through 1929). Jolley topped the league in hitting and RBIs (163) in 1927, when teammate Lefty O'Doul was league MVP. Smead won the PCL Triple Crown (.404, 45 homers, 188 RBIs) in 1928 and belted 35 homers in 1929.

The major leagues had taken notice. Babe Pinelli, the umpire and former player, admitted "Smead wasn't much of a guy with the glove, but…there wasn't a pitcher born that Jolley felt he couldn't knock his brains out." Something would have to be done about his defensive play, however. Cardinals coach Johnny Riddle once said Jolley fielded "like a kid chasing soap bubbles."

But new White Sox manager Donie Bush persuaded Charles A. Comiskey to pay the $50,000 to bring Jolley to Chicago, and Smead batted cleanup in the 1930 Opening Day lineup at old Comiskey and went 2-for-5. He went on to appear in all but two games, drove in 114 runs and batted .313. In 1931, though, health troubles held him to 54 games and 110 at-bats, as 32 of his appearances came as a pinch-hitter. But he did hit .300. Jolley appeared in 12 games with the White Sox the next April (.357, 7 RBIs), but they dealt him to the Red Sox for catcher Charlie Berry and outfielder Jack Rothrock.

In the end, though, his defense is what keeps his legend alive. Back in those years, Fenway Park had a terraced left field that forced the outfielder to run uphill to get to the wall—a forerunner of "Tal's Hill" today at Minute Maid Park. Manager Bush and his coaches worked tirelessly with Smead during Chicago's first 1930 visit to Boston on having him go up the incline to catch flyballs. Then the game started, and Jolley handled two flyballs perfectly. On the next one, though, the wind blew the ball back toward the infield, and Jolley dived from the top of the incline, missed the ball and slid all the way along the grass on his chin. Between innings, he was razzed pretty well in the dugout. He blamed it on the skipper: "Donie showed me how to get up the hill but he never told me how to get down."

Another time, supposedly, he was in left field for a game against the A's in Philadelphia when Bing Miller smashed a line-drive single headed right at Jolley. The ball shot through his legs for an error, and Jolley whirled around to play the carom off the wall. The ball scooted back through his legs for error No. 2. Smead then hustled after the ball, picked it up and fired it over the third baseman's head for the third error on the play. Meanwhile, Miller circled the bases.

It might be true; it might not be. This *is* true, however: In four seasons of outfield play in the majors, Smead Jolley did manage to make 44 errors.

52 Black Jack: 'Nuff Said

The 1987 Minnesota Twins were headed to the postseason and, as it turned out, a World Series title. They led the AL West by 3½ games with 17 to go, and this night they would be going up against a kid right-hander for Chicago named Jack McDowell, making his major-league debut just three months after helping Stanford win the College World Series.

The Twins never had a chance. McDowell, demonstrating to all why GM Larry Himes had taken him with the fifth pick in that June's amateur draft, shut out Minnesota for seven innings on four hits, striking out three and walking none. Bobby Thigpen finished up the 6–2 victory.

"This was pretty much a dream come true," McDowell said. "I have to keep my head on straight. I still have to prove myself. I know I'm not here to stay."

He was there to stay by 1990, though, when he was 14–9 for a young Sox team that won 94 games but was beaten out by Oakland for the AL West crown. By 1991, McDowell, the 6'5", 180-pounder with the mean streak and the meaner split-finger pitch, was posting a 17–10 record and 3.41 ERA. Next year he was 20–10, 3.18, and in 1993 he was 22–10 and 3.37, threw 250-plus innings for the third straight season, and won the AL Cy Young Award.

"I really looked around to see how guys who won played at this level," McDowell told an interviewer. "I saw that the successful pitchers threw a lot of innings. That's what I decided I needed to do. I had 15 complete games that year, which today is a couple years' worth. When it was my turn to pitch I wanted to take the ball, pitch, and finish what I started.... That really helped the team, too, because the bullpen guys got the day off. A lot of fans don't know how important that is."

If a fan wanted to find out about the makeup of Jack McDowell, all he'd have to do is get a tape of Jack's 20th win back in 1993 at the Metrodome in Minneapolis. Frank Thomas homered in the first inning for a quick 1–0 lead, and McDowell had his run. Kirby Puckett opened the Twins' fourth with a double and moved to third on Kent Hrbek's flyout to center. But Dave Winfield struck out and Shane Mack popped out to second.

In the sixth, the Twins still down 1–0, Chuck Knoblauch singled and went to third on a single by Jeff Reboulet. Here McDowell bore down—he struck out Puckett and Hrbek and got Winfield on a flyball to Lance Johnson in center. The hosts had another great chance in the seventh, when Mack singled, stole second, and took third on Chip Hale's single to center. It was McDowell time again. Lenny Webster struck out and David McCarty grounded to Ozzie Guillen, who turned it into a double-play. "Black Jack" then retired the final six batters in order.

In the ALCS that followed, the Sox fell four games to two to defending world champ Toronto, and McDowell was roughed up in both of his starts: 9 innings, 18 hits, 10 runs. The funk continued into 1994, when, in late June, he was 3–7 with a 5.42 ERA. The hot Sox pitchers were Wilson Alvarez, Jason Bere, and Alex Fernandez. McDowell was almost the forgotten man.

Some joked that he hadn't been the same since the previous November, when he and Eddie Vedder, his good buddy from the rock music world, had leaped to each other's defense during a 4:00 AM brawl outside a New Orleans bar. McDowell was knocked out during the incident and was treated for a cut lip and scalp lacerations. He wasn't injured, but the incident couldn't have endeared Jack to Jerry Reinsdorf. Nor could his performance up to that point in 1994.

And then he ripped off one of those streaks that the great ones always seem to do. In his remaining 10 starts (the strike ended the

Black Jack leaves Game 5 of the 1993 ALCS.

season August 12), Jack threw six complete games, including two shutouts, and went 7–2 with an ERA of 1.81. In 84⅔ innings, he gave up 74 hits and only 14 walks and struck out 71.

After the 1994 season, McDowell was traded to the Yankees for lumbering outfielder Lyle Mouton but, bothered by injuries, he never again was the top-flight pitcher he'd been in Chicago.

McDowell is still a musician with a rock band called Stickfigure. The group was formed in 1992, following a tour with his former band, V.I.E.W., as the opening act for The Smithereens. Songwriting is what brings him joy these days, as does coaching high school baseball and getting his players to think championship.

"Winning the College World Series was by far the most memorable and important event in my baseball career," he said. "I never won a World Series title, so the college thing stands as the one best event.

"I always tell my players that every individual year can be improved upon. The only end-all achievement is winning a championship because at that point, there is nothing left to accomplish."

53 A Big Day In Sox History

A Hall-of-Fame career got off to a rather quiet start back on Wednesday, September 10, 1930. Lucius Benjamin Appling, known as Luke, made his major league debut as the White Sox's shortstop in seventh-place Chicago's 6–2 loss to last-place Boston at old Comiskey Park.

Edgar Munzel, a young sportswriter for the *Chicago Herald*, watched the import from Atlanta and decided it was too early to count him out or count him in. "There was another newcomer in the Sox front yesterday," wrote Munzel, who 43 years later, when with the *Sun-Times*, presented the 1972 American League MVP award to Dick Allen on the same field. "Luke Appling, the shortstop from Atlanta, made his bow. He gathered one hit but had little to do afield, so judgment must be reserved."

The kid shortstop, batting sixth and playing that day behind another Hall of Famer, Sox starter Red Faber, had just that one single in four at-bats. For Atlanta, then in the Southern Association, Appling that summer had batted .326 in 104 games with 19 doubles and 17 triples. He also had committed 42 errors. He therefore had lots to work on that month, but after getting into just five more games, in which he went 7-for-22 and committed three more errors, he suffered a broken finger in a morning workout and missed the rest of the season—which amounted to 11 games.

So the first hint of the "Old Aches and Pains" Appling persona that fans grew to love had surfaced for the first time. Then came more trouble in 1931.

Appling, during the exhibition games, got rave reviews from the press and was named the starting shortstop. But, during batting practice on Opening Day, he was struck in the elbow by a wild pitch while he was waiting in the batting cage for his turn to hit. His elbow swelled so much he could barely lift a bat, but he played anyway—and went 0-for-4. After an 0-for-28 stretch, Appling found himself on the bench. He eventually wound up playing 96 games but he hit only .232 and committed 42 errors in 76 games at shortstop.

New manager Lew Fonseca worked with Luke in spring camp of 1932 and slowly but surely began rebuilding Appling's confidence. His batting average improved to .274 by season's end. After an Appling error cost the Sox a game early in 1933, Fonseca told him he was going to be the starting shortstop the rest of the season. Appling's confidence returned and he finished at .322.

And then developed the legendary Luke who always hit well over .300—and who was always hurt and who became the champ at fouling off pitches.

"When Appling was around, the real blunder was to ask him, 'How do you feel?' It would sometimes take half an hour before he stopped telling you," said New York writer Maury Allen. He once told manager Jimmy Dykes he couldn't play because he was "dying." Of course he was exaggerating, but Appling did play most of his career with a chronic ankle injury and won his batting title in 1943 despite an eye infection, the flu, and several pulled muscles.

Maybe the eye problem was the result of watching all those pitches. No one fouled them off like Luke, who sometimes did so with good reason.

Said Chicago broadcaster Jack Brickhouse: "I remember one day during the early part of the war—Harry Grabiner was the general manager—and Luke wanted a dozen baseballs for a Red Cross raffle back home in Atlanta so they could raise some funds. And Grabiner turned him down: 'Not on this one, Luke.' Luke said, 'Okay.' Now about 10 minutes later, they pass the word to Grabiner: 'You'd better come out and watch batting practice.' Luke fouled off about 15 pitches into the stands, and finally Grabiner yells to him: 'You got 'em, Luke! You win—you got the balls.'"

54 Ernie Banks, 3B, Chicago White Sox?

It is certainly possible that Mr. Cub, Ernie Banks, might never have played for the Cubs.

It is also quite possible he would have followed Luis Aparicio, Nellie Fox, and Minnie Minoso in the lineup of the White Sox.

There also is the possibility Ernie would have followed Bill Veeck to Baltimore with the St. Louis Browns—had American League owners voted to keep Bill as head of that franchise, and had Veeck been able to get his hands on $31,500.

Then again, what might have happened is exactly what did happen: AL owners blocked Veeck's planned move to Baltimore, got him to sell to a Baltimore group and then bid him a "tearful" farewell and wished him their best in all future endeavors. As for the Sox, apparently some lousy scouting reports made Ernie sound like perhaps the equal of Freddie Marsh, the club's top utility infielder in 1953. And the Cubs, getting Veeck's highest recommendation, signed Banks in September 1953.

Part of the story was the slowly deteriorating relationship between Sox GM Frank Lane and manager Paul Richards. Richards believed he'd had as much to do with the franchise's remarkable turnaround as had Lane. That might have been stretching the truth a bit, but what mattered was that Paul had begun looking for work elsewhere. He couldn't get a raise or an extension—though Lane insisted he wanted Richards to stay in Chicago. On September 14, 1954, Richards accepted the job of both field and general manager of the new Baltimore club.

So where does Banks come into play?

Fast-forward to May 21, 1956. Richards was still with the Orioles; Lane had left the Sox for the St. Louis Cardinals. On this day, Lane's replacements—Chuck Comiskey and his brother-in-law, John Rigney—traded third baseman George Kell, outfielder Bob Nieman, and pitchers Connie Johnson and Mike Fornieles to the Orioles for outfielder-first baseman Dave Philley and pitcher Jim Wilson. Lane's reaction was to tweak Richards: "Comiskey got the best of Richards." When Richards heard that, he stormed, "If you leave Lane alone, he'll trade a first-place club into a sixth-place club." He ripped most of Lane's Chicago deals and then dropped a bombshell.

Three years earlier, Richards claimed, he had pushed hard for Lane to get Banks, but at that time, he and Frank weren't getting along that well and Lane was paying little heed to Richards' suggestions. (It's difficult to believe Lane wouldn't be interested in Banks: Lane had brought Negro leaguers Bob Boyd and Sam Hairston into the organization in 1950 and Connie Johnson in 1952.)

In a 1990 interview in Kansas City, Johnson, a former Kansas City Monarchs teammate of Ernie's, remembered the story this way:

"In my first year in Chicago (1953), Richards had [coach] Luman Harris talk to me. He said, 'We need a third baseman. Do you know any in the Negro leagues?' Right away, I say, 'Ernie Banks of the Kansas City Monarchs.' See, Ernie had told me, 'Hey Johnson, you get me a job up there in Chicago!'

"I told the Sox, 'He's a shortstop, but he can hit. And anybody who can play short well, they can play third.' So they scouted him, and the scout comes back with this report: 'Well, he's a pretty fair hitter, but he can't move to his right too good. He's just a mediocre ballplayer.'

"Can you believe that? Three years later, I'm traded to Baltimore, and Luman Harris is a coach there. He says, 'Man, Banks just hit another one—for the wrong Chicago team!'

"But Ernie didn't care. He did pretty well for himself with the Cubs."

And the chances are the North Side was where Ernie was headed all along. If Veeck wasn't going to be able to afford him, he would make sure his old friends at Wrigley Field got first crack at him.

Essentially, he wote in his autobiography, "I lost Ernie Banks for want of $31,500. Bill Norman was scouting the Kansas City team in the American Association for us. And while he was there, he stayed over to watch the Negro Leagues team, the Kansas City Monarchs. Bill called, in great excitement, to tell me that the Monarchs' shortstop, Banks, was tremendous. I knew Tom Baird, the Monarchs' owner, fairly well and I asked him what he wanted for Banks.

"Thirty-five," he said.

"I said, 'Gee, I don't have $35,000. I'll give you $3,500 now and the $31,500 when you catch me."

He began to laugh. "That's the way I'm doing business myself, Bill," he said. "I have to get $35,000 for Banks to pay my own debts."

"Listen," I said, "just please don't sell him in our (American) league. Norman tells me he's tremendous."

"All right," Baird said, "where do you want him to go?"

Veeck's answer was the Cubs. And that's who landed him.

That Scoreboard Did More Than Just Keep Score

Considering the way the White Sox have *not* been hitting the baseball the last few seasons, maybe the time has come to return to yesteryear and get that big scoreboard in center field working for the home team once again.

When the Sox played their home games in the old ballpark across 35th Street, the big board—built in 1951 and then greatly modified in 1960 by Bill Veeck and then again in 1982 by new owners Jerry Reinsdorf and Eddie Einhorn—sometimes had more to do than just stand out there and look impressive.

No, the scoreboard, when needed, also did helpful things such as aid in the relaying of stolen signals. Such activity goes back to the mid-1950s, when Frank Lane was general manager in charge of mischief. Then came Bill Veeck, who presided over a 1960 team that went 51–26 at home, and although no one ever questioned him about it, could Veeck not have had a little fun going on, with the board's help, during the South Side Hit Men's marvelous mashing season of 1977? And there had been accusations by a man who would know—then-Milwaukee Brewers GM Lane—in 1972, when the Sox at one point were 44–14 at home.

For the White Sox, the cheating began in 1955, when Lane at last grew weary of other teams getting away with it. He had seen Cleveland doing it, as far back as 1949, when Veeck was owner and Lou Boudreau the manager. He had gotten reports that Detroit had secreted non-playing personnel up in the Tigers' scoreboard. And in 1955, he had caught the Kansas City A's, then managed by Boudreau, stealing signs as well.

Said Lane in 1978, "What we were doing then is what the White Sox have been doing for years—stealing signs from the board. Veeck denied it. Chuck Tanner [Sox manager in 1972] denied it. But they did.

"What we did, we put Del Wilber, our bullpen coach, in the scoreboard with a pair of binoculars," Lane said. "At that time, the board listed the number of the pitcher and the catcher. [Catcher] Sherm Lollar 's number was 10. Now Wilber, with the binoculars, would catch the sign. If it was for a fastball, they'd wiggle the 'one.' If it was a curve, they'd wiggle the 'zero.'

"Not everyone would take the signs. I think the only guys who did were George Kell and Bob Kennedy. And that first homestand, about 8–10 days, Kell and Kennedy just wore it out."

Lane's claim that Veeck continued the practice in Chicago in 1960 was confirmed some years ago by former pitcher Al Worthington, picked up by the Sox for relief help down the stretch in 1960.

"Up on the scoreboard," he remembered, "this light would come on if the pitch was going to be a breaking ball—it flashed on and off. If it was a fastball, there was no flashing. I'd heard about it from a couple other ballplayers. I'm not sure who was up there in the board, but I think it was Dizzy Trout."

Trout, the former big-league pitching star, worked for Veeck then in the Sox's community relations department.

"It bothered me," Worthington said. "I talked to Al Lopez about it. I talked to Bill Veeck and [Sox veep] Hank Greenberg. They wanted me to go along with it. And I didn't want to go along with it. To me, that was cheating. So I packed my bags and flew home. I was with them six days."

Lane was with the Sox long enough to know something fishy was going on in the scoreboard in 1972, when he ran the Brewers. "I'm convinced thay have someone up in the scoreboard stealing signs. But I don't blame them. When I was here [as GM], we had someone up there. And unless you catch them red-handed, it's the toughest thing in the world to prove."

So let's get that scoreboard busy again. The author, for one, is tired of all those 1–2–3 innings.

56 The "All-M" Infield of 1971

This was going to be a little tidbit about a foursome of White Sox infielders that played together for a few weeks at some point back in the '40s. And one of the players represented what was to be the trick portion of the answer.

Well, the trouble with the whole thing is that research turned up no seasons with the right combination. There *were* four White Sox infielders in 1941, for example, with last names starting with

"K"—third baseman Bob Kennedy, first baseman Joe Kuhel and second basemen Don Kolloway and Bill Knickerbocker. But because Luke Appling played every day at shortstop, this group could not be the right answer. And so it went, for several hours.

In the meantime:

The "trick" part of the answer was to have been Cass Michaels, who early in his career played under his real name: Cass Kwietniewski.

With the "4-K" infield tale not working out too well and another chapter beckoning, memories of the unexpectedly exciting and competitive 1971 White Sox paid a visit. That was it! The "4-M" infield of 1971 helped turn that season around—"Melton, Morales, McKinney, and May, the infield from third to first"—and they were liked not only because of the alliteration but because the four of them, as a unit, made the routine plays on defense and did their jobs at the plate.

When the season started at Oakland on April 7, the infield consisted of Bill Melton at third, rookie speedster Bee Bee Richard at short, ex–Red Sox Mike Andrews at second and Carlos May, formerly the left fielder, at first base. Manager Chuck Tanner stayed with Richard, the Sox's No. 1 draft pick in 1970, as long as he could. But even Tanner couldn't accept the fact that just about every other groundball to shortstop was going to be misplayed. And Andrews was just beginning to have the back problems that would eventually cost him his career. He was still hitting well, but he barely could cover more ground than a tortoise.

McKinney, meanwhile, was unbelievable as a pinch-hitter that season, going 11-for-19 (.579) , including game-winning hits in the season-opener in Oakland and the home opener against Minnesota in front of 44,250 at a revved-up old Comiskey Park. So on June 30, with the Sox at 29–42, Tanner started—as a unit for the first time—McKinney at second, Rich Morales at short, Melton at third, and May at first. The club began winning and, from that point on and using that infield alignment the majority of the time, posted a 50–41 won-lost record.

And make no mistake: Andrews and Richard didn't just sit around twiddling their thumbs. Andrews began playing first base when a left-hander pitched for the opposition, and he continued to hit: He ended that year with a .282 batting average, .400 on-base percentage and 12 homers in 109 games.

Richard was given some opportunities to play center field and lots of chances to pinch run. One of the most exciting plays of the season took place one July evening in Chicago when the Sox and A's were tied 1–1 in the seventh and Richard, pinch-running for Ed Herrmann, was at second base with one out. McKinney batted for the pitcher, Tommy John, and drove a flyball to fairly deep center. As Bee Bee tagged up at second, Oakland's Angel Mangual made the catch and conceded him third base. Richard, looking for more than that, never broke stride at third and raced home, sliding in with the go-ahead run. Bart Johnson shut down the A's in the eighth and ninth to save the 2–1 triumph.

Now, about that "All-K" infield…. It'll have to wait.

57 Turning the Tables on the Hated Yankees

Back in the years when both the White Sox and New York Yankees were pennant contenders, the games, especially those played in Chicago, would follow a script that never did seem to change.

Generally, it went like this:

Sox take early lead, maybe 2–0 or 3–0, then fail to capitalize on excellent chances to expand that lead, leaving door open for New

York to rally with a couple runs in eighth and a couple more in ninth to win 4–3 or 5–4.

But once in a great while, the roles were somewhat reversed: The Sox would be the team trailing throughout and then come back to pull out the stunning victory.

One was a game played on Saturday, September 10, 1955, in Yankee Stadium. This was the year of the AL pennant race involving four teams: these two combatants plus defending AL champ Cleveland and, for a while, surprising Boston. After the previous day's tough 5–4 loss in the Bronx, the Sox trailed first-place Cleveland by 3½ games and New York by three.

They gave it their best shot. Manager Marty Marion used 20 players to Casey Stengel's 21 in a game that lasted 3:59 and attracted 31,486. Chicago's best pitcher, lefty Billy Pierce, lasted far less: an inning and a third. It was 6–1 New York after two. The season seemed lost.

The Yankees were up 7–3 in the seventh when Bob Nieman singled to right and South Side native Bob Kennedy, already 3-for-3 with two runs driven across, homered into the left-field seats, and now it was 7–5.

Suddenly the contest was in the ninth inning, and Yankee reliever Bob Grim seemed in complete command, especially when Minnie Minoso popped out and Nieman flied to right. Kennedy drew a walk and Les Moss, who long since had replaced Sherm Lollar behind the plate, hit a grounder to Andy Carey at third, and Carey booted it. Two on and two out. Chico Carrasquel grounded a sharp base hit to left, scoring Kennedy to make it 7–6. After Jim Rivera walked, Walt Dropo, not starting this game because of a 1-for-18 skid, stepped up to face Grim. And Dropo lined the first pitch past Grim's head and into center field to send pinch-runner Bobby Adams and Carrasquel home, and the Sox led 8–7. And Dropo was now 25-for-64 (.391) against the Yankees in 1955 with six homers, 18 RBIs, a .466 on-base percentage, and a .719 slugging average.

It wasn't over yet. Minoso dropped Hank Bauer's liner toward left-center to allow Mickey Mantle to score the tying run in the Yankees' ninth. Then, first baseman Eddie Robinson dropped Phil Rizzuto's throw on Dixie Howell's bases-loaded, two-out grounder in the 10th, Minoso scored and it was 9–8 Chicago. Minnie then caught Gil McDougald's pop to shallow left, and the White Sox were still alive—barely.

On Friday night, September 21, 1962, the Yankees were closing in on their third straight pennant while the host White Sox still had their eyes on the third-place Los Angeles Angels, just 2½ games ahead of them.

The Yankees led this game, too, by a 6–1 score, but this time the Sox had only one chance left—the home ninth—to catch up. Here's what happened:

Nellie Fox singled to left, as did Camilo Carreon, and pinch-hitter Bob Roselli doubled to right-center to score Fox and send Carreon to third. Lefty Marshall Bridges relieved Bud Daley and walked Luis Aparicio to fill the bases. Joe Cunningham doubled down the left-field line, scoring three runs and leaving "Smoky Joe" at second. It was 6–5 and no one yet was out. Floyd Robinson was walked intentionally, and Al Smith, facing right-hander Jim Coates, doubled past third to score Cunningham, Robinson stopping at third. The ballpark was alive, with 32,711 yelling for one more run. Jim Landis was walked to reload the bases. To hit for Mike Hershberger, Al Lopez sent up Grover "Deacon" Jones, a 28-year-old minor-league hitting machine who finally had made it back to the South Side after signing in Frank Lane's office in June 1955.

He was 6-for-18 so far with the Sox, and here he swung and lined a ball to the gap in left-center for a 7–6 Sox victory. "That was awesome," he recalled. "Big crowd. The Yankees. Pinch-hitting with the bases loaded…."

And there still is nobody out.

58 How Good Was Magglio?

Talk about a guy who could get out of bed on Christmas morning and hit line drives—Magglio Ordonez was that guy.

And yet, for what seemed like the longest time, it was almost as if the White Sox didn't know what they had in "Maggs." While other minor-league outfielders zipped through the Chicago farm system, Ordonez took his time—either that, or the farm office never truly thought he was major league material.

After Ordonez made stops in Hickory, Prince William and Birmingham, the Sox decided to go ahead and promote Ordonez to Triple-A Nashville in 1997—even though he hadn't truly torn up the Southern Association during his tour of duty with the Barons. There he had a steady, excellent season—so steady and excellent that he won the American Association batting championship with a .329 average. For good measure, he collected 29 doubles, 14 home runs, and 90 RBIs.

Some still had doubts, however. When the need had arisen for outfield help in Chicago earlier in the 1997 season, the Sox had sent for, first, Mike Cameron and, next, Jeff Abbott, Ordonez's Nashville outfield mates. But one night after he had made his Sox debut in late August 1997 against the Astros on the South Side, he did not complain about being a bit of a forgotten man.

"You have to be patient and stay ready," he said. "I'm just glad they're giving me the opportunity now."

Ordonez certainly capitalized on that opportunity. In his first game in a Sox uniform, he was up three times and had two singles, one a line shot off the wall in left, a bullet that got out there so fast, the runner ahead of Maggs had to hold up at second base.

Magglio Ordonez watches a two-run homer clear the center-field fence.
(Getty Images)

The next night, he hit his first major league home run—a two-run shot off Houston's Jose Lima. Ordonez paused just a bit to watch his homer. He had led all 1996–97 winter-league players in that department with seven in Venezuela, plus there were the 14 he'd hit in Nashville.

This, though, was the major leagues.

"Playing in Venezuela the last couple of winters really helped me," he said. "I got to face Wilson Alvarez and Ramon Garcia, guys like that. And it taught me how to hit the breaking pitch."

As a pinch-hitter two days later, on Labor Day in St. Louis, he hit lefty Tony Fossas' breaking pitch about 400 feet to the bleachers in left-center to give the White Sox a 5–4 lead in the ninth. The Sox held on, and so too did it look like Ordonez was going to hold on to the right-field job in Chicago. Already he was 5-for-8 with a couple home runs in three games. Ordonez held onto it through June of 2004. He had collided with second baseman Willie Harris on Omar Vizquel's short pop fly to right during the May 19 game that year at Cleveland. The collision wound up costing him two trips to the disabled list and two surgeries—one of them done in Austria—on his left knee.

Before he was injured, he had strung together, from 1999 through 2003, batting averages of .301, .315, .305, .320 and .317; home run totals of 30, 32, 31, 38 and 29; and RBI years of 117, 126, 113, 135 and 99. Yes, Magglio was pretty good.

The knee surgeries also cost him a World Series ring: The Sox felt they could not wait for the results of his final knee procedure. They had to proceed, they said, with their off-season plans. So Ordonez watched the Series from his home in Venezuela—and eventually signed with Detroit.

"It's hard to see your [former] teammates win the World Series," he said. "You spend your whole career there and—I left one year early. I didn't know they were going to win the World Series."

As it happened, though, his new team made it to the World Series the very next year. The Tigers did not win it all, however. Even so, White Sox fans had to be smiling when Magglio Ordonez hit the ALCS-winning home run that October evening in Motown.

59 The Youngest Starting Pitcher Ever

Some of those fortunate enough to still have in their possession Topps 1958 Baseball Card No. 129 only recently realized why the card is, in a way, rather special.

The card is of former White Sox left-hander Jim Derrington, the photo of him having been taken during the 1957 season, when he was 17. He was one of the last of the '50s bonus babies and, at 6'3", 195, one of the biggest. The Los Angeles native signed with the Sox in September 1956, and manager Marty Marion named him to start the season finale September 30 in Kansas City.

When he threw his first pitch that day to the Athletics' Vic Power, the 16-year-old made history: He was—and remains—the youngest pitcher to start a regular-season big-league game. (The late Joe Nuxhall, then 15, was the youngest pitcher to *appear* in a big-league game.)

In that 1956 finale, Derrington pitched six innings and gave up five earned runs, nine hits, six walks, and a balk—and left after home runs by Power and Lou Skizas put K.C. up 6–3 after six. Jim also singled to right his second time up, becoming the youngest player to get a base hit in an American League game. That he was up against big-leaguers and not high school or American Legion competition didn't concern him.

"I was always used to playing against much better competition," he once told an interviewer. "I played semipro ball with my dad when I was 13. If I hadn't been wild, I would've won [that first start]. I felt confident.

"I could throw hard, real hard. There were no radar guns in those days, but I wish there were. It would have been interesting."

The following year, Derrington was in 20 games and pitched 37 innings, going 0–1 with a 4.86 ERA under a new manager, Al Lopez. Lopez gave the kid lefty five starts, four of which lasted no longer than three innings. However, on Saturday night, August 10, before 31,470 at Comiskey Park and with the Sox still just four games back of the first-place Yankees, Derrington showed what the future might hold. He zipped through a lineup that included two of the AL's best hitters—Harvey Kuenn and Al Kaline—and took a no-hitter and a 3–0 lead into the sixth. But with one out, Bill Tuttle doubled to "cancel the postgame show." Tuttle stayed at second, though, as Kuenn flied out and J.W. Porter grounded out.

In the seventh, Derrington allowed a single to Kaline but nothing else and still led 3–0. He walked Red Wilson to open the eighth and then gave up a homer to Reno Bertoia. With the score 3–2, Lopez went out and took the ball from the 17-year-old, who walked to the dugout as 31,000-plus stood and cheered. And then staff ace Billy Pierce, making a rare relief appearance—so badly did Lopez want to get Derrington a "W"—was tagged for four runs in the ninth and the Sox lost 6–4.

The nice folks at Topps offered encouragement by having the following printed on the back of that 1958 card: "The Sox feel that this will be a big year for young Jim."

Derrington struggled, though, in 1958 when he was 10–8 at Colorado Springs but his ERA was a loud 7.06. With a weak Charleston club in 1959, he had the same record (10–8) but sliced his ERA to 3.68 and struck out 134 in 176 innings. "After my second year in the minors," he said, "I was really pitching well."

He was scheduled to start the opener for the Sox's Triple-A San Diego club in 1960—at age 20—when he hurt his arm in an exhibition game with Sacramento. He had torn all the ligaments and tendons in his left elbow. "The doctor told me I'd be able to throw again, but not like I had."

Derrington took a year off from pitching and instead played the outfield at Charleston in 1960, then pitched in 1961 at Lincoln, where he tried to re-invent himself as an off-speed pitcher. After that season, he gave up the pursuit. He was 21.

"A lot of people said it came too soon, that I wasn't ready for that kind of pressure," Derrington said. "But I don't know. I was throwing as hard as I could. I knew I could play at that level. I do know that for all the kids who play baseball, the biggest dream you ever have is to play in the big leagues, and that dream came true for me.

"All things considered, I wouldn't change a thing."

60 The Nights Were Long at Old Comiskey

It is rather hard to believe, but until the White Sox made the change in 1955, night games at Comiskey Park started at 8:30 p.m. A normal, 2-hour–15-minute ballgame before 1955 would have had you out of your seat by, say, 10:45, in your car by 10:55 and home perhaps by midnight—depending on how far away you lived.

So when Chicago American sports columnist Warren Brown began referring to Comiskey Park as Get Home Late Park, he wasn't being critical so much as he simply wished to make a point: Boy, some of these nights are really, really long.

After what went on at 35th and Shields on Thursday and Friday nights, July 12–13, 1951, Brown would have had every right to call the place Get Home Extremely Late Park.

Here's what happened:

First, it's important to point out that the All-Star break had just ended and play was resuming on Thursday night, July 12. The surprising Go-Go White Sox, as they had come to be known, were in first place, a game ahead of Boston, two ahead of New York and four ahead of Cleveland. The Sox, White and Red, were to play a twi-night doubleheader Thursday evening. First game would start at 6. Second game would start 25 minutes after Game 1 ended.

The only problem was that the second game went 17 innings and lasted 4 hours 1 minute.

Some highlights:

In Game 1, Boston's Mel Parnell opposed his former Red Sox teammate, Joe Dobson. The teams traded zeroes until one out in the seventh, when Boston's Billy Goodman walked and scored on a homer to left by Clyde Vollmer. In the eighth, little lefty Marv Rotblatt, a lifelong Chicagoan, gave up a two-out double that scored Johnny Pesky, who had walked.

Now it was 3–0. It was still 3–0 when the White Sox came up in the ninth. Don Lenhardt walked, Jim Busby singled to right, and so did Phil Masi to fill the bases with no outs. The crowd of 52,592 was, one could say, alive. Harry Taylor, a right-hander, relieved Parnell, and Paul Richards sent lefty-hitting Eddie Stewart up to bat for Chico Carrasquel. Stewart grounded out to second, a run scoring and men moving to second and third. Al Zarilla hit for Rotblatt and he too grounded out to second baseman Bobby Doerr, a run scored and Masi moved to third.

That brought up Bob Dillinger, who sent a groundball to Doerr, who fired to first to end it.

Boston had a rookie lefty, Leo Kiely, going against that year's ERA champ, Saul Rogovin, in Game 2. Chicago scored twice in the seventh to go up 4–3, Nellie Fox's single breaking the tie. Boston came right back to tie it on Dom DiMaggio's RBI single, and the game stayed tied until the 17th, the home team having loaded the bases with one out in the 12th but failing to score.

In the Boston 17th, Lou Boudreau singled, went to third on Goodman's one-out single and scored on Vollmer's sacrifice fly. Naturally, the Sox went down 1–2–3 in their half. The scoreboard clock read 12:40-something: Some bulbs, not used to having to work so late, had burned out.

Rogovin hadn't burned out, however. He pitched all 17 innings.

The next night, Billy Pierce opposed fellow lefty Mickey McDermott—before only 25,211. This time the game went 19! And McDermott went 17. This one was tied 2–2 in the 19th, but Vollmer singled in the tie-breaking run and Fox's error brought in another run. It was past 1 a.m. by then, so those who had stayed this long were now departing.

Floyd Baker's pinch single, a hit by Dillinger and Fox's hit off the pitcher, Taylor, filled the bases with no outs. Stewart batted for Busby and singled to left, scoring two and tying the game. Ray Scarborough relieved Taylor, and Zarilla beat out a bunt toward the mound. With the bases filled again, Lenhardt flied deep to center to score Fox, and the White Sox, after 4:47, finally had a victory.

Wonder what time Warren Brown got home that night.

61 Even This Bunch Had Its Moments

The battle cry of the Boston Braves down the stretch in 1948 was: *"Spahn and Sain and pray for rain."*

That was the year Warren Spahn and Johnny Sain often pitched with just two days' rest and led the Braves to the World Series.

The 1970 White Sox, one could tell early, were going to have an awful season, because of the lack of pitching other than that provided by starters Tommy John and Joe Horlen—and reliever Wilbur Wood. Hence, the following little rhyme began making the rounds:

"Tommy and Joe and pray for snow."

Others didn't make it into the newspapers or simply didn't catch on:

"Arrigo and Sisk: Why take the risk?" and *"Secrist or Virle—they'll make you hurl."*

Jerry Arrigo and Tommie Sisk had experienced success before in their careers. They would not do so in 1970. Nor would either Don Secrist or Virle Rounsaville. No, the 1970 Sox were not exactly pennant contenders, but they *could* hit. Catchers Duane Josephson (.316) and Ed Herrmann (.283, 19 homers in 297 at-bats) finally began coming into their own. At 36, Luis Aparicio, in his final year in Chicago, batted .313. First baseman Gail Hopkins hit .286. Carlos May, miraculously returning from having blown off his right thumb during Marine mortar training the previoius August, batted .285 with 12 home runs. Ken Berry batted .276 and won a Gold Glove for his brilliant play in center. And then there was Bill Melton, who broke the club home run record of 29 and wound up with 33.

They had their fun, too, mixed in with all the losing. Herrmann and Melton drove a white, souped-up 1929 Ford—called "The Big White Machine"—around the park after the weekly victory. But the most fun they had came on May 31 in Boston, when they jumped all over their former teammate, Gary Peters, at Fenway Park and pounded out a 22–13 victory.

The fun started almost immediately, as the White Sox scored six in the first, sending Peters to the clubhouse far earlier than he had any right to expect. Little Walter Williams started it with a double off the Green Monster, and he scored on the first of five hits by Aparicio, who took second on an error by center fielder Carl Yastrzemski. Rookie first baseman Ossie Blanco, who had become, for no apparent reason, a favorite of manager Don Gutteridge, singled to left, Looie came across and it was 2–0. After Peters fanned May and Josephson, Melton singled Blanco home.

Buddy Bradford walked, and both he and Melton scored when "Yaz" dropped Bobby Knoop's flyball for his second error of the inning, Knoop reaching second base. Sox pitcher Jerry Janeski singled to score Knoop, and Lee Stange entered to relieve Peters. It was now 6–0, and Peters had given up three, four, five, and six runs in the first inning of each of his last four starts.

"Maybe I'll start (reliever) Sparky Lyle next time," joked Boston manager Eddie Kasko, "and bring Gary in for the second inning."

When the Red Sox got uncomfortably close, down 11–7 after five, the White Sox went back to work and put up a 7-spot. May led off with a hit to left, Josephson doubled him to third, and both scored on Melton's double to left. When Bradford walked, Bill Lee was replaced on the mound by Jose Santiago, who was promptly greeted by Knoop's double that plated Melton and sent Bradford to third. After pitcher Floyd Weaver popped to right, Williams singled to drive in Bradford as Knoop stopped at third. Now it was 18–7, and the Sox could breathe a bit easier.

The Chicago Sox had some more Fenway fun later in the year—on August 19, to be exact, when, after trailing 5–2 entering the ninth, they scored 11 runs and won 13–5. Berry, Melton, and Aparicio each got two hits in the inning.

62 Getting Even with L.A.

This was supposed to be a fun weekend to begin with. With the Los Angeles Dodgers scheduled to be facing the White Sox in interleague play at U.S. Cellular Field June 17–19, the Sox figured it would be nice to bring back some of the few remaining players from the 1959 Sox, the Dodgers' opponents in the 1959 World Series.

Before the Saturday night game, the Sox honored 11: Billy Pierce, Jim Landis, Bob Shaw, Jim Rivera, Barry Latman, Jim McAnany and Rudy Arias—plus four who had spent almost all of that season in the minors: first baseman Ron Jackson, pitcher Claude Raymond, third baseman J.C. Martin, and outfielder Joe Hicks. (Not that it mattered, but very few in the stands or press-box were aware that McAnany had hit an even .400 and Hicks .381 for Colorado Springs in 1958.)

Then the 2005 Sox took the field, decked out in 1959 uniforms. But, of course, the unies didn't match the numbers the 1959 players had worn. So running out to left field was Scott Podsednik as Dick Donovan (No. 22), Aaron Rowand as third-base coach Tony Cuccinello (33) and Carl Everett as Harry "Suitcase" Simpson (8) in right. At third was Joe Crede as big, hard-throwing right-hander Early Wynn (24). Juan Uribe was at shortstop, wearing 5, the number of 1959 third baseman Bubba Phillips. Tadahito Iguchi, wearing pitcher Ken McBride's 15, was playing second and Sammy Esposito—oops, Paul Konerko—at first (No. 14). Designated hitter Frank Thomas had No. 35, Bob Shaw's old number, and pitching was Freddy Garcia, wearing the number of Al Lopez's bench coach, Johnny Cooney (34).

Alas, only A.J. Pierzynski (12) didn't have a match, but that was all right. He was going to stand out in a different way this night.

As the game began, the Sox had a 44–22 record and solid lead in the AL Central—5½ games on Minnesota and 8½ on Cleveland. But for most of the night, they certainly did not resemble World Series contenders. First, they were mesmerized through the first six innings by Dodgers right-hander Elmer Dessens, who had just come off the disabled list. All Dessens allowed were two hits and an unearned run—and a walk to Pierzynski, who scored in the third to cut the L.A. lead to 2–1.

The situation appeared bleak when Duaner Sanchez came on in the seventh and struck out Konerko, Everett and Rowand, and in the visitors' eighth, when Garcia wild-pitched a run in. So it was 3–1 when the Sox came up to bat in the ninth. Dodgers closer Yhency Brazoban, unscored upon in his last six outings, awaited them. He walked Iguchi, but now there were two outs and "Gooch" was still on second. Here Everett lashed a base hit to right, Iguchi scoring. Willie Harris, running for Everett, stole second, and, on a 2–2 pitch, Rowand lined a single to left, Harris scored and the game was tied. And 36,067 people were getting the feeling.

Next was Pierzynski, in a 1-for-20 skid. After his foul pop fell just out of the reach of first baseman Hee Seop Choi, he went the other way and hit a shot into the seats in left-center to give the Sox a 5–3 triumph.

"People bring up questions about us," A.J. said. "But we're not beating ourselves, and we do the little things very well. We were down to our last strike a couple of times tonight, but we don't quit. As soon as the ninth came, we said, 'Let's find a way.'"

And they did, just like their honored guests had done so often 46 years before.

63 Really? 53,000 on a Tuesday Night?

The White Sox of 1954 might have been among the top 10 in franchise history if it hadn't been for some truly devastating injuries. It was the best club Paul Richards managed during his four years in Chicago and was the best one Frank Lane generally managed during his seven years there.

Richards' outfield was headed by left fielder Minnie Minoso, who had his greatest year in 1954: 29 doubles, 18 triples, 19 home runs, 116 runs batted in, 119 runs scored, and a .320 batting average. Next to Minnie in center was Chicagoan Johnny Groth and, in right field, was Jim Rivera. He also had an All-Star infield with George Kell at third, Chico Carrasquel at short, Nellie Fox at second and Ferris Fain at first. Sherman Lollar was the No. 1 catcher.

Virgil Oliver "Fire" Trucks, a 20-game winner in 1953 and on his way to another big year in 1954, was the leader of a pitching staff that also included Billy Pierce (recovering from some arm soreness), Bob Keegan, Sandy Consuegra, rookie Jack Harshman, and relievers Harry Dorish and Morrie Martin and swing man Don Johnson.

With the pitching and offense clicking, the White Sox were in first place most of June, and the deal for Kell had fired up the fan base. When that trade went down, Sox fans got out their pocket schedules and circled two series: July 9-10-11 against Cleveland and July 27-28-29 vs. New York. And then they went and bought their tickets.

What they couldn't have known was that, by the time the games were actually played, Kell would be sidelined till early August with a twisted knee and Fain would be out for the rest of the season with a more severe knee injury. And yet, the Sox were hanging tough that last week in July when the Yankees came to town. That is one reason—others were the age-old Yankee mystique and the warmth of the beautiful summer evening—that people kept coming and coming that Tuesday night.

So, on July 27, 1954, a standing-room-only throng of 53,067 showed up ready to do some yelling. They got their chance in the first inning, when Minoso crushed one of Harry Byrd's pitches into the center-field bullpen on one hop for a ground-rule double. Up now was the former Cubs manager and first baseman, Phil Cavarretta, hitting .329 in 76 at-bats since signing in late May as a free agent. Cavarretta lined a single to center, scoring Minoso, and took off for second when he noticed Mickey Mantle's throw from center couldn't be cut off. Catcher Yogi Berra's throw to second was just a split second late. Jim Rivera followed with another single, and "Cavvy" beat another Mantle throw home, and the score was 2–0.

Meanwhile, Trucks was firing heat at Yankee batters, shutting them down on five singles over nine innings. He struck out four and walked only two and worked quickly: The game was over in 2 hours 15 minutes.

"Ted Williams," Trucks once said, "always gave me credit, said that for consistency, for throwing hard over the whole nine innings, I was always at high velocity. Of course, I was strictly a fastball pitcher, anyway. I never really had a great curveball. I had a decent slider and, under Paul Richards, I developed a pretty good change-of-pace. And that helped extend my career a few years."

Richards was off to Baltimore by mid-September, and Trucks' manager was to be Marty Marion, his skipper in 1953 with the Browns before they traded him to Chicago.

"He [Marion] didn't pitch me like he should have in 1955," Trucks said. "He'd skip me...and I didn't like that. He wasn't my kind of manager."

But, for the 53,067 people who watched him baffle the Yankees that July night, Virgil Trucks surely was their kind of pitcher.

64 The Cell: A Quick Sell

Here are a few facts and figures about U.S. Cellular Field, often called "The House That Frank Built," sometimes known as "James R. Thompson Stadium at Reinsdorf Park," or, as it was originally called, "New Comiskey Park," or, also, "The Ballpark On 35th," but mostly, "The Cell."

These notes were culled from the club's own publications, and many are quite interesting.

The total construction cost was $137 million.

The total renovation cost (to date) reads "approximately" $90 million. Oh, if only they'd have done it right the first time....

The ballpark originally stood 146 feet high, from the roof peak to the playing field; the height now, since the top eight rows of the upper deck were lopped off, is 130 feet.

The Cell is the first new sports facility built in Chicago since Chicago Stadium opened its gates in 1929.

It also was the first new baseball-only facility since Royals Stadium (now known as Kauffman Stadium) opened in 1973. Fifteen others have opened since 1991.

Groundbreaking took place on May 7, 1989, and the ballpark officially opened on April 18, 1991.

Approximately 100,000 cubic yards of concrete were used in the building process.

The ballpark has been used in these motion pictures: *Little Big League, Major League II*, and *My Best Friend's Wedding*.

It has been the site of concerts by The Rolling Stones (2002) and by Bruce Springsteen (2003).

The main concourse is 40 feet wide, compared to about eight feet at old Comiskey and about five at Wrigley Field.

The ballpark has 12 escalators and 15 elevators, as well as 40 public restrooms.

It has more than 400 wheelchair-accessible seats.

Of course, there is an exploding scoreboard, which is loaded manually but is set off by computers.

The stadium also has a Mitsubishi DiamondVision screen that is 53 feet wide and 28 feet high.

The press box, which was relocated to the first-base side a few years back, has 100 seats and 32 plasma TVs.

About that playing field: The infield consists of dirt brought across the street from the old ballpark; the base of the field is made up of four inches each of drainage tiles, pea gravel and sand; the playing field is made up of bluegrass sod, with three different blends of grass.

And finally, here are some of the best additions to the park since renovations began in 2001:

A new out-of-town scoreboard was added above the right-field concourse in 2009 to allow fans to follow other games, providing ball-and-strike count, number of outs, who's pitching and who's batting.

The installation of dark-green seats was completed by the opening of the 2007 season. Funny, but the almost-empty upper deck still looks almost as empty with the green seats as it did with the blue ones.

Eight rows and 6,600 seats were removed from the upper deck in 2004, and the original sloped canopy roof was replaced by a flat one, helping to contain crowd noise.

A vertical screen was installed in 2002 behind home plate, enabling more fans to injure themselves—or at least lose their beer—by trying to make diving, sprawling catches of foul balls.

Actually, that change was among the very best.

65 Washington Slept Here

The title of this chapter also is word-for-word what appeared on one of the all-time great homemade signs ever to be unfurled at Comiskey Park—or any ballpark, for that matter.

It is funny and yet it is sad as well. That's because it was aimed at a ballplayer who could have been a real Chicago favorite but maybe did not want to be one or perhaps never thought he was talented enough to be one.

It tells the Chicago chapter, anyway, of the Claudell Washington story, a tale about an Oakland native who played in the World Series with his hometown team at age 20—and played well, too, going 4-for-7 (.571) in a five-game blitz of the Dodgers. At age 21 in 1975, he was an every-day outfielder for the A's, batting .308 with 77 RBIs and 40 stolen bases.

That might have been the problem.

Washington, with that big a year for a division champion and doing so at such a young age, may have set the bar too high for himself. Also, he brooded over being traded from the A's to Texas before the 1977 season, this after A's owner Charlie Finley had assured him there was no chance he'd be traded. He had a decent year for the Rangers in 1977, but by the following May he was brooding again; the Rangers traded him to the last-place White Sox in the Bobby Bonds deal, at a time Claudell was nursing a bad ankle that had put him on the DL. The Rangers, too, had told him he wasn't going to be dealt. Washington's response to the deal, made on a Tuesday, was to not report to the Sox till that Saturday. He showed up at the Oakland Coliseum an hour after the game had ended—with a Chicago loss.

Said Claudell to manager Bob Lemon: "I overslept."

He caught up on his sleep soon enough, but his ankle really didn't fully heal until that winter, so his 1978 season was not, he would insist, a true picture of what he could do, both at the plate and in the outfield. Fans only could see an outfielder who didn't seem interested in chasing down balls hit in the gap or giving it his all on balls driven toward the wall. The seeds for the banner no doubt began germinating during that period.

Months later, he explained a few things. "I didn't come over here to the White Sox with a positive attitude. I was depressed. But I've grown up. I never had anything against this club. It's just that I thought I had played good enough baseball that somebody would want to keep me."

At that time, in the sometimes rarefied air of spring training, he predicted what he would do in 1979.

"If I don't get hurt," he said, "I'm going to hit .300, steal 50—maybe 60—bases. And I'm going to play in the 'Midsummer Classic.' "

Well, he didn't come close to all that, but he had a good season: He batted an even .280 with 33 doubles, 5 triples, 13 homers and 66 RBIs—ad 19 stolen bases. And, on July 14, two nights after "Disco Demolition," he had one of the biggest games of his career as the Sox hammered Detroit 12–4 at Comiskey Park.

In the third inning, facing Tigers starter Steve Baker with the bases empty, he hit his eighth homer of the year to tie the game

1–1. In the seventh, leading off against Milt Wilcox, he drove No. 9 into the lower deck in right. And in the eighth, with Dave Tobik now working for the Tigers, Claudell came up with two men on and launched his third of the night and 10th of the year for a 12–4 final.

He had gone 3-for-5 with five RBIs. Was he in Chicago to stay?

The answer is in the chapter title.

By next June, he'd been traded to the Mets for a minor-league pitcher. Washington then played for the Braves, Yankees, and Angels—seven teams all told. His lifetime batting average? .278.

That's nowhere near what a lot of people had expected, but he had an okay career. No doubt he can sleep well.

66 "Psycho" Really Was

"Psycho" is what they used to call Steve Lyons, the eccentric former super utility man of the White Sox during the final years of old Comiskey Park. He got the nickname from a teammate in the Red Sox system who watched Lyons throw a few minor temper tantrums and some bigger ones, too—like chucking equipment onto the field after doing something really awful, like grounding out to the second baseman to end an inning with a runner on third.

He will be remembered in White Sox Country as (A) the player the Sox received from Boston in the Tom Seaver deal in 1986, (B) the man who, as the Sox's late-inning defensive replacement at first base, recorded the final putout in the last game at old Comiskey, and (C) the guy who, knowingly or not, dropped his pants on the field during a game in Detroit in 1990.

In this particular episode, Lyons slid head-first into first base in a bid for an infield single. Umpire Jim Evans called "Safe!" Tigers pitcher Dan Petry disagreed. They then argued over the matter. Lyons, absorbed in the discussion, felt dirt trickling down the inside of his pants. Apparently forgetting where he was, he unbuckled his belt, dropped his pants and bent over to brush away some dirt. Then, suddenly realizing his blunder, he looked skyward as if to ask, "What did I just do?"

Fans laughed at the sight of Lyons wearing nothing but a white athletic supporter over a pair of white longjohns. He quickly pulled his pants back up.

"I could feel dirt running all down my legs," Lyons said. "I just kind of forgot where I was."

Lyons, who was forced at second on a grounder by the next batter, got a round of applause from his teammates as he walked into the Chicago dugout.

"I don't have anything to be embarrassed about, but it's embarrassing that I did it," Lyons said. "When I got back to the bench, girls were waving money at me."

He said it was unintentional, that he wasn't thinking about where he was or whether the television cameras were on him. "I may be off the wall, but I'm not stupid," he insisted.

Within 24 hours of the incident, Lyons did approximately 20 radio interviews and seven live TV spots.

"We've got a pitcher, Melido Perez, who earlier this month pitched a no-hitter," he said the next night. "And I'll guarantee you he didn't do two live shots afterward. I pull my pants down, and I do seven. Something's pretty skewed toward the zany in this game."

"Six guys have thrown no-hitters this year," Sox pitcher Jack McDowell noted. "Only one guy's taken off his pants."

Psycho.

"He loves that name," said Jeff Torborg, then the Sox manager. "That ought to tell you something."

So may this:

As a rookie with the Red Sox in 1985, he was on second base and Marty Barrett on first with two out in the ninth and Boston down by two to Milwaukee. The batter was Wade Boggs, who was hitting .400 at the time. Lyons took off for third and was thrown out to end the game.

"In a way," he said, "I'm glad I pulled my pants down. I'd just as soon be remembered for that than for trying to steal third with Wade Boggs up and two out in the ninth."

Give him credit, though, for being the type of player who would try to help out everywhere. He added catching to his list of positions in 1988 after then–White Sox manager Jim Fregosi strongly suggested it. Lyons made two appearances as a catcher and started 102 games at third base, two at second, eight in center, and five in right.

Fregosi was asked what Lyons did best. His response: "TV interviews."

67 1960: Getting It Straight

Bill Veeck still gets beaten up over the way he "bulwarked," as he put it, the White Sox for a run at a repeat American League championship in 1960. He has his detractors; he has his backers.

Both sides are correct. It all depends on perspective.

Here was Bill's. He certainly hadn't brought it up publicly, but he was beginning to have some doubts about just how much longer he was going to be around—not just around ballparks, but *around*. He had enjoyed immensely the run to the 1959 title, and he wanted desperately to win again, And he wished to do so with a team that he would have put together—not one that Frank Lane, Chuck Comiskey, Al Lopez, and John Rigney had put together. And so he set about putting together *his* club.

His detractors did not have Veeck's perspective. They looked around and saw a 1959 Sox team that, yes, had several oldsters but also had some young ballplayers who were the envy of most of baseball. Keep this bunch together, tweak here and there with a trade, and, so the theory went, "the White Sox may not repeat and may not win in 1961, but look out in 1962, 1963, 1964, and beyond."

But Bill Veeck ran the club. His approach was going to win out. And so he began thinking about who he might make available and who he wished to pursue from other teams.

"The statement Bill had made," Billy Pierce recalled, "was that the 1959 team wasn't *his* team. He wanted to repeat in 1960 with *his* team." Added Al Lopez: "Bill made the remark, 'If Lopez could win the pennant with *that* club, I'm gonna get some hitters in here and he'll win the pennant next year easy.'"

His first post–World Series move was to send former bonus-baby first baseman Ron Jackson to Boston for lefty Frank Baumann, 26 and showing improvement. Next, at the winter meetings in Florida, he brought Minnie Minoso back to Chicago from Cleveland (plus catcher Dick Brown and two more lefties for Lopez's lefty-less bullpen: Don Ferrarese and Jake Striker). Veeck gave up third baseman Bubba Phillips and two of the younger set: first baseman Norm Cash, 25, and catcher Johnny Romano, 25, who had led the AL in pinch-hitting as a rookie (8-for-13, .615).

Next was the trade of 20-year-old Opening Day left fielder Johnny Callison, the crown jewel of the farm system, to the Phillies for thumper Gene Freese, a third baseman with power (23 homers in 1959) but whose fielding was erratic at best.

Then, in April, in the final days of spring training, Veeck sent catcher Earl Battey, 25, and a good-looking minor-league first baseman, Don Mincher, to Washington for a longtime Veeck

Freese Frame: Coming Clean on Gene

When it started, or where, no one seems to know, but whenever the White Sox's 1960 disappointments are discussed, Gene Freese invariably is grouped with Roy Sievers as one of Bill Veeck's ancient, lead-footed, base-clogging additions who was going to further slow down the Go-Go Sox.

The truth is that Freese turned 26 in January 1960, stole himself 10 bases and, as Veeck had anticipated, was no defensive genius but had the kind of pop that the previous year's Sox club had none of at the third-base position.

Freese did his part in trying to keep the 1960 Sox in the race until the final weeks. He batted a solid .273 with a pile of extra-base hits: 32 doubles, 6 triples and 17 homers. And he drove in 79 runs.

That winter he went to the Cincinnati Reds in a three-way deal that netted the Sox two pitchers: Cal McLish and a blazing-fast lefty named Juan Pizarro. And Freese? He wound up in the World Series.

favorite, Roy Sievers. And then, the day before the season began, 23-year-old right-hander Barry Latman went to Cleveland for the once-brilliant lefty Herb Score. Also, in May, Veeck purchased from Washington a dependable starter/reliever in Russ Kemmerer.

The team struggled through late June (30–29 on the 20th) before beginning to jell. They won 14 of 20 heading into the All-Star break, won eight straight and took first place on the weekend of July 22–24 by winning three of four in New York. The Yankees, Sox and Orioles took turns in first place throughout August. Then, with two weeks to go, the Sox were two games behind. But then the Yankees won their last 15 straight. Goodbye, pennant.

While holdovers like Nellie Fox, Sherm Lollar, Jim Landis and pitchers Dick Donovan and Turk Lown fell off sharply from 1959, Veeck's acquisitions had kept the club in the race. Minoso hit .311 with 20 homers and 105 RBIs, Roy Sievers (.295, 28, 93) carried the club in July, and Freese drove in 79 runs though missing time with an injured foot. Also, Al Smith, who moved to right field from left to make room for Minnie, hit .315. Baumann led the league in ERA and Score strung together one low-hit game after another in July and August.

Add the brand-new exploding scoreboard and the record Chicago baseball attendance of 1,644,460, and 1960 was a fun season. The next year, as Veeck's detractors knew, would not bring more of the same.

68 The Blackout Game

"Good guys wear black," or so the White Sox ad campaign went a few years back. And now, the evening before the American League Central tiebreaker game, the Sox front office was calling for all fans of the "good guys" to wear black as well.

It was Monday night, September 29, 2008, and White Sox fans were whooping it up. Their off-and-on heroes had defeated Detroit 8–2 just a couple hours earlier in front of 35,923 at The Cell, the big blow having been a record fourth rookie grand slam by Alexei Ramirez, the so-called "Cuban Missile." The victory had moved the Sox into a one-game, winner-take-all showdown Tuesday night at home for the AL Central title against the Twins, admired by Sox manager Ozzie Guillen but universally hated by most all real Sox fans.

The marketing department, headed by Brooks Boyer, had gotten the concept off the ground within minutes of Monday's victory. Then, within an hour, word came that the tiebreaker was a complete sellout. Radio ads were already being heard, asking that fans wear black to the game. Added Boyer: "We will have 40,000 'Sox Pride' black rally towels, and hopefully, 40,000 fans using them in support of the team. Hopefully, it'll be pretty darn intimidating, and the Twins can see how it's done Chicago style."

The game, of course, wouldn't have been necessary if the Sox had won just one of their three games with the Twins up in the Metrodome the week before. The Sox, however, simply couldn't win in that place. Then they had come home for a season-ending three-game series with Cleveland and were just pounded in the first two contests.

On Sunday, Minnesota and Scott Baker blanked Kansas City 6–0. The Sox, who now *had* to win, had saved their best, Mark Buehrle, for last. He gave up a Jhonny Peralta home run in the second, but the Sox scored three times in their half, the key hit Paul Konerko's 22nd homer. Jermaine Dye added a two-run single in the seventh, after which Matt Thornton and Bobby Jenks each threw an inning of scoreless relief, and the Sox won 5–1.

Next came Monday afternoon's rain-delayed makeup game with the Tigers, whose manager, former Sox third-base coach Jim Leyland, made the mistake of bringing in ex-Sox reliever Gary Glover to face Ramirez with one out and the bases filled in the sixth. Glover, some recalled, had given up the longest home run by an opponent at The Cell, a 495-foot blast by Oakland's Eric Chavez a few seasons back. Ramirez hit the first pitch from Glover into the left-field seats, 35,923 went nuts and this one was over.

Bring on the Twins.

John Danks, working on three days' rest, gave up just two hits and three walks in eight innings. He got help from Ken Griffey Jr., whose throw from center field in the fifth cut down Michael Cuddyer at the plate, A.J. Pierzynski hanging on to the ball despite the impact of the collision. The black-jacketed 40,354 let out with a roar—of relief.

The game was still scoreless when the beloved Jim Thome led off the home seventh with a monstrous 460-foot home run to straightaway center, only the third hit off Twins starter Nick

Fans "black out" U.S. Cellular Field for the AL Central tiebreaker game on September 30, 2008. (Getty Images)

Blackburn. One run was all that was needed. Danks gave way to Bobby Jenks for a 1–2–3 ninth, the game ending with a diving catch by Griffey's replacement, Brian Anderson.

The White Sox had become the first team in baseball history to win their final three games against three different opponents.

"I think I'll sleep tonight," said Sox general manager Kenny Williams. "I haven't slept too well for a while."

Now, Tampa Bay awaited.

69 Those Rivals from the North Side

There were all sorts of stories in the Chicago papers' sports sections this past season about the formerly red-hot rivalry between the White Sox and their pals from the North Side, the Cubs. Where had the intensity gone? Where had the crowds gone, for that matter? There weren't even 30,000 for either of the two matchups on the South Side.

Several reasons were posited, but often the most obvious was missing from the discussion. And that is simply this: The two teams were dreadful in 2013, which had not been the case in recent years. The Sox generally have had winning teams since 1997, the first year of interleague play, and have been truly bad only twice: in 2007 and this past season. The Cubs have had fewer winning years since 1997 but they've had their share. The games naturally mean more when both are having good years.

And maybe two series of three games each was becoming too much of a good thing. The setup used in 2013 and which is also on the schedule for 2014 (two games Monday and Tuesday May 5–6 at Wrigley Field followed by two May 7–8 at The Cell) isn't much of a solution either. Having the series *that* early in the season, and on weeknights at a time when schools are still in session, makes little if any sense.

Another factor: One of the teams actually made it to the World Series quite recently—and won it. Having experienced that, Sox fans who formerly thought of the Cubs series as being *the* highlight of the season no longer think that way. However, there is still reason to believe that, some day in the not-too-distant future, Major League Baseball will get it right.

Till then, there are the newspaper clippings from an era gone forever, when the Sox and Cubs would play the "City Series" at

5 Wonderful Cub Defeats

June 28, 2002: The White Sox were down 8–0 to Kerry Wood by the third inning on the South Side. Then Paul Konerko took over—he had a 4-for-4 afternoon and smashed two home runs—-and the Sox won 13–9.

June 8, 2001: Carlos Lee was a career Cub-killer. One of his more memorable blows came in the 10th inning this night, when, with the score 3–3 and the bases loaded with two out, "El Caballo" belted a grand slam for a 7–3 victory.

June 13, 1999: After a three-hour rain delay, play resumed in the eighth and Mike Caruso hit a liner just over the wall in right for a two-run homer, and the Sox won 6–4 to complete a sweep at Wrigley Field.

May 20, 2006: A.J. Pierzynski tagged up, came rumbling home and collided with the Cubs' Michael Barrett—but was safe when the ball popped loose. A.J. slapped home plate for emphasis, which Barrett didn't enjoy. So the Cub catcher punched him in the face, igniting an on-field brawl. Once order was restored, Tadahito Iguchi hit a grand slam. Sox won 7–0.

July 1, 2006: With two on and two outs in the top of the ninth, the Cubs leading 6–5 and Ryan Dempster on the mound, Pierzynski stepped up and crushed one onto Sheffield Avenue for an 8–6 Sox triumph.

Wrigley Field and old Comiskey Park at the same time the World Series was taking place. The first series was held in 1903; Sox domination, a lessening of interest with each passing year, and finally World War II combined to end the event in 1942. All told, the Sox won 18 out of 25 City Series. None was held in 1906, 1907, 1908, 1910, 1917, 1918, 1919, 1929, 1932, 1935, or 1938—years when one or both teams were in the World Series—or in 1920, when the Black Sox scandal story was just breaking.

There were the Boys Baseball Benefit Games that were played during the season—usually under the lights at Comiskey Park—from 1949 through 1972. This period included the Sox's 17-year string of winning seasons, and yet Ernie Banks and the invariably second-division Cub teams (pre–1967) generally came out the winners. There were exceptions, of course. In 1960, Herb Score signaled he was ready for a heavier workload by blanking the Cubs 7–0. In 1964, a standing-room-only crowd of 52,712—hundreds stood behind ropes in right field—watched the Sox hammer the Cubs 11–1. And in 1965, Juan Pizarro, recovering from arm trouble, indicated he was just about ready to go again when he went five innings of one hit ball in a 6–1 Sox victory before 37,526.

Usually, though, the Cubs would bring up someone from the minors—like 18-year-old Dick Ellsworth, who shut out the Sox in the 1958 game—and the Sox would have no chance.

But the real fun started in 1997, when the advent of interleague play suddenly meant that the games counted in the standings. The ensuing years have brought Sox-Cub games with on-field brawls, fights between teammates, fisticuffs in the stands, game-ending pickoffs, walk-off home runs, grand slams, extra-inning thrillers, sellout crowds, and, through 2013, a total of 49 victories for the Sox to 45 for the Cubs.

It will be fun again soon enough.

70 How the Sox Landed Al Lopez

Good timing and the help of an old friend combined in the off-season of 1956–57 to bring to Chicago the brightest manager in baseball at the time and the only manager to beat out Casey Stengel in a pennant race.

Alfonso Ramon Lopez, seventh son of a seventh son, born and raised in the Ybor City section of Tampa, was thinking about his future on this final weekend of the 1956 season. He had just turned 48 the month before. He had enjoyed, for the most part, managing the Cleveland Indians these past six seasons—especially 1954, when his team won 111 games and beat out the Yankees and his former manager, Stengel, by eight games.

But something wasn't right.

Attendance had dropped precipitously in 1955, when Lopez's Tribe, making a strong bid to repeat, led the American League entering the final two weekends and still drew only 1,221,780 in that huge, 72,000-seat Municipal Stadium. The Indians were a solid 88–66 in the just-completed 1956 season, but attendance dropped again, this time to 865,467. Al didn't like the trend.

"It started in 1955," he told an interviewer. "With two weeks to go, we came home tied for first place (with New York) and we had a night game with Detroit. We went to the ballpark and there were 6,000 (actually 14,639 paid) people in the stands. I thought to myself, 'My God, this doesn't look good. If the fans start getting down on your club, you're gonna be in trouble.'"

The Tigers swept the Indians three straight, the Yankees grabbed the lead, and the Tribe finished second. During the final week of the '56 season, Lopez told Tribe VP Hank Greenberg he was resigning at season's end. The Sox front-office tag team of

Yikes! Dykes Won a Lot of Games

Jimmy Dykes, who managed the White Sox from 1934 until his firing in 1946, amassed more victories (899) than any other Sox manager, including Al Lopez (840). Lopez's winning percentage (.564 over nine seasons and parts of two others) overwhelms Dykes' .489, however.

Dykes was a favorite of J. Lou Comiskey from the day he reported to spring training in 1933 as one of the three newcomers from Connie Mack's Philadelphia A's. Comiskey had shelled out $150,000 for third baseman Dykes and outfielders Mule Haas and Al Simmons, the All-Star slugger and Milwaukee native.

Working wonders with players—especially pitchers—who were thought to be washed up, Dykes took the Sox from a 53–99 record and last (eighth) place in 1934 to 81–70 and third place in 1936 and 86–68 and third place again in 1937.

He kept his teams loose with stories of the greats he had played with and against, like Babe Ruth, of whom he said: "All the lies about him are true."

brothers-in-law Chuck Comiskey and John Rigney had decided that 1956 was to be Marty Marion's final year of managing in Chicago—even though the Sox had been 91–63 and 85–69 in Marion's first two years and he had another year to go on his contract. Still, Comiskey and Rigney went to work on Lopez.

"After I resigned," Lopez said, "Hollis Thurston, a White Sox scout, called me from Los Angeles. I remember it was on a Saturday night—the season was over the next day. I hadn't heard from him in quite a while. He and I had been roommates in Brooklyn, real close friends. He said. 'Al, I understand you're not going back to Cleveland.' 'No, Hollis, I've already told Hank I'm gonna quit.' 'Would you be interested in managing the White Sox?' 'Hollis, I don't have anything in mind. But what are they going to do with Marty Marion? I think Marty's got another year on his contract.' 'Well, they asked me to call you.' 'Well, you tell them I'd be glad to sit down and talk with them.'

"After the season was over, I was home maybe a week to 10 days when I got a call from John Rigney and Chuck Comiskey asking if I'd want to come up to Chicago to talk to them and meet Mrs. Comiskey. I said, 'Yeah, I would.' They told me to catch a plane and come in under an assumed name, so none of the writers would find out. I said, 'John, I don't like this—you've got a manager under contract already.' He said, 'Al, whether you come here or not, Marty Marion is through here. We're gonna make a change.' So I flew up to Chicago, they picked me up at the airport, took me over to see Mrs. Comiskey. We talked, I signed, they took me back to the airport, and I flew back to Tampa—all in the same day."

So Al Lopez had the White Sox job and Marty Marion had no job. But Marty didn't seem to mind.

"I hated the travel," he once said. "I'd been in baseball since 1936 and I'd traveled a lot. I'd love coming back home here to St. Louis. I had four daughters and I always wanted to be with them. The reason I got fired in Chicago was, whenever we had an off-day, I was always running back here to be with my family. The White Sox didn't like that."

They *would* like the way Al Lopez operated—especially in 1959.

71 Lights! Camera! White Sox!

They were linked together for so many summers during the 1960s that it should not have been surprising to see their names in the credits of two of the best baseball movies ever produced.

Don Buford signed with the White Sox out of USC in 1959. Ken Berry signed with the Sox out of Wichita State in 1961. Buford spent 1962 at Savannah, Ga., and hit .323. Berry spent the first two months of the 1962 season at Visalia in the California League before moving up to rejoin Buford in Savannah, where he hit .368 in 76 games. They were teammates at Triple-A Indianapolis in 1963, when Berry slumped to .234 and Buford batted .336 with 41 doubles and 42 steals.

Buford made it up to the Sox to stay in 1964, Berry in 1965. And though they aren't that proud of it, they led the Sox in batting average in 1967, each having hit .241.

They both coached and managed in the minors; indeed, Berry managed Robin Ventura at Double-A Birmingham in 1989, the latter's only season of minor-league ball.

Now, name the movies that listed them in the credits:

Correct! Don Buford (along with his college coach, USC's Rod Dedeaux) was the baseball coach/instructor for *Field of Dreams*, the 1989 Phil Alden Robinson classic. And Ken Berry is listed as both baseball coach/instructor and also "Heckler," for the scene when Berry trades a word or two of profanity with Sox slugger "Shoeless Joe" Jackson, in the 1988 film adaptation of Eliot Asinof's *Eight Men Out*.

For *Field of Dreams*, Buford and Dedeaux were flown in to Dubuque to help make the final cuts and then work with those who had survived them. Buford admitted he had been impressed.

"I guess I wasn't surprised at the quality of players," he said. "Semipro is a big part of baseball, and here you have aspiring players playing through school, and some of them played some minor-league ball and have continued to play.

"It doesn't get out of the blood quick, I tell you. We saw some talent."

Quite by chance, Berry landed his position in *Eight Men Out*.

He had managed Kansas City's club in the Midwest League against former big-leaguer Don Leppert of the Minnesota system. The two had become friends, and Leppert called him one day and asked him if he'd like to help out on a movie. Leppert couldn't do it because he had been assigned to manage in the Arizona Fall League.

"So he gave me the number of the person to call," Ken said. "I did and got to be technical adviser. It took about two months, and I had a great time."

Some of the actors involved in that movie, especially Charlie Sheen, had been around the game and had played it competitively. There were, however, other good baseball players besides Sheen, who is also remembered as "Wild Thing" reliever Rick Vaughn in *Major League.*

"D.B. Sweeney knew what he was doing," Berry said of the actor who played Jackson. "He had a good idea of how to play the game. John Cusack [Buck Weaver] was pretty athletic. It's just that era-wise he wasn't quite right. He was trying to do a lot of things that just didn't happen on a ballfield in the '20s. He did make some athletic stops at third base in the movie—he'd just dive fully extended and make the catch. I was hitting those balls to him off camera with a fungo bat, and I was hitting them good."

"I enjoyed working with John Sayles. He was a good director. He'd give me the scenes that we needed to shoot and we'd work on them. I remember one where Sheen had to make a catch and hit the unpadded portion of the park we were shooting in. I showed Charlie how to make the catch and then spin into the wall so that he really wasn't hitting it that hard.

"So we did the shot and Charlie unfortunately forgot about spinning and just slammed right into the wall. He also tore up his leg pretty good when he caught it on [something] sticking out from the door. One other thing about Charlie stands out: I was throwing the ball and he had to dive and make the catch. On one play he did it fully extended directly over his head. Just remarkable."

Remarkable: the perfect word to describe those "temp" jobs Don Buford and Ken Berry had a few years ago.

72 The Cubs Weren't Always Kings at the Gate

Going into the 1993 season, the White Sox had outdrawn the Cubs in 24 of the previous 43 years, going back to 1951. Now you can change that to read: Going into the 2014 season, the White Sox have outdrawn the Cubs in only 24 of the previous 63 years.

That's what happens when the Cubs outdraw the Sox 21 years in a row—oh, and by the way, draw 3 million people eight straight years.

For fans who went to their first baseball games in the decades of the '50s and '60s, all this is sometimes difficult to grasp. After all, you remember when Wrigley Field was simply another old ballpark. Who knew the old place that featured little more than Ernie Banks, the Smokie Links cart, and "crowds" of 6,000 or so not only would still be standing but would today be a museum, loaded not only with Iowans but, truth be told, folks from all over the country—and beyond?

But it's all true, which is fine. The only problem is that there are those who think it was always this way. Like former Cubs manager Dale Sveum, No. 42 on his back but hardly No. 1 in your hearts during his brief South Side stay in 1992.

"That's just the way it's always been," Sveum said last season. "The Chicago Cubs are the Chicago Cubs. People are going to come to Wrigley all the time."

To help Sox fans to keep their sanity in the face of such misinformation, we present two examples from the 1960s. These are two game dates—one from 1961, when both teams had disappointing seasons, and another from 1963, when both teams—yes, even the Cubs—enjoyed successful ones. Both teams happened to be home at the same time: on June 21, 1961, because of a scheduling quirk, and on May 9, 1963 because the Sox were making up a game rained out on April 29.

1961: The Dodgers, favorite opponents of many Cub fans because of the Jackie Robinson years but also the 1959 World Series, were in town for a weekday doubleheader on the North Side. Many in the crowd of 12,364 were there to see the further development of two special young Cubs: third baseman Ron Santo, 21, and rookie outfielder Billy Williams, who had just turned 23. But this afternoon, Stan Williams and Johnny Podres were tough on everyone in the Cubs' lineup, although Billy Williams did manage to go 3-for-8 on the day, which ended with the Dodgers having swept a pair, 4–1 and 4–2, to move within one game of the first-place Reds. The seventh-place Cubs fell to 22–39 and 16½ games out.

At Comiskey Park, the suddenly hot White Sox, a team depending on aging veterans who had started quite slowly, took on second-place Cleveland that evening in a twi-night twin bill. With a crowd of 45,125 roaring all night, the Sox destroyed Tribe pitching and won 15–3 and 11–1 for their fifth and sixth consecutive victories (See "A Homestand to Remember"). They were still down in sixth place (32–34) but had knocked Cleveland out of second.

1963: The Cubs, at long last, were looking like contenders because, of all things, terrific pitching—from the likes of Dick Ellsworth and two former St. Louis Cardinals, Larry Jackson and Lindy McDaniel. But the fans hadn't caught on yet: Witness the Thursday afternoon turnout of 5,961 for a match with Roberto Clemente and the Pirates. Even so, Ellsworth threw a two-hitter and beat the Bucs 3–1 in exactly 2 hours. The Cubs (16–11) were in second place, just two games behind the Giants.

Meanwhile, on the South Side, the Sox and Yankees hoped the predicted night-time rain would hold off so they could get in this hastily arranged makeup of the rained-out April 29 game. They did. Ron Hansen doubled off Ralph Terry in the second inning to drive in Pete Ward and Dave Nicholson, and Ray Herbert, like Ellsworth, fired a two-hitter and the first-place Sox (15–10) beat the second-place New Yorkers 2–0 in just 1:51. And the paid attendance? 32,405.

So, no, this *isn't* "the way it's always been."

Birth of the Midsummer Classic

Even as late as 1933, the biggest name in baseball, even to his fellow players, was still Babe Ruth. If Arch Ward's inaugural All-Star Game was going to be the hit everyone was hoping it would be, then Ruth needed to be *the* star.

He was now 38, yes, but he was on his way to a season most players could only dream of: 34 homers, 103 RBIs, .301 batting, .442 on-base, and .582 slugging average.

"We wanted to see the Babe," admitted St. Louis Cardinals pitcher Bill Hallahan, the National League's starter in that very first Midsummer Classic on July 6, 1933. "Sure, he was old and had a big waistline, but that didn't make any difference. We were on the same field as Babe Ruth."

Ruth didn't disappoint. He was the key to the American League's 4–2 victory, going 2-for-4 with a home run—off Hallahan.

However, if Babe Ruth was the game's No. 1 star, then the No. 2 star had to be the visionary Arch Ward, sports editor of the *Chicago Tribune* and a man with more political clout than most politicians. Ward wore many hats, working throughout his lifetime as a writer, editor, public relations director, and broadcaster. Mainly, though, he was a master promoter.

In This Park, the Fans Cared

By the time the game's third batter came up to hit, the place was awash in boos.

American League starting pitcher Dave Stieb had made an error on Steve Sax's roller to start this 50th Anniversary All-Star Game at old Comiskey Park. Sax then stole second. Stieb then rushed in for Tim Raines' tap and fired to first. But Rod Carew missed the ball and Sax scored from second and Raines went all the way to third.

Two batters, two errors, one run in, and a man on third with nobody out.

Chicago fans hadn't paid this kind of money to see *this*. They let themselves be heard. The players seemed genuinely stunned. There's no booing at an All-Star Game, is there? Well, there is when you've lost 11 in a row like the AL had. And when it's July 6, 1983, 50 years to the day of the first one of these.

The message got through. With the AL ahead 2–1, the home team went to work in the third against Giants lefty Atlee Hamaker. Jim Rice led off with a laser into the lower deck in left. Later in the inning, Robin Yount was walked to load the bases. That's when Fred Lynn hit the first All-Star Game grand slam, a shot to right. It was 9–1 Americans. It was only the third inning. And, it was about time.

"Arch definitely belonged among the great sports editors of his time, probably as much for his promotions as his writing," said the late Cooper Rollow, one of Ward's successors. "He was on a handshake basis with the great sports names of his day, maybe more so than the people in his own department. He was a real good guy, garrulous, a good mixer."

Ward, 36 in 1933, had dreams of becoming a ballplayer (he was a big White Sox fan), but he was slow and had poor eyesight. So he chose to be a sportswriter. He joined the *Tribune* staff in 1925 and became its sports editor five years later and held the position until his death in 1955.

By 1933, Ward had established a reputation for himself as one of the best in the business. He also had ties with a most powerful figure in Chicago, *Tribune* owner and publisher Col. Robert McCormick. That same year, in celebration of Chicago's centennial, the city held a World's Fair, called "A Century of Progress." Highlights included a selection of "Dream cars" from all the major auto manufacturers, a "home of tomorrow" exhibit, and singer Judy Garland.

Mayor Ed Kelly discussed with McCormick the possibility of using a sporting event to coincide with the World's Fair. McCormick went to Ward, who knew exactly what he wanted to present: a major league baseball All-Star Game, pitting the biggest stars of the American League against the biggest stars of the National League.

Making the Trip Even More Worthwhile

The seven White Sox who were winning pitchers in All-Star Games:

Edgar Smith, 1941: Gave up 2-run homer to Arky Vaughan in 8th as NL upped lead to 5–2, but was pitcher of record when Ted Williams hit 3-run shot in 9th for 7–5 AL win.

Early Wynn, 1958: Retired Frank Thomas, Bill Mazeroski, and Del Crandall in 6th, then was lifted for pinch-hitter Gil McDougald, who singled in go-ahead run in bottom half.

Ray Herbert, 1962: Pitched 3 scoreless innings (3rd through 5th) and was in game when Leon Wagner's 2-run homer put AL up 3–1. AL went on to win 9–4 at Wrigley.

Jack McDowell, 1993: Entered in 5th with game tied 2–2, retired Darren Daulton, Ryne Sandberg, and Marquis Grissom in order. AL then scored 3 to take lead for good.

James Baldwin, 2000: Came on in 3rd and gave up game-tying home run to Chipper Jones, but was lifted for pinch-hitter as AL scored 2 in next inning to go ahead to stay.

Mark Buehrle, 2005: Started the game and pitched the first 2 innings and allowed 3 hits but also struck out 3 and threw a double-play ball and left with 1–0 lead.

Chris Sale, 2013: Pitched the second and third innings and retired 6 hitters in succession, striking out 2. Was in game when AL scored its first run in 3–0 triumph.

The *Tribune* would underwrite the game against any loss, Ward told AL president Will Harridge, whose office was right down Michigan Avenue from Tribune Tower, and its sports department would tabulate the votes from fans to select the teams' starters. Ward, despite some NL resistance, managed to pull the team owners together to make the game happen.

With the support of major league baseball secured, Ward then announced the game to the public on May 19 in his column. This was the official kickoff of the campaign to promote the dream game.

The *Tribune* and more than 50 other newspapers around the country printed a total of 8 million ballots, of which 550,000 were filled out and turned in. Ward regularly announced voting results, continuing to build interest in the contest.

The game, played at Comiskey Park in ideal weather, brought out a capacity crowd of 47,595 fans.

Why Comiskey Park and not Wrigley Field? Larger seating capacity, of course (by at least 5,000–6,000), but remember, too:

Arch Ward was a White Sox fan.

74 A Cub Hero Becomes a Sox Favorite

The news came on the heels of the announcement that the 1954 White Sox had made a big deal with Boston that was bringing perennial All-Star third baseman George Kell to Chicago. Now, a day later, the story was out that Frank Lane and Paul Richards were bringing in another big name to help the South Siders reach their pennant goal.

He was Phil Cavarretta, a Cubs fixture since 1934, National League batting champion in 1945, NL Most Valuable Player the same year, and Cubs player-manager from 1951 through the final week of 1954 spring training, when he was handed his walking papers by owner P.K. Wrigley.

"Just before we broke camp," he said years later, "I went in and talked to Mr. Wrigley, like I'd do every year, to go over the ballclub and what we needed and what he could expect. And I guess he didn't like what I told him. And they let me go."

It wasn't long before the former manager of the North Side ballclub got a phone call from the current manager of the South Side ballclub. "I was sitting at home in Dallas, and Paul Richards called me up and said, 'You think you can still play?' And I said I feel good, 'cause I worked hard and was in pretty good shape—I'd been player-manager. So he said, 'Well, come on up. We'll work you out, you can take some batting practice, and we'll see what happens.' Well, they liked what they saw, and I signed with them."

The Sox got far more from Cavarretta than they'd had any right to expect. He was hitless in three at-bats on a long road trip, then came home and singled in a run as a pinch-hitter during a win over Philadelphia, was awarded with a start the next afternoon against the A's and had a single and a walk in four trips.

The next night, before 45,216 at Comiskey Park, he led off the ninth inning against the Yankees with a pinch home run that cut New York's lead to 7–5 in a game the Sox lost 7–6. Soon he would be doing more than pinch-hitting.

"I was gonna fill in for them, pinch-hit a little and back up Ferris Fain, who was a very good first baseman," he said. "Then he tore up his knee sliding into home, and I got to play quite a bit, and did pretty well. You know, you're 38 years old, you're just going out there and trying to help the club any way you can. And I was able to do that."

Indeed, he hit .316 in 71 games plus two other homers—one a grand slam against the Red Sox at Comiskey Park.

The story was a bit different for another Cubs legend who, 20 years later, said he would not approve a trade to the California Angels but would accept a move to the White Sox. Ron Santo the nine-time All-Star third baseman, was about to try on red-pinstriped uniforms. The Sox sent Steve Stone and three others as payment.

One problem: The Sox already had an All-Star-caliber third baseman in Bill Melton. What about Melton? Tanner said Melton would play some third base as well as first base and DH—as would the team's first baseman, Dick Allen. Santo had another concern: He didn't want to be stuck as a designated hitter. Tanner assured Santo that he'd get plenty of time in the field. Santo took him at his word.

He signed a contract for two years at $120,000 a year and reported to the Sox's Sarasota, Florida, camp. As Santo tells the story, he walked out onto the practice field and Tanner greeted him warmly, putting his arm around him.

"I know what you can do. You just have a good spring," Tanner told him. Then came Chuck's bombshell.

"By the way," he said. "Would you stay away from third base?"

"What?" Santo said.

Tanner scratched his spikes in the dirt. "Melton's a little nervous about you coming over," he said at last.

Santo's shoulders sagged. "I didn't say anything more," he said. "I coulda had a talk with Melton, you know? Tanner was bullshitting me on the very first day. I just knew right then and there, that was my last year in baseball."

Dick Allen was the kingpin of those White Sox. He was the highest-paid player in baseball and had carried the Sox in 1972—and in 1973 until he broke his leg. He and Santo didn't exactly blend together well. One day in Minnesota, they almost came to blows. Allen quit the team in September; Santo retired after the season, which hadn't been a good one: .221 average in 117 games with 5 homers, one an inside-the-parker when Boston's Tommy Harper was knocked unconscious when his head hit Comiskey's brick outfield wall as he went for Santo's drive.

He did repeat something Cavarretta had done, though: He hit a grand slam against the Red Sox at Comiskey Park.

75 Professor Berres: Master of Zeroes

White Sox pitchers have thrown shutouts in both ends of double-headers 15 times. That total isn't likely to change very soon, mostly because of the paucity of doubleheaders. During the '50s and '60s, the White Sox actually scheduled at least two twilight-night doubleheaders each year. Luis Aparicio's return to Chicago for the first time in another team's uniform was on May 1, 1963, at a Wednesday night twi-nighter against Baltimore.

Another reason we're not likely to see many more doubleheader shutouts is a shortage of pitchers who can throw a shutout. And if you do uncover someone capable of throwing one, he'd likely only be allowed to go seven or eight innings, tops.

In any event, the list of White Sox pitchers' doubleheader shutouts currently numbers 15—from September 6, 1905 against Detroit through September 10, 1967, also against Detroit. Five of the twin shutouts, not surprisingly, took place before 1920 and the advent of the lively—or, better, the livelier—ball. Almost 25 years passed until the next one, in 1940 (Ted Lyons and Jack Knott shut out Boston at Fenway) and the next, in 1941 (Thornton Lee and John Humphries blanked the A's in Chicago).

The Berres Seven
A list of the seven doubleheader shutouts recorded during Ray Berres' watch as White Sox pitching coach (1949–66):

Date	Pitchers	Scores	Opponents
5/15/49	Bill Wight/Al Gettel	10–0, 2–0	Cleveland
5/25/52	Joe Dobson/Marv Grissom	3–0, 1–0	Detroit
6/14/53	Billy Pierce/Sandy Consuegra	6–0, 1–0	Boston
6/15/58	Jim Wilson/Dick Donovan	3–0, 4–0	at Baltimore
6/5/60	Russ Kemmerer/Frank Baumann	2–0, 2–0	Kansas City
7/5/64	Juan Pizarro/Joe Horlen	2–0, 5–0	Cleveland
5/30/66	John Buzhardt/Jack Lamabe	1–0, 11–0	at Boston

NOTE: Lamabe's shutout was a one-hitter.

That leaves eight. And here's what's remarkable about these eight: Seven of the twin-bill shutouts were registered in the period 1949 through 1966—when the White Sox pitching coach was Kenosha's own Ray Berres. The eighth doubleheader whitewash job was turned in by Joe Horlen and Cisco Carlos against the Tigers during the 1967 pennant scramble. Berres had worked since 1961 with both right-handers, more closely with Horlen because he was always on the varsity roster.

All of Professor Berres' students heard the same lectures. "What he basically taught," Bob Shaw, one of Berres' brightest pupils once said, "was quite simple: Get the hand out of the glove, keep your weight back, get your arm up. It wasn't all that elaborate. Just basic fundamentals and he knew them, and there are really very few people in the country who know what they are."

Years ago, in his home in Twin Lakes, Wisconsin, Berres spoke to a class of one on his area of expertise.

"I always worked toward a delivery that was conducive to throwing strikes. I preached delivery and keeping the ball low. If you have the proper delivery, the pitch will be low, or you'll have command of it. My argument was, you can never practice theory unless the mechanics of pitching are ironed out. To tell a guy to throw a ball low and away, and it goes high and away, there's something wrong with the mechanics. Pitching should really be simple."

"Dr. Ray" was effective teaching those pitchers originally signed by the White Sox as well as those who had pitched elsewhere and now were losing their effectiveness. The doubleheader shutout chart includes both types. One was Juan Pizarro, a hard-throwing lefty who had drained the Milwaukee Braves' patience.

"Pizarro," Berres remembered, "pitched with an arched back and a rushed delivery, and consequently all he could throw was one fastball after another. And his best pitches, with the most velocity and the most movement, were out of the strike zone. Well, you might as well throw it out the window. It took a long time to convince him to change his delivery just a little bit."

The change came quite by accident. Berres noticed it in the bullpen, where Pizarro was throwing a couple final pitches just as a game was ending. Said Berres, "He'd gone from arching his back and rushing to the plate like before to just laying back and throwing it. And when he got it, he said, 'Why didn't you tell me?' I said, 'My God, every day I've been telling you!'"

An interviewer mentioned Ray Berres' name to Pizarro a few years ago at an O'Hare area restaurant. Juan's eyes lit up. "Ray Berres, that was my man," he said, smiling. "He's the one who taught me how to throw strikes."

The Professor's prize pupils don't forget.

76 Some Pre-Cell Sox Teams That Could Hit

Researchers are surprised to learn that the normally light-hitting White Sox of 1901–1990 B.C. (Before Cell) occasionally did field some offensive-minded clubs—such as the 1951, 1955, and 1960 teams that led the American League in batting average; the 1977 South Side Hit Men who smashed both the team's home run record as well as the city's single-season attendance mark; and, finally, the 1983 club that topped the majors in runs scored.

Those teams did put up some impressive hitting stats, but in addition to them, some might be stunned to see some of the numbers recorded by the Sox of 1920 and 1936.

First, let's go back to the 1919 team, eight members of which decided they could make some pretty good money if they made odd plays in the field during the World Series and lost on purpose to a weaker Cincinnati Reds team. It was basically the same team that had won the World Series two seasons before; the 1917 Sox led the majors in runs scored, stolen bases (219) and team ERA (2.16).

Thus it figured that the 1919 White Sox would be among baseball's best. They led the AL in batting average (.287), runs scored, and bases stolen.

The 1951 "Go-Go Sox" of Paul Richards shocked the baseball world for the first half, anyway, before almost coming back to Earth by season's end. Minnie Minoso, Nellie Fox, and Jim Busby—all of whom had been batting in the mid- to upper .300s in late May and through June—faded somewhat but still had to be happy with their improvement, both teamwise and individually. As a team, they hit an AL-best .270 and were No. 1 in steals (99).

By 1955, the Sox weren't running as much, but they led the AL in batting average (.268) thanks to George Kell (.312), Fox (.311), and Bob Kennedy, who hit .304 after his May 30 arrival. The team that ranked highest in the most categories was the 1960 club, which ranked No. 1 in batting average (.270), on-base percentage, and stolen bases (122); and second in slugging and runs scored.

Dwarfing the best Chicago offenses of the decade 1951–60, however, was the 1977 clobberin' crew, whose .278 was good enough to lead the league some years but was only fourth that season. Led by Oscar Gamble (31 homers), Richie Zisk (30), Eric Soderholm (25), Chet Lemon (19), and Lamar Johnson and Jim Spencer (18 each), the Sox belted 192 homers, second highest total in the league.

Minnie Minoso crosses the plate and is congratulated by Nellie Fox. (Getty Images)

The 1983 team was another White Sox team that bashed the opposition into submission. Their total of 800 runs scored led both leagues; they stole 165 bases (led by Rudy Law's club-record 77); and they drilled 157 home runs, with rookie Ron Kittle (35), Greg Luzinski (32), Carlton Fisk (26), and Harold Baines (20) leading an assault on Comiskey Park's outfield roof.

The home run, however, was not what made the offenses of 1936 or 1920 go. The third-place 1936 team (81–70) scored 920 runs, fourth-best in the AL), and hit line drives everywhere. Zeke Bonura (.330) drove in 138 runs with only 12 home runs, for instance. Luke Appling, league batting champ with his .388 mark, drove in 128 runs with only 6 homers. Second baseman Jackie Hayes hit .312 and had 84 RBIs. And we didn't yet mention left fielder Rip Radcliff (.335, 31 doubles, 7 triples) and center fielder Mike Kreevich (.307, 32 doubles, 11 triples).

And finally, there's the 1920 Sox team that was a half-game behind first-place Cleveland in the final week when Charles A. Comiskey announced his "Black Sox" suspensions. Joe Jackson's numbers are ridiculous: 42 doubles, 20 triples, 12 homers, 121 RBIs, .382 average. Eddie Collins collected 224 hits and batted .372 with 38 doubles and 13 triples; Happy Felsch (40 doubles, 15 triples, 14 homers, 115 RBIs, .338 average) had his greatest year, and Buck Weaver batted .331 and drove in 74 runs.

Oh, and remember: The 1920 White Sox boasted four 20-game winners: Eddie Cicotte, Lefty Williams, Red Faber, and Dickie Kerr.

What a team. And what a shame.

77 Pitch at Risk to Zisk—and Gamble and Lemon and...

Baseball was stunned. Bill Veeck's 1977 White Sox, picked by some experts to finish in seventh place (also called last) in the AL West, were pounding baseballs against and over fences all through the league and getting just enough pitching (especially from Steve Stone, Francisco Barrios, Ken Kravec, and closer Lerrin LaGrow) to stay in the race.

A team with little pitching and with a defense that could charitably be termed "suspect" was capturing a city's imagination. Something mystifying was going on. "I think," said slugging right fielder Richie Zisk, "that Bill Veeck has sold his soul to the devil."

Veeck denied that thought but did admit he was enjoying himself. Here was a team he had put together, and it was mashing the ball and getting surprisingly good pitching and, get this, making all the routine plays in the field.

Here were some of the heroes as the Sox, by mid-May, had posted a 20–11 record:

- Zisk, the slugger acquired from the Pirates for pitchers Goose Gossage and Terry Forster;
- Chet Lemon, second-year center fielder whose home run total would go from four the year before to 19;
- Eric Soderholm, the former Twins third baseman, finally healthy enough after leg surgery to swing a bat and, when necessary, to field a few groundballs;
- Alan Bannister, former Phillies prospect, on his way to a 40-error season at shortstop but a consistent .300-plus hitter until the final few weeks;

- Jim Spencer, the holdover first baseman who saved Bannister 10–15 more errors with his glove and who, on May 14, had driven in eight runs in an 18–2 late-morning rout of the Indians;
- Steve Stone, right-handed pitcher who had gone to the Cubs in the Ron Santo trade and developed arm trouble, but throwing well again and owner of a 6–3 record.

June was marked by fun home series with the Yankees (the Sox lost two of three but Zisk put one in the center-field bleachers, a shot of 475 feet) and with the A's, whom the Sox beat three of four. Special anthem singer before the Sunday doubleheader? Lamar Johnson, who then hit two homers to give the Sox a 2–1 victory. At that point, the Sox and Twins were tied for first in the West.

The big month was July, when leadoff man Ralph Garr got hot and the Sox went 22–6. The Twins came to town the first weekend of that month and limped away after losing four straight. The Sox won 5–2 Friday night, 13–8 Saturday as Spencer drove in eight more runs with a couple homers, and then 6–0 and 10–8 in Sunday's twin bill. Total paid attendance for the weekend was 96,564, with the fans joining organist Nancy Faust to sing "Na Na! Hey Hey! Kiss Him Goodbye!" to one pulverized Minnesota pitcher after another as they made their way back slowly to the visitors' dugout. Also that weekend, the fans cheered the many Sox home run hitters so loudly and for so long that the home run hero would have to come out of the dugout and wave to the crowd before they would stop their adoring cheers. Thus, the curtain call at old Comiskey got its start.

The final weekend in July was pivotal. The Sox led the second-place Kansas City Royals by 3½ games as the series began. The series drew 131,276. There were 45,919 on hand for the wild Friday night game, when the Sox, down 8–6 in the seventh, rallied to win 11–8 as eardrums throughout the ballpark were abused.

The home clubhouse was almost as loud. Said Zisk: "I can't believe it. I can't believe it. I can't believe it. I've never seen anything like this before. Not the crowd, not the game. That crowd is unbelievable. That game is unbelievable. We're unbelievable."

The Sox won again Saturday 6–4 before 34,945 and then, before a Sunday throng of 50,412, Jorge Orta, Lemon, and Garr pulled out the opener 5–4 in 10 innings. Hal McRae hit a homer in the Royals' 8–4 win in Game 2 and mocked Sox fans with some odd antics during the game and ripped the Sox afterward, labeling the curtain calls "bush."

Of course, now all of baseball therefore is "bush," but back then McRae's comments took a little air out of the Sox balloon. Their 5½-game lead was soon gone, and though they continued to battle, the Sox finished third, 90–72 and 12 games behind Kansas City.

78 Harshman Still Has It

Back in June of 1994 at U.S. Cellular Field, White Sox right-hander Jason Bere was striking out Oakland A's at a furious clip. He had just fanned Brent Gates and Ruben Sierra to end the top of the eighth, giving him 14 K's on the night. He had allowed only two hits but had walked six, and the Sox led just 1–0.

The Sox strikeout record was 16, set in 1954 by Jack Harshman. Manager Gene Lamont decided it would be best not to worry about the club record but instead worry about the 1–0 lead.

So Roberto Hernandez was brought in to pitch the ninth, and Bere watched from the bench. Moments later, Bere had upped his won-lost record to 8–1.

A year later, Bere again threatened the record—sort of. He struck out the Twins' Marty Cordova for his 14th "K" of the game to start the ninth, but then allowed a walk and a single. Out of the game he came. The record was still intact.

Since then, lefty Chris Sale has come close, having struck out 15 Tampa Bay batters on May 28, 2012, but he left after 7⅓ innings. He had walked only two and given up three hits, but the Sox figured he had thrown enough pitches. Sale was rewarded with his sixth win.

And again Jack Harshman's record was alive.

It has been for a while now—since July 25, 1954, when Jack fanned 16 Red Sox in the first game of a Sunday doubleheader at Fenway Park. That afternoon, Harshman, then in his first year as a big-league pitcher, struck out one in the first, three (Harry Agganis, Jackie Jensen, and Del Wilber) in the second and two in the third.

Then came trouble.

Jimmy Piersall and Ted Williams singled to open the fourth, and after Agganis fanned, Jackie Jensen walked to fill the bases and Wilber followed with a double, scoring two and leaving men at second and third.

Sox catcher Matt Batts, on signal from manager Paul Richards, went to the mound to find out how Harshman was feeling. Said Harshman, "If Richards wants me out of here, he'll have to come and get me."

After an intentional walk to Ted Lepcio, Harshman got both Milt Bolling and pitcher Willard Nixon on strikes, and he was back in the groove.

His teammates got the two runs back for him in the fifth, and two more welcome runs came across in the seventh on an RBI single by Phil Cavarretta and a squeeze bunt by Jim Rivera that scored Minnie Minoso. Harshman now led 5–2.

In the Boston seventh, Billy Consolo, Piersall, and Williams all struck out, and the press box sent out the word that Jack had tied Big Ed Walsh for the club strikeout mark of 15. In the Boston eighth, Harshman received no help from the Carmines. Agganis bounced out, Jensen popped to Batts and Wilber grounded out.

Lepcio, opening the Red Sox ninth, swung and missed for strike three, and Harshman had the record to himself. Don Lenhardt popped out and Karl Olson flied out to Minoso in left to end it.

Harshman had his seventh win—and the Chicago White Sox's strikeout record for pitchers. And if anyone should break it, he won't know. Jack Harshman passed away in August 2013 at age 86, 59 years to the month that he pitched his finest game: a 1–0 victory in 16 innings over the Tigers' Al Aber, also a lefty.

That night, he and his wife celebrated with dinner out at the Chez Paree. "I dropped eight pounds in the game," he said, "but I put away enough steak to get it all back."

79 Slamming the Yankees

The best kind of home run, other than a game-winner, is a grand slam. For those White Sox fans who fell in love wih the game during the time when the Sox and Yankees would meet 22 times per season and, later, 18 times, the best grand slams were those hit against New York.

Tireless research has produced the accompanying chart that shows the dates and locations of the games and names of the grand gentlemen who struck these blows for truth, justice, and the Chicago way.

Of the 19—the latest, by the way, having been launched just two seasons ago (August 2012) by Kevin Youkilis—two stand out for their special importance and deserve separate recognition.

May 16, 1953: This was the year the White Sox more or less had nominated themselves to win the pennant. They had made a big trade in January for tough customer/two-time batting champion/on-field brawler Ferris Fain. They had added veteran third baseman Vern "Junior" Stephens, a noted longball hitter from the Boston Red Sox.

The teams had met already for three games in Chicago, two of them won by the White Sox. Now, here in New York, the visitors had beaten New York 7–5 on a Thursday, scoring twice in the ninth off Johnny Sain on RBI singles by Sam Mele and Nellie Fox.

Friday's game was rained out, and New York's Vic Raschi had a two-hitter and a 3–0 lead as Saturday's finale moved to the ninth. But the Sox managed two hits and two walks to chase Raschi, who left the bases filled with two out for sidearming Ewell "The Whip" Blackwell, the pitcher manager Casey Stengel wanted to face Stephens, who had hit 10 career grand slams.

But manager Paul Richards wanted the lefty-swinging Tommy Byrne, former Yankee pitcher, to hit against the sidearming right-hander. At this point in his career, Byrne, KO'd by the Yankees in the series opener, was probably a better hitter than he was a pitcher.

While Bob Elson wondered aloud on WCFL radio, "Where's Junior?" Byrne was moving toward the batter's box. And then came the P.A. announcement from Bob Shepard: "For the White Sox.... batting for Stephens.... Numbah twenty-seven.... Tommy Byrne!.... Numbah twenty-seven." That brought a roar from the crowd of 22,966 as they realized who was in that Chicago uniform.

Byrne was swinging a bat and reminding himself, "He throws a sinker, and he's got a good one." He decided to take a pitch or two. The 2–1 pitch was called a strike. "And it was that sinker," he said, "and I thought it was gonna hit me in the knee." The count was 2–2. "And the next pitch comes in, and I just swung and let that bat fly, and that damned thing went into the right-field seats. Oh, it was a line drive, went up in there about 25 rows.

Sox Grand Slams Against the Yankees

Player	Date	Location	Pitcher	Inning	Result
Happy Felsch	6/2/18	Chi	Slim Love	5	W, 6–2
Eddie Collins	6/5/19	NY*	Ernie Shore	8	W, 5–1
Bibb Falk	7/11/24	NY	Joe Bush	3	L, 12–9
Al Simmons	6/27/34	NY	Lefty Gomez	4	L, 8–7
Eddie Stewart	5/18/51	NY	Spec Shea	8	W, 7–4
Tommy Byrne	5/16/53	NY	Ewell Blackwell	9	W, 5–3
Jim Rivera	6/5/55	Chi	Tommy Byrne	1	W, 5–3
Harry Simpson	6/27/59	Chi	Bob Turley	8	W, 5–4
Wes Covington	5/28/61	NY	Bob Turley	3	W, 14–9
Gary Peters	5/5/68	Chi	Al Downing	4	W, 5–1
Russ Snyder	6/11/68	NY	Bill Monbouquette	3	W, 9–5
Dick Allen	6/4/74	NY	Pat Dobson	5	W, 9–2
Harold Baines	8/9/84	NY	D. Rasmussen	6	L, 7–6
John Kruk	7/5/95	Chi**	Brian Boehringer	1	W, 11–5
Harold Baines	5/4/96	NY	Jim Mecir	9	W, 11–5
Robin Ventura	8/13/96	NY	David Weathers	5	W, 8–4
Jose Valentin	6/18/00	NY	O. Hernandez	1	W, 17–4
Frank Thomas	8/26/03	NY	Roger Clemens	5	W, 13–2
Kevin Youkilis	8/21/12	Chi**	Ivan Nova	5	W, 7–3

Notes: * indicates game played at the Polo Grounds; all other New York results at Yankee Stadium.

** indicates game played at U.S. Cellular Field; all other Chicago results at old Comiskey Park.

"I remember Minoso jumpin' up in my lap and kissin' me when I crossed home plate. Everyone went crazy."

To complete the story, the Sox won 5–3.

June 27, 1959: Going into this Saturday matchup of the four-game weekend series, both teams were 36–32 and tied for third place. But they were going in opposite directions: The Yanks, 8–4 winners the night before, had won nine of their last 12; the Sox had lost seven of their last 10. Now New York and Bob Turley led 2–1 with two outs and bases empty in the eighth inning of Saturday's game; the Sox were going to lose for the fifth straight time to the Yankees. And then the inning, the game, the series, and, one could say, the season turned around.

Fox walked and raced to third on Earl Torgeson's single, and then Sherm Lollar walked to fill the bases. The batter was Harry "Suitcase" Simpson, a former Yankee. Turley tried to get a fastball in on his hands, but missed his target. Simpson didn't miss the pitch, driving the ball off the facing of the upper deck in right-center for his fifth career slam. The Sox led 5–2 and held on to win 5–4. They swept the next day's doubleheader, too.

Said "Suitcase" that day: "I was just swinging and I got lucky. It felt good, really good, to hit it in a spot like that."

80 The Last Game at Old Comiskey Park

A perfect autumn afternoon…a sellout crowd…Chuck Comiskey throwing out the ceremonial first pitch…Minnie Minoso bringing out the last lineup card…a White Sox victory…by the traditional Sox score of 2–1.

What more could you ask for at a funeral?

Of course, you couldn't keep the celebrities out of the park, people like Goldie Hawn, Kurt Russell, and Ron Howard. But there was no point being down on them. They were there, weren't they? There were lots of other places they could have been this weekend. Instead, they chose to be with 42,846 other people to commemorate the end of an era and the approaching wrecking of our summer home away from home.

The banners were out, of course:

Goodbye, Old Friend

Pitch at Risk to Fisk

Washington Slept Here

Among the best new signs this year was a takeoff on the Sox's 1990 ad campaign, which said, "Years from now, you'll say you were there: The last historic season at old Comiskey Park."

The new sign simply read:

Years From Now, You'll Park Here.

As for the game, with the Sox opposed by Seattle, it was another opportunity for Jack McDowell to show that he was on his way to becoming the top-flight pitcher he was to become—17-game winner in 1991, 20-game winner in 1992, a 22-game winner in 1993, and Cy Young Award winner in 1993.

There was no score after five, as a journeyman named Rich DeLucia matched Black Jack pitch for pitch and annoyed expression for annoyed expression. Then, leading off the sixth, Ken Griffey Jr. (Years From Now, He'll Play For The Sox) tripled to right and scored when McDowell let loose with a wild pitch.

The Sox tied and went ahead in their half of the sixth. Lance Johnson led off with a triple, and with everyone in the place hoping to see him pop one, the old guy, Carlton Fisk (Years From Now, But Not Many, He'll Be In Cooperstown), struck out. But the new guy, Frank Thomas (Years From Now, So Will He) just up from Double-A Birmingham two months ago, singled in the tying run.

Up stepped Dan Pasqua, and he lined a bullet to left that hit in front of Ken Griffey Sr. and bounced weirdly past him, Thomas scoring and Pasqua winding up on third. But first-year players Robin Ventura (Years From Now, He'll Manage The Sox) and Sammy Sosa (Years From Now, He Won't Know English) failed to get the runner home.

Soon it was the ninth, and Steve Lyons had taken over at first base for Thomas and Bobby Thigpen had relieved McDowell in

New Comiskey Park sits empty next to old Comiskey on September 30, 1990, the last game at the 80-year-old stadium.

quest of his 57th save. Moments later, Harold Reynolds grounded out, Scottie Fletcher to Lyons, and the Sox had won the last game at old Comiskey, 2–1. Their record was an impressive 93–66 and they had drawn, in the last year of the old park, 2,002,357.

They all took a walk around the park, waving up to the fans, none of whom wanted to leave the place. The players? That was a different story. Most couldn't wait till they could move across the street. But not all. Said Fletcher, a member of the 1983 AL West championship club:

"I think next year, when we go into the new park and we don't see this park standing here, it will really hit us, what it was all about."

Last player to leave was Fisk, who was still a bit disappointed in his 0-for-4 afternoon. But then he turned wistful when someone asked him about memories of old Comiskey.

"Memories are between your ears," he said. "You take those wherever you go. They'll always be there."

81 The First Game at New Comiskey

As Harry Caray most assuredly would have said had he still been broadcasting White Sox games, "The less said about this one, the better."

He might well have mentioned that Carlton Fisk, still spry at age 43, had extended his early-season hitting streak to seven games, and that Robin Ventura, the kid third baseman starting his second season in the big leagues, collected two hits to raise his batting average to .346.

And he would have had to mention that Sox starting pitcher Jack McDowell had lasted only 2⅔ innings, and had given up five hits, three walks, and six earned runs—including two home runs.

And then, too, he would have had to give the final score: Detroit 16, White Sox 0.

Everything had started out so well, too. Jim Thompson, the governor who had made sure the downstate politicians voted yes on the construction of a new home for the White Sox—in Chicago, and not Florida—threw out the first ball. Appearances were made by Mayor Richie Daley and U.S. Vice President Dan Quayle, Sox fans since they were kids, when their favorites included Nellie Fox, Minnie Minoso, Billy Pierce, Luis Aparicio & Co. The Oak Ridge Boys, pals of Fisk, sang the national anthem.

Maybe that's when they should've called the whole thing off.

They did not, however, and the game began. There were no problems until the third inning, when Travis Fryman walked, stole second, went to third on an infield out, and scored on Alan Trammell's single. Trammell then singled and stole second, Lou Whitaker also walked and Cecil Fielder hit the first of four Tigers home runs. It was 4–0.

Then Pete Incaviglia walked, Mickey Tettleton hit into a force-out, and Rob Deer hit a home run. Now it was 6–0. Sox manager Jeff Torborg here decided "Black Jack" would be safer in the club-house, and so ended McDowell's afternoon.

At least that presented McDowell time to get acquainted with the spacious new facilities. "The trainer's room is so far away I called a cab," he said. Where, someone asked, was the McDowell who in his first two starts this season (the Sox opened the season going 6–1 on the road) had thrown complete games and struck out 20 in 18 innings?

"I didn't feel good at all," he responded, "which is unusual because I had felt good for a long period of time. They hit the ball. And I didn't have my (split-finger pitch)."

When it was over, the Tigers had totaled 19 hits and had belted two more home runs—a second by Deer and one from leadoff man Tony Phillips. Deer and Fielder each drove in four runs, Phillips and Trammell each collected four hits, and Whitaker was 3-for-3 with the one walk.

With McDowell gone so early, Torborg had the chance to give Brian Drahman and Kenny Patterson some work. The manager said there was only one other positive he could take away from the home opener.

"The last out."

Fisk summed up the problems still facing the Sox as they continued to get used to their new playground.

"The distractions—Where do you park? What exit do you take? How do you get to the clubhouse?—those were a problem. It takes getting used to. It's not really home yet."

It did not take long, though, to become home. During the 1991 season, the White Sox won 25 games in their last at-bat, and the great majority of them were at their brand-new home.

82 Now *That's* How to Open a Season

Charlie Finley figured this way:

His Oakland A's were opening the 1971 season on Monday, April 5, at Washington. Then, they were coming home for games Wednesday and Thursday with the lowly Chicago White Sox, whom his A's had beaten 16 of 18 in 1970 and no doubt were going to be hapless again, seeing as they were practically a whole new team with an entirely different staff.

With such a weak sister scheduled to be Oakland's opponent at its home opener, Finley figured he wouldn't exactly be packing them in. And for the game on Thursday afternoon? He was thinking 3,000 tops. So why not have a doubleheader for Opening Day? Even with Chicago as the visiting club, Finley thought a crowd of 30,000 might be a strong possibility.

He needed permission, which he then received, from the league office to make the switch. It was all set. The A's and White Sox in an Opening Day doubleheader. Surely, the A's and Finley saw a sweep. For the first three innings on that cool but sunny day, things were looking that way. Reggie Jackson's sacrifice fly in the first and Sal Bando's two-out, three-run homer in the third off Tommy

When the Sox Swept the Yanks on Opening Day

The White Sox had seen their season opener postponed by rain and/
or cold four times. Now the schedule had taken them to New York,
where they were going to try, try again to get this 1982 season
underway with a Sunday doubleheader and show off their new threads
and new lineup all in one fell swoop.

The fifth time was the charm.

The Sox swept a pair from the Yankees, 7–6 in 12 innings in the
first game and a snappy 2–0 victory in Game 2, with Britt Burns (six
innings) and rookie Mexican reliever Salome Barojas teaming up for
the shutout.

Barojas, the spring-camp sensation, had never seen New York
City, let alone Yankee Stadium. But if he was nervous, he didn't show
it, as he faced the minimum for his first big-league save.

Among the heroes:

Ron LeFlore, who had three hits in Game 1 and singled in the
game-winner off Goose Gossage;

Tony Bernazard, who doubled in the tiebreaking run in Game 2;

Steve Kemp and Tom Paciorek, who each had four hits on their
first day with the Sox.

John gave the A's and Catfish Hunter a 4–0 lead. Had this game
been played in 1970, Oakland would've won 12–1. But this was
1971. This, the A's would see, was a different White Sox team—
and not just because of their flashy new uniforms.

In the fourth, rookie shortstop Bee Bee Richard singled
and after two other 1971 new faces—Jay Johnstone and Mike
Andrews—popped to third, holdover Bill Melton belted a home
run to cut the lead in half. And in the fifth, little Walt Williams
homered and Richard delivered a two-out RBI single to tie it. "Bee
Bee played as though he's been in the big leagues four or five years,"
his manager, Chuck Tanner, said afterward.

Dave Duncan's two-out RBI single in the sixth broke the tie,
but the Sox bounced right back. With two on and two out in
the seventh and lefty-swinging Lee Maye announced as the hitter

for John, A's manager Dick Williams removed Hunter from the contest and switched to lefty Paul Lindblad. Now Tanner had the matchup he wanted; he sent Rich McKinney to the plate to bat for Maye, and the right-handed McKinney lined Lindblad's first pitch to left-center for a base hit, scoring first Williams and also Ed Herrmann, who kept on running as the ball skipped past center fielder Rick Monday for an error.

Now it was 6–5 Chicago, and there it remained. Vicente Romo, acquired just 10 days earlier from Boston for catcher Duane Josephson, threw three scoreless innings to close it out, striking out Campy Campaneris and Felipe Alou to end it with the tying and winning runs aboard.

Herrmann was impressed. "He's just got a great repertoire, that's all," he said of Romo. "Four speeds on his curve, two kinds of sliders, and a fastball that sails."

In Game 2, the Sox gave 21-year-old Bart Johnson a 3–0 first-inning lead on Johnstone's homer off starter Rollie Fingers and Carlos May's two-run triple, which should have been a home run but for the fact King Carlos failed to tag the plate while jubilantly jumping up and down with his teammates.

After Oakland tied it up in the fourth, Andrews' two-run double to left-center put Chicago ahead 5–3 in the fifth. The Sox busted it open in the sixth. After two were out, Richard doubled in a run and Johnstone and Andrews walked to load the bases. Here, ex-Sox reliever Bob Locker entered the fray, and Melton lit him up for a grand slam. The Sox were safely ahead 10–3; they would win 12–4, Johnson going all the way and striking out nine, including Jackson four times.

The Sox were 2–0 against Oakland. In one day they had equaled their 1970 victory total against the A's. And they had helped Charlie Finley a little: Paid attendance, 23,838.

83 The Pursuit of Larry Doby

The White Sox first began expressing interest in trading for Cleveland center fielder Larry Doby, the first African American to play in the American League, as far back as the December 1952 baseball winter meetings in Phoenix. That's when Sox GM Frank Lane was thinking about doing an Eddie Robinson-for-Ferris Fain deal—a trade of first basemen, one of them (Robinson) a long-ball hitter and the other (Fain) a singles-and-doubles hitter coming off his second straight AL batting title.

He did manage to pull off the Robinson-Fain deal, but now Lane's team was lacking a power hitter from the left side. More talks with Cleveland ensued. Nothing came of those talks, except that Lane was amenable to making Sox shortstop Chico Carrasquel the key man going to the Indians in any Doby trade. Lane and Tribe GM Hank Greenberg discussed versions of a Doby-Carrasquel deal over the next three years, to no avail. Finally, after Lane had left Chicago for St. Louis in late September 1955, Chuck Comiskey and John Rigney conferred with Greenberg and, at long last, came up with their man.

The Sox welcomed Doby to Chicago and sent Carrasquel and center fielder Jim Busby to Cleveland. The new Chicago shortstop was to be a 21-year-old Venezuelan named Luis Aparicio. Doby's leg injuries had limited him to 131 games in 1955, but he did hit .291 with 26 homers and 75 RBIs. Carrasquel had landed in manager Marty Marion's doghouse with some rather lackadaisical play and a .256 batting average. Busby, who had come back to his original team in early June 1955, had hit only .243 but would provide the Tribe with speed and terrific outfield play. Aparicio, of course, would be a revelation at shortstop and on the bases.

Not everyone in Cleveland was sorry to see Doby depart. Wrote Franklin Lewis of the *Plain Dealer*: "He has been a controversial athlete. Highly gifted, he was frequently morose, sullen, and upon occasion, downright surly to his teammates."

His new Chicago employers were overjoyed to have him. Said Comiskey, "The search is over for a long-ball hitter. We've certainly needed a consistent one, and we've been eyeing Doby for some time." Added Marion, "The guy used to murder us when we played Cleveland. He'll make a big difference in the number of one-run and two-run decisions we used to lose."

A check of the stats, though, showed that in 1955, Doby had hit .250 in the Tribe's 11 games at Comiskey Park with one homer and three runs batted in. And in Cleveland's pennant year of 1954, Doby had batted .231 with one homer and four RBIs in 11 games at Comiskey Park. Was Doby worried at all about the change in home ballparks and how it might affect his power numbers?

"White Sox Park [he called it] was a little bit tougher than Cleveland to hit in," he told an interviewer in 1976, when he was the Montreal Expos' hitting coach. "You had to hit it a pretty long ways to get a home run in Chicago. But I didn't think about that too much—until I got there. And then I saw that balls that would've been home runs in Cleveland were outs at White Sox Park."

That, and some nagging hamstrings, helped keep him from hitting his first Sox homer until June 13, the team's 45th game. "You had to get in the frame of mind where you don't think about that," Larry said. "You try to hit the ball as hard as you can hit it and let the results take care of themselves."

As the 1956 season progressed, Doby learned how to handle it. Chuck Comiskey never doubted that he would.

"You know, when we dealt for Larry, we weren't worried about him. We knew he'd come through," Comiskey said.

He began turning it around during a 12–2 homestand (June 15 through June 27) that included the memorable four-game sweep of the Yankees. Doby, in the 14 games, was 16-for-48 (.333) with 6 homers, 13 RBIs, and 18 runs scored. In the Yankee series alone, he was 7-for-16 (.438) with 3 homers and 7 RBIs.

The 1956 Sox disappointed their fans and the front office by finishing third at 85–69. Doby could hardly be blamed: He finished at .268 with 24 home runs and 102 RBIs.

84 Let's Play Several!

The season after the White Sox won 99 games and the American League West race by 20, they staggered to the finish line with a remarkably awful record of 74–88.

This was basically the same team as the 1983 AL West champs, but the "Winning Ugly" heroes either were hurt or had hurting seasons in 1984. It wasn't so bad in the first half, but it wasn't really that good, either. Even so, the White Sox were 44–40 and in first place in the West at the All-Star break, having won their last seven (and nine out of 10).

Sports talk in Chicago centered around the very real possibility that both the Sox and Cubs were going to win division titles that year, and that, according to the schedule used in past seasons, the playoffs were to open in the home park of the NL East champion and the home of the AL West champ. Just think: The Cubs against San Diego on the North Side in the afternoon followed by the White Sox and Detroit on the South Side at night. Talk about the baseball capital of the world....

Suffice it to say the Sox did not hold up their part of the bargain. Kansas City came out of nowhere to win the division with a very poor record (for a division champ) of 84–78. Thus, had the White Sox just played ordinary baseball after the break—say, 41–37—they'd have finished a game better than Kansas City.

But that apparently was too much to ask for. There was little chance that the Luzinskis, the Hoyts, the Fisks, the Kittles, the Bannisters, the Pacioreks, and the rest could play up to even 75 percent of their capabilities. And so the 74–88 record for the 1984 would-be repeat champs.

Still, this team took part in one of the season's memorable games on the nights of May 8 and May 9, which should give you an idea of what kind of ballgame this was.

Extra innings? You bet. Like 16 extras, in fact. And the man who broke it up—in the 25th inning—was the first player selected in the June 1977 amateur draft precisely because he was going to be that kind of ballplayer who delivered in these kinds of moments.

Harold Baines, still just 25 years old at the time, blasted a Chuck Porter 2–0 fastball some 420 feet over the center-field-bullpen fence at old Comiskey Park to give the Sox a 7–6 victory over the Milwaukee Brewers in the longest game time-wise (eight hours six minutes) in major league history and the longest innings-wise in AL history.

Tom Seaver pitched the 25th inning of the suspended game, which had been halted the night before by curfew with the game tied 3–3 after 17 innings. Then, after Baines' homer took care of that game, Seaver went out to pitch the regularly scheduled contest. He took a 5–3 lead into the ninth, but was tagged for Robin Yount's solo homer with one out. Manager Tony La Russa called for Salome Barojas, who, after giving up two hits, got Ted Simmons to ground into a game-ending double play.

"I didn't feel comfortable coming in in relief," Seaver said. And he was fairly certain he knew why he wasn't comfortable: He hadn't pitched in relief since 1976.

"My adrenaline was pumping in the 25th inning, but I could feel I wasn't in total control. I treated it like I was coming back from a rain delay. I had no other reference point."

The Sox could have lost the marathon game in 21 innings. Ben Oglivie's three-run homer off Ron Reed put the Brew Crew up 6–3, but the Sox tied it in their half. Carlton Fisk singled in one run, and Tom Paciorek singled with the bases filled to make it 6–6 and set the stage for Baines.

Did he get all of it? he must have been asked. And you know the answer:

"Evidently."

85 Roland Got 'em Rollin'

Some of this, class, you may already know, and is strictly for review. But there is some material that, hopefully, is completely new to you.

Roland Hemond came to Chicago's South Side in September 1970 along with a fellow 41-year-old, Chuck Tanner, ready to roll their sleeves up and go to work in an attempt to fix the train wreck known as the Chicago White Sox.

They had worked together in the Angels' farm system, Hemond as director and Tanner as the organization's extremely successful Triple-A manager. They spent the last month of that season watching the 56–106 Sox show why they were 56–106. They saw rather quickly that, though this team had some hitters, it had almost no speed and—outside of young Bart Johnson, 20, and lefty Tommy John, 27—a similar shortage of good arms on the pitching staff.

Hemond couldn't wait to get started. By mid-December he had landed speedy outfielder Pat Kelly from Kansas City; 23-year-old right-hander Tom Bradley (11–1 under Tanner that season at Triple-A Hawaii), outfielder Jay Johnstone and catcher Tom Egan from the Angels and second baseman Mike Andrews and short-stop prospect Luis Alvarado from Boston. Later, left fielder Rick Reichardt and reliever Steve Kealey arrived from the Angels and reliever Vicente Romo from the Red Sox.

"We felt we had to use in deals the two players who had had their best years—Luis Aparicio (to Boston) and Ken Berry (to the Angels). They were the only players who could bring you some value. And we were adding youth to the club. The deals worked. We added 23 victories to the club that first year (and the Sox went from last to third place).

More were added the next year, after Hemond had landed slugger Dick Allen from the Dodgers for John and then, the same day, getting starting pitcher Stan Bahnsen from the Yankees for Rich McKinney, who struggled mightily in New York. The Sox took second in the AL West in 1972 and might've finished first had defending AL homer champ Bill Melton not missed more than half the season with back trouble.

The Sox were even better in 1973, but injuries to Allen and Hemond's newest acquisition, center fielder Kenny Henderson, ruined the season. And during the Reinsdorf ownership, after he had gathered together the pieces (Carlton Fisk, Greg Luzinski, Floyd Bannister, Tom Paciorek, Julio Cruz, etc.) for a world championship club, the team was ousted by Baltimore from the 1983 ALCS in four games as three of the big guns (Fisk, Luzinski, and Harold Baines) combined to go 7-for-48 (.146).

But Roland Hemond didn't go off somewhere and cry. They didn't make 'em that way where he came from.

He was born on October 26, 1929, in Central Falls, Rhode Island, a textile-mill community next to Pawtucket. His father,

Ernest, was born and raised in Rhode Island; his mother, Antoinette, moved to the area from a suburb of Montreal.

"We were French-Canadian," he said. "Actually, I didn't speak English until I was about 6 years old. It was a typical French community in the city—those three- and four-story tenement houses built close to the textile mill. People couldn't afford cars when they first arrived so they would walk to work and they built houses close to the textile mills.

"I can still speak French and occasionally do when I get calls from newspaper people in Montreal."

In fact, when the White Sox and Montreal made a trade at the 1984 winter meetings in which the Sox sent French-Canadian reliever Bert Roberge and infielder Vance Law to the Expos for pitcher Bob James and second baseman Bryan Little, Hemond announced it to the startled media in French.

"I'd asked John McHale, the president of the Montreal Expos at the time, 'Hey, how about if I announce it in French and we'll shock all the baseball people.' People got a big kick out of it. That's probably the first time in major league baseball history that a deal at the baseball convention was announced in French. "

That idea was likely hatched in a long-ago late-night confab in the Bards Room at old Comiskey Park, where Bill Veeck—Roland's boss for five years—would hold forth till all hours. Remembered Roland, "Somebody asked me one day what my hours are. I said, 'Nine to five. Nine in the morning till five A.M.'"

It was Hemond who, during Veeck's first day as the Sox's "new" president in December 1975, set up a "trading post" in the hotel lobby the final day of the winter meetings, with a sign reading: "Open for Business."

"We made four deals in the final hour and 15 minutes of the convention," Roland said, smiling, remembering the deals that netted Ralph Garr, Clay Carroll, Jack Brohamer, and Buddy Bradford, among others. "That was exhilarating—real joy. Conventioneers were cheering. Like show biz. And people who frowned on it at the time now tell me, 'Hey, that was great.'"

Roland Hemond has been in baseball since 1951. He can relax now and look back on a marvelous career and use those very same words to sum it up:

"Hey, that was great."

86 Did Joe Borchard Choose Poorly?

There's the question of the day, and really the answer is a simple "No." That's because either way you look at it, Joe Borchard was going to come out a winner.

His dilemma after completion of his junior year at Stanford was this: He was an excellent college quarterback who stood 6'5", weighed 225 pounds, had a great arm, and had been told by several NFL scouts he would go high in the 2001 NFL draft.

Also a slugging outfielder, he had just been chosen in the June 2000 amateur draft by the White Sox, who had selected him in the first round, the 12th player drafted.

If he were to choose baseball, which he did, he was to receive a bonus of $5.3 million, plus a regular salary. (The $5.3 million bonus was the highest given a drafted player until Justin Upton raked in $6.1 million from the Arizona Diamondbacks in 2005.) Football was no sure thing money-wise, nor health-wise, though there's no doubt he would have been taken care of financially, as are most NFL quarterbacks. It did seem unlikely, however, that he would have been given a signing bonus of $5.3 million.

In the end, Joe was happy with his choice of baseball and confident he had given it his best shot. When he decided to retire in June 2011, Borchard, whose final stop had been the independent Bridgeport (Connecticut) Bluefish, told an interviewer:

"I just wanted to see if I could play at a level that is acceptable to me. And I think I gave it a fair shake. It just wasn't in the cards. So that's kind of the way it goes.

"It's unfortunate on a number of different fronts, but at the end of the day, I have to make the best decision. And I think this is it."

Borchard's most significant playing time with the White Sox came in the 2004 season, where he received 201 at-bats. He hit .174 that year with 9 home runs and 20 RBIs. His most notable feat? On August 30, 2004, he hit the longest home run at U.S. Cellular Field, a 504-footer off Brett Myers, then with the Phillies.

The Sox dealt him to Seattle for pitcher Matt Thornton in March 2006 in an exchange of first-round disappointments. Thornton became one of the game's top lefty relievers, while Joe moved on to the Marlins and then the Braves and Giants, for whose Triple-A affiliate, Fresno, Borchard hit for the cycle in a May 2010 game against Colorado Springs.

Borchard, 32 when he announced his retirement, figured that he could no longer justify being away from his family—namely, daughter Ellie, son Charlie, and wife Erin.

He played winter ball in the Dominican Republic and Puerto Rico in an attempt to improve his game. In the end, the level of success he hoped to see simply was not there.

In 301 big-league games with the Sox, Mariners, and Marlins, Borchard hit .205 with 26 home runs and 77 RBIs. He hit a combined .268 with 154 home runs and 516 RBIs in 908 games in the minor leagues and in independent ball. He just never was quite able to make consistent contact.

"It certainly wasn't because of a lack of effort," he said. "When you kind of look at things objectively, I'm really the same player I've always been. At some point, you feel like you're just beating your head against the wall. It's time to allow that to run its course and move on to the next thing."

Borchard played in more than 1,200 games in his career. He walked away, he said, with no regrets.

"You do this for 12 years and really see every end of the spectrum, it seems like," he said. "I really gave it every chance possible. At the end of the day, you really have nothing to be ashamed of.

"It's just things go a certain way and that's it, and it's time to move on and get into whatever's next."

87 Basebrawl at Its Best

A delightful, sunny Saturday afternoon turned ugly rather quickly.

White Sox starter Jim Parque hit Tigers third baseman Dean Palmer with a pitch only minutes after the Tigers' Jeff Weaver had nailed Carlos Lee.

Palmer perhaps didn't realize that that's the way the game has always been played and took off for the mound, slowing down only to fire his helmet at Parque's head.

Soon there were some 60 grown men—half in Detroit Tigers gray, the rest in White Sox home unies—scurrying all over the field. Some were attempting to be peacemakers. The majority seemed to have malice in their hearts.

Detroit was getting buried again (its record to that point was 4–11). This afternoon, April 22, 2000, the Tigers were already down 8–1 when the real hostilities broke out.

When Part 1 of the festivities ended, both sides had long casualty lists. The Sox's included reliever Keith Foulke, who emerged with bloodstains and a gash under his left eye that required five stitches. "I've never seen a (baseball) fight so dangerous," said Detroit batting coach Bill Madlock.

After Round 1 ended, four Tigers (Palmer, Weaver, reserve catcher Robert Fick, and reliever Danny Patterson) and two Sox (Bill Simas and Magglio Ordonez) were tossed. Then, in the ninth, manager Jerry Manuel and pitcher Tanyon Sturtze were thumbed when Sturtze's third pitch of the inning hit Deivi Cruz. Soon after that, Bobby Howry drilled Shane Halter, Howry accepted Tiger pitcher Doug Brocail's invitation to "let her rip," and Round 2 was underway.

Punishment soon was meted out. Nine Tigers were suspended for a total of 54 games; seven Sox were banned for 28.

Yankees at White Sox, June 13, 1957: First-place Chicago and second-place New York at old Comiskey Park on a Thursday afternoon, the series' rubber game, Billy Pierce vs. Sox-killer Art Ditmar. The Sox had two on and two out in the opening inning. The batter was Larry Doby. Ditmar's first pitch was up and in—really up and in. The pitch sailed past catcher Elston Howard and back to the screen. The runners, Minnie Minoso and Nellie Fox, each moved up a base. Ditmar came in to cover the plate, where Doby was waiting. Angry words were exchanged and, all of a sudden, down went Ditmar, victim of a Doby left hook.

Then things really got exciting. Walt Dropo, the Sox's "Moose," and Bill "Moose" Skowron were first on the scene, cast in the role of peacemakers. That didn't last long. "Doby dropped the bat and went after Ditmar," Skowron said years later. "And I happened to dive and caught Doby—I made a good tackle—and I got him down. Then Billy Martin started hitting him, and then Walt Dropo thought I was hitting Doby, so he pulled me off him—almost pulled my pants off. And Enos Slaughter thought Dropo was hitting me, so then he got into it. And Dropo just beat the heck out of Slaughter."

Said Dropo: "I had nothing against Slaughter. I just figured, 'The next guy comin' out here is gonna get it,' and he came barreling out there. He was the first one out. Well, the thing became a fiasco. I tore his shirt off, gave him a couple good shots. But those things are impulsive things. I had no hostility toward Slaughter. I didn't even know the guy. "

Order had been restored when, without warning, Martin and Doby started up again, and the fight between those two became one involving several. Finally, the umps made their move: Doby and Dropo ejected, along with Martin and Slaughter. Ditmar, who threw the pitch that started it all, was allowed to stay. New York went on to win 4–3.

Cubs at White Sox, May 20, 2006: With one out and no score in the second, lefty Rich Hill walked A.J. Pierzynski, Joe Crede, and Juan Uribe to load the bases. On Brian Anderson's fly to left, Pierzynski tagged up and scored, running over catcher Michael Barrett at the plate. Barrett didn't take kindly either to that or to A.J.'s emphatic slap of home plate. So, naturally, he punched the Sox catcher in the face.

That triggered a benches- and bullpens-clearing melee that got the two catchers plus Anderson and the Cubs' John Mabry ejected—and served to ignite some action in the stands. When calm returned, Scott Podsednik walked, filling the bases again, and Tadahito Iguchi crushed a grand slam to left-center. The Sox went on to win 7–0.

88 Paulie's Memorable Milestones

Mike Cameron was a solid ballplayer. He struck out an awful lot—176 times one year—but he could play center field quite well, and he could run (eight seasons with 20-plus steals). And, though he never hit for average (.249 lifetime), he did hit for power (eight years of 20 or more home runs).

Yet there was a feeling that, when White Sox General Manager Ron Schueler traded Mike to the Cincinnati Reds for 1997 Baseball America Minor League Player of the Year Paul Konerko, the deal would turn out to be a very good one for Chicago.

And not just because the date of the deal—November 10, 1998—fell exactly 50 years to the day that the Sox stole Billy Pierce from the Detroit Tigers. It turned out so well because the Sox got themselves a serious, totally professional hitter, a superb teammate, an All-Star, a World Series hero, the team captain for 10 years running, and the man considered the face of a franchise.

The following are the milestone home runs in Paul Konerko's career. Noticeable early will be his attitude toward the home run and its relative importance.

No. 100

June 22, 2002: During what proved to be an otherwise lost weekend in Atlanta, Paulie hit homer No. 99 off Braves lefty Damian Moss and No. 100 off right-hander Kerry Ligtenberg during the Braves' three-game sweep.

The man now wearing No. 14 with the Sox sounded much like the fellow who wore No. 14 in the '70s: Bill Melton, who used to complain that he was hitting nothing but meaningless home runs—"counterfeit" homers, he called them.

"Friday's home runs weren't the most meaningful home runs," Konerko noted. He added that that had been a recent pattern, one he did not find impressive. On June 11, Konerko hit his second home run of the game against the New York Mets as the Sox built a big lead. On June 14 against the Cubs, his two homers drove in all the Sox runs in an 8–4 loss. And then came the two against the Braves on Friday, when the rest of the club managed just two other hits in a 15–2 loss.

"I'm not here to hit for power," he said. "I'm here to drive in runs and have good quality at-bats, and that doesn't always mean hit home runs. They're nice, but I want to be a good hitter first and have power come secondary."

No. 200

August 13, 2005: 'Twas the Pale Hose vs. the Carmine Hose at Fenway Park, with both teams chasing berths in the upcoming playoffs. Things were not going too well for the visitors, who, after waiting out a lengthy rain delay, were trailing 5–0 in the seventh.

Konerko, the White Sox's first batter after the rain delay, crushed a 1–2 pitch from Tim Wakefield over the Green Monster in left. It was Konerko's 30th home run of the season and the 200th of his career. He had homered in each of the first two games of the series, the first two of his career at Fenway Park.

"It's cool, but there are a lot of guys walking around with more than 200 home runs, so it's not that cool," Konerko said. "It's my seventh year, so it shows some consistency getting there. But it would have been nicer to do it if it came during a better game—in a win or something."

No. 300

April 13, 2009: Konerko especially enjoyed this milestone. First, Jermaine Dye stepped up against Detroit starter Zach Miner in the second inning at Comerica Park and launched his 300th career

Paul Konerko congratulates Jermaine Dye on hitting his 300ᵗʰ career home run on April 13, 2009. Paulie would immediately step to the plate and deposit his 300ᵗʰ career homer in the seats as well.

home run. Then Paulie went up to the plate and he, too, hit No. 300. They had just become the first teammates to hit century milestone home runs in the same game, according to Elias Sports Bureau.

And the Sox went on to win 10–6.

"It's amazing we hit our 300ᵗʰ in the same game," Konerko said. "It's even more amazing that it was back-to-back. I'm thinking 10, 20 years from now, we'll be able to say that, which is kind of cool."

Then he noted how far away he and Dye were to catching teammate Jim Thome, who had 543 long ones at the time and finished his career with 612.

"I'm proud of it. But then you're in the dugout, reflecting for a few minutes, and then you look over at Jim, and you realize what he's done, and you say, 'Let's go play defense.'"

No. 400

April 25, 2012: With the Sox down 2–1, Konerko hit A's closer Grant Balfour's first pitch of the ninth inning over the left-field wall at the Oakland-Alameda Coliseum. Unfortunately, the Sox blew any number of scoring opportunities after that and lost 5–4 in 14 innings.

Said P.K. of No. 400: "Everybody likes round numbers, and when I'm done playing it might hit home. When you're in the grind, you don't think about it. But yeah, it's nice. It's cool. I'll tuck it away for now."

It was also his 2,000th base hit in a White Sox uniform.

89 It's Well Worth the Climb

If you haven't seen this, you really should. Next time you're at U.S. Cellular Field go up to the 500 level and check out the terrific-looking murals that adorn the walls. They provide a superb, decade-by-decade photographic look at the history of the city of Chicago and of the White Sox.

You can start anywhere, but it's recommended you start with the murals for the years 1900–1910 and then work toward the present.

On the 1900–1910 wall, you'll see Engine House No. 40 right next to a team photo of the 1901 White Sox, the first American League championship team. There's a shot of the Water Tower as well as the Pullman Clock Tower and the corner of State and Van Buren. Featured too is a shot of South Side Park in 1909, a year before it was replaced by the first Comiskey Park, which opened July 1, 1910.

Other highlights from 1900 through 1910 include a photo of the "Hitless Wonders," the 1906 world championship team that defeated the Cubs in six games, plus shots of pitcher Ed Walsh, the Cottage Grove streetcar, and a 1908 shot of Riverview.

Move on to the decade 1911–1920, where photos of "Shoeless" Joe Jackson share space with a 1915 amateur game in Ashburn Field at Crawford Avenue and 87th Street. The 1917 entry of the U.S. into World War I brought pictures of ballplayers in military uniform, marching on the field. Giant photos of Ed Cicotte and Buck Weaver appear, as does one of a bus dropping off riders at Orchestra Hall, another of the Randolph Street Market, and one of Michigan Avenue, looking north, in 1917.

You get the idea. In the background, a city landmark or a portion of a city neighborhood, overlaid with photos, action and posed, of White Sox personnel. The '50s section, for instance, has as its backdrop the "L" coming around a curve into the station at 40th and Indiana, a shot of State Street at night in 1958, a view of Clark and Madison in 1958, and a 1953 photo of "6 Corners"— Milwaukee Avenue, Cicero Avenue, and Irving Park Road. And in the midst of all that are images of Al Lopez, Billy Pierce, Early Wynn, Sherm Lollar, Ted Kluszewski, and Luis Aparicio and more—plus Al Smith getting the famous beer shower in the 1959 World Series.

The '70s (or Bill Veeck) portion of the display, in addition to the personalities, like Dick Allen, Bill Melton, Carlos May and, from later in the decade, Chet Lemon, Oscar Gamble, Richie Zisk, and organist Nancy Faust, also includes a shot of Mayor Richard J. Daley throwing out the ceremonial first pitch at the 1976 opener. Also commemorated is Belly Dancers Night as well as Beer-Case Stacking Night, with the team of Bart Johnson, Ken Brett, and Goose Gossage doing rather well.

That's just a glance though; there is so much more. Next time the Sox fall hopelessly behind—say, 2–0 in the fifth—take a walk up the ramps or ride the escalator up to the 500 level and check out a slice of Chicago history.

It is well worth the climb—and there is no climb if you're already sitting up there.

90 Best Seats in the House?

They certainly were that night.

Section 159, Row 7, Seat 4. And Section 101, Row 1, Seat 13.

The night we refer to is Sunday, October 23, 2005, the evening of Game 2 of the 2005 World Series.

Two of the biggest moments in White Sox history, stashed into a segment of about 1 hour 15 minutes. Could this really be done by the White Sox?

First, in the bottom of the seventh inning and Houston leading 4–2, the Sox loaded the bases with two out. Paul Konerko was the batter. Reliever Chad Qualls entered, took his warmups, and looked in for the sign. He threw one pitch—a sinker that didn't sink. Konerko swung and the ball went flying toward the seats in left. The place erupted. Grand slam! The Sox led 6–4.

Next, the Astros showed why they were in the World Series. A pinch single by Jose Vizcaino off Sox closer Bobby Jenks tied the game in the ninth inning at 6–6, again with two out. Houston was going to be a problem.

But not for long. Scott Podsednik, one of the keys to the 2005 Sox offense with his 59 stolen bases and .290 batting average—but zero home runs—came up with two out in the Chicago half of the ninth to face Astros closer Brad Lidge. The count on "Pods" went to 2–1, and then he unloaded on a Lidge fastball.

The ball was driven deep to right-center. The fans couldn't believe this was happening. Sox center fielder Aaron Rowand couldn't, either. "No," he said to teammate Brian Anderson. "No way."

But when the ball disappeared over the railing, and he and his teammates jumped out of the dugout and onto the field and made a beeline for home plate, Rowand was no longer saying, "No way."

Those magical seats again: Section 159, Row 7, Seat 4. And Section 101, Row 1, Seat 13. The first location is where the Konerko shot landed; the second is where Podsednik's blast touched down. Next time you are out at the ballpark, take a walk on the outfield concourse and pay a visit.

The seats remain the original blue color, so they stand out pretty well.

As they should.

91 A Definite Must-Have

This is something every Sox fan should have.

It's Major League Baseball's official *2005 World Series Chicago White Sox Collector's Edition*.

The collection consists of seven DVDs, starting out with the play-by-play telecast—commercial-free—of the final game of the Division Series against defending world champion Boston. It's a chance to see "El Duque," Orlando Hernandez, perform his magical relief act one more time. Next is the finale of the ALCS against the Angels in Anaheim, when Jose Contreras went the distance, Joe Crede homered and drove in three runs, and the Sox won their first AL pennant since 1959.

Then comes one DVD for each of the four World Series games—again, commercial-free. Just the dulcet tones of Joe Buck and Tim McCarver. If you've forgotten, the Sox won all four.

The final DVD is entitled "2005 World Series Bonus DVD" and shows the clubhouse victory celebration at Minute Maid Park, victory parade footage, and players' speeches, as well as interviews with Ozzie Guilen, A.J. Pierzynski, Series MVP Jermaine Dye, Paul Konerko, and many others.

On the cover of each disc are tidbits of information that some professors would insist be committed to memory. Some examples:

The Sox hit .259 with runners in scoring position during the regular season. In the three ALDS games with Boston, they hit .417 in those situations.

Geoff Blum became the second player in history to homer in his first career World Series at-bat during extra innings; the other was Dusty Rhodes of the Giants in 1954.

And this one that's a little bittersweet:

Bobby Jenks was the first rookie pitcher on the mound for the final out of the World Series since the Dodgers' Larry Sherry closed out Game 6 of the 1959 Series against the White Sox.

The set may be a bit pricey. But you should really have it. It's especially valuable during lengthy losing streaks.

92 Nellie Land

Should your travels ever take you through south-central Pennsylvania and to historic Gettysburg with its many points of interest, carve out a little time to visit close-by Nellie Fox Territory. Chambersburg, Pennsylvania, itself the scene of a key Civil War battle and the only major northern community burned down by Confederate forces during the war, is the town where Little Nell and his family lived during his career. It's just 25 miles west of Gettysburg on U.S. Hwy. 30. St. Thomas, where he was born and raised—and where he is buried—is just another 10 minutes down U.S. 30.

By the way, Nellie Fox Bowl, the 20-lane alley that Nellie and a business partner first opened in Chambersburg in 1956, is still open and doing a brisk business. (One wonders—would it be drawing even more customers if the name of the place were "Nellie's Alleys"?) Bowling and hunting and fishing were Fox's off-season pastimes.

One of Nellie's best friends was former New York Yankees fireballer Bob Turley. Both owned bowling alleys, Turley's in Bel Air, Maryland. And Nellie's team each year would bowl, in a home-and-home event, against the team from Turley's place—one each in Chambersburg and in Bel Air. But nothing, Billy Pierce said, could top hunting and fishing.

"He loved it," Pierce, his longtime roommate, said. "He didn't like to mingle with crowds and he didn't like big cities too much. His favorite thing to do when the season was over was to go home to hunt and fish. He'd get lost in the woods out there in the wintertime."

And that's why Bill Veeck, on Nellie Fox Night in August 1959, presented Fox with a somewhat surprising gift.

"We gave him a boat that night, a 26-foot sailboat," Veeck recalled, smiling, years later. "There was no water, of course—except for a little creek—within 100 miles of his house. Ultimately, he sold the boat and bought some land he had wanted. We would've given him the land, of course, but you can't tow a piece of land into a ballpark."

If you have the time—and are fairly silly—you might want to recreate the hour-long ride from St. Thomas to Frederick, Maryland, that a 16-year-old Nellie Fox and his father made back in the spring of 1944 in the family pickup truck. Local legends disagree as to whether the 5-foot-6-inch, 140-pound Nellie or his dad did the driving, and also as to who was smoking the huge cigar in the truck—he or his dad, or both. What matters is the trip was made to the Philadelphia A's wartime spring-training camp and that A's owner and manager Connie Mack was impressed by Nellie's all-out style during workouts that day. He called Jake Fox over and said, "Your boy seems to have baseball in his blood. Why not leave him with me?"

That's what Jake Fox did. And a Hall-of-Fame career commenced.

93 Pudge's Playgrounds

Any vacation through New England should include a side trip to the wonderful (in summer) and beautiful (in autumn) Land of Fisk. The "pilgrimage" should first take the traveler to Bellows Falls, Vermont, on the west bank of the Connecticut River, which separates Vermont from New Hampshire, its neighbor to the east.

The town of Bellows Falls—not to be confused, of course, with Bedford Falls—is where Carlton Fisk was born on the day after Christmas in 1947. Which explains everything. Now we know why he so often seemed to be in a foul mood. You would be, too, if you never received birthday presents because your big day was too close to Christmas for the family to afford to celebrate Christmas and a birthday.

That's likely why, when the Fisks moved across the river to Charlestown, there were no reports of a kid running through the streets of his old hometown and yelling, "Hello, Bellows Falls!! Merry Christmas, Movie House!! Merry Christmas, Emporium!! Merry Christmas, you wonderful old Building and Loan!!"

No, Fisk was to be the product of Charlestown, not Bellows Falls. He, his older brother Calvin, younger brothers Conrad and Cedric, and sisters Janet and June made a name for the Fisk family beyond Charlestown, population of which at that time was fewer than a thousand. The old high school, open to pilgrims of course, is now Charlestown Middle School, located on the busiest street in town at 307 Main Street. The Fisk home was just north of the middle school's athletic field. (The new Charlestown High School is on the edge of town.)

"Pudge," so nicknamed by his folks, who remembered him being a chubby 1-year-old, was Charlestown High's most valuable player in baseball, soccer, and basketball his senior year. Actually, it was his prowess in the latter—although he did play baseball, and quite well—that earned him an athletic scholarship to the University of New Hampshire in Durham. The campus, by the way, is a picture-perfect place to stop on the trip to Portsmouth and the seacoast.

About Portsmouth: It's a historic little port city that has cobblestone streets and a charming downtown with shops and restaurants that overlook the harbor. Also on the water's edge is Prescott Park, a fine place to just rest for a few minutes.

As for Fisk, he and his wife, Linda, also a New Hampshire native, now split time between Chicago's southwest suburbs and their newest home, in Bradenton, Florida.

Finally, some notes to take along on your journey:

American League Rookie of the Year in 1972 with Boston, Fisk signed as a free agent with the White Sox in March 1981. He retired in 1993 after almost 13 years in Chicago and was inducted into the Hall of Fame in 2000. Fisk's uniform numbers (27 with Boston, 72 with Chicago) have been retired by both the Red Sox and the White Sox; he's one of only eight players so honored by two or more teams. A life-sized bronze statue of Fisk was erected at The Cell in 2005. In 2006, the Sox presented him with a World Series ring in honor of their 2005 championship run.

94 He Never Squealed —and Now He Can't

The "he" in the chapter title is George "Buck" Weaver, the outstanding third baseman of the 1917 and 1919 American League champion Chicago White Sox who spent almost every waking hour telling anyone who would listen that he was innocent of any wrongdoing in the 1919 World Series.

He did so because he probably was.

His sin? Sitting in on meetings where Chick Gandil and Swede Risberg would try to explain why the Sox players weren't getting the money they'd been promised from as few as one gambling syndicate to as many as three.

That "sin," however, is what cost him his true livelihood. Several years later, you could have found Buck Weaver doing various painting jobs in City Hall and/or the County Building,

Buck Weaver poses in the dugout at Comiskey Park before a game in 1918.
(Getty Images)

among other locations. During breaks, he would spell out to listeners young and old why he was not guilty.

He died in Chicago on January 31, 1956, and is buried in Mt. Hope Cemetery in the Morgan Park neighborhood on the Far South Side, just off 115th Street. The grave is in Section 35, and his stone simply reads "HUSBAND George D. Weaver 1890–1956."

For those wondering, Weaver hit .324 during the Series, played errorless ball at third base, and drew praise from several sportswriters for his excellent play in the midst of the chaos that was the White Sox those two weeks.

When the World Series ended, several suspicious reporters wrote of their doubts as to whether or not the Fall Classic had been legitimate. Several others, however, praised Weaver for his efforts all along during the Series. Ross Tenney of the *Cincinnati Post* wrote:

"Though they are hopeless and heartless, the White Sox have a hero. He is George Weaver, who plays and fights at third base. Day after day Weaver has done his work and smiled. In spite of the certain fate that closed about the hopes of the Sox, Weaver smiled and scrapped. One by one his mates gave up. Weaver continued to grin and fought harder....Weaver's smile never faded. His spirit never waned....The Reds have beaten the spirit out of the Sox—all but Weaver. Buck's spirit is untouched. He was ready to die fighting. Buck is Chicago's one big hero; long may he fight and smile."

All told, Weaver applied six times for reinstatement to baseball before his death at age 65 from a heart attack—or, maybe more accurate, a broken heart.

"There are murderers who serve a sentence and then get out," he once told a reporter. "I got life."

95 A Sadly Typical White Sox Tale

Be sure that, at some point, you rent or purchase the DVD of the 1949 motion picture *The Stratton Story*, starring Jimmy Stewart as Monty Stratton, the young White Sox pitcher who appeared to be on the verge of stardom only to have his career cut short by a hunting accident.

You think about Monty Stratton, and how good he was, and how good he might have been. You think about other accidents suffered by young White Sox players across the decades: Paul Edmondson, a pitcher, killed in an automobile accident in February 1970; Carlos May and the mortar accident at Camp Pendleton in August 1969; Mike Degerick, 20-year-old pitcher struck in the head by a line drive in April 1963, who pitched three innings total (all in 1964) thereafter.

Monty Stratton, though, was the first to be victimized.

In 1937, his second year in the big leagues, he went 15–5 with a 2.40 ERA and made the American League All-Star team. In 1938, injuries (especially Luke Appling's broken ankle) wrecked a season of high expectations for the Sox. Still, Stratton was 15–9, though his ERA jumped to 4.01.

Then came the accident.

The date was November 27, 1938. Stratton was hunting rabbits on his farm in Texas when he fell, the impact making his holstered pistol go off. The bullet hit his right leg, damaging a main artery enough to make doctors decide he needed to have the leg amputated immediately.

Monty worked with the Sox the next two years as a coach and batting practice pitcher. In 1939, Sox ownership sponsored a charity game in Comiskey Park between the Sox and Cubs, the proceeds (about $28,000) all going to Stratton. In the day's most memorable moment, he threw from the mound to demonstrate that he could still pitch. He had difficulty in transferring his weight to the artificial leg.

During the war years, he spent a good deal of time learning how to pitch despite his prosthetic leg. After the war, he organized semipro teams and pitched with them and also pitched in the low minors. In fact, in 1946 he was 18–8 in 27 starts for Sherman of the Class C East Texas League. He never again approached those kinds of numbers.

The movie is fairly faithful to the real story. It's certainly worth a look. And you might recognize the following big-leaguers (and Pacific Coast League stars who eventually made it to the big leagues) at various times in the movie: Joe DiMaggio, ex-Cub slugger Hank Sauer (as a Yankee player), Gus Zernial (then with the Sox), Catfish Metkovich (as a Sox player), ex-Sox Al Zarilla (as a Yankee), ex-Cub Lou Novikoff (as a Detroit Tiger), and the longtime manager Gene Mauch (Southern All-Stars).

96 Just Do It

Go to SoxFest. At least once.

It's not all just waiting in line with a program or yearbook or bat or photo to get signed by a utility infielder or relief pitcher who might not even make the club —although that is part of it, certainly.

It's more a celebration—well, there won't be much to celebrate at the 2014 SoxFest. It's more a confirmation that the White Sox still value their fans and are still thinking about winning championships, however absurd that sounds as this is being written. It's a reassurance that baseball season is coming, that pitchers and catchers will be reporting in a couple of weeks and that it is a new season, brimming with hope—you hope.

And there is something to be said about the often-informative, often-entertaining seminars—especially when they involve Kenny Williams and fans who give him little if any credit for the club's successes through the last several seasons.

There is always some down time to stop and get acquainted with Gene Honda, the Sox's and Hawks' public-address announcer—he's also the man at the P.A. mike for the NCAA's Final Four. There's also time to go check for bargains at the garage sale. And there are rows upon rows of Sox memorabilia for sale or trade—quite a bit of it never before displayed. So if you're looking for a sharp color photo of Wes Covington in a White Sox uniform (he was only here a month) or if you are still trying to fill out a complete 1953 Bowman's Sox set and the only card you need is a Sam Dente, this is the place to be.

Best of all, you never know who might get on the elevator with you. One time, when SoxFest was held at the Hyatt Regency on Wacker Drive, a guy held the elevator door for whomever that was who was hurriedly approaching, hoping he wouldn't have to wait for the next one. The man got on. He was Hall of Famer Larry Doby, good ol' No. 14, hero center fielder of the elevator rider when the latter was eight years old, way back in 1956. He introduced his wife and son to Doby, who, as it happened, was not only staying on the same floor but was right across the hall.

So did they have a good time? Hall, yes.

97 Will They Get Around to Appling?

A highlight of every trip to The Cell should be a leisurely stroll on the outfield concourse in order to view the statues that honor various legends through White Sox history.

As of this writing, there are eight men so honored. Starting in left field and continuing beyond center field to straightaway right, the statues represent these Souh Side greats:

Frank Thomas, Minnie Minoso, Carlton Fisk, Billy Pierce, Nellie Fox, Luis Aparicio, club founder Charles A. Comiskey, and, out in right field, Harold Baines.

The next former White Sox great in bronze?

No doubt the decision already has been made, and this corner predicts it's going to be Luke Appling, "Ol' Aches and Pains" himself, the master great-pitch spoiler who once fouled off 24 consecutive pitches from then-Yankee Red Ruffing. Appling won two batting titles (1936 and 1943) and in one season (1936) drove in 128 runs despite hitting only 6 home runs all year.

Another possibility is the one and only Ted Lyons, who played his entire career with the Sox and yet still won 260 games. He also gets points for managing the White Sox—a hopeless assignment in the years he did it (1946–48)—scouting for the club (he signed, among others, Joe Horlen and Ken "The Bandit" Berry), and for managing, for the season's final six weeks, the 1955 Memphis Chicks (who included Luis Aparicio and Sammy Esposito in their number) to the Southern Association championship.

And here are a couple rather frivolous suggestions from the Peanut Gallery:

A statue depicting a real moose posing with the two slugging Sox first basemen nicknamed "Moose": Bill Skowron and Walt

Dropo—Skowron, the ex-Yankee star, because he finally was able to convince his new Chicago teammates in 1964 that the Yankees were not gods, and Dropo for hitting .391 with 6 homers and 18 RBIs in the Sox's 22 games against the Yankees in 1955.

A statue commemorating three great pinch-hitters from the South Side past, kneeling or standing in the on-deck circle, bats in hand: Smoky Burgess, Ron Northey, and Jerry Hairston. Only trouble with that one is that "Ol' Smokehouse" and "Round Ron" never would fit in the same on-deck circle.

Incidentally, all of the concourse statues but one (Charles A. Comiskey's) were designed by Julie Rotblatt-Amrany, a relative of the late Marv Rotblatt, a left-handed reliever for the 1951 Go-Go Sox. Another of her credits at U.S. Cellular Field is the white bronze and black granite "Championship Moments" monument at the main entrance. The monument and the surrounding "Champions Plaza" are certainly worth a look during your next trip to the ballpark.

98 Take a Trip to Spring Training

For many, many years, the author's family spent part of its spring break in the Ft. Lauderdale area. The baseball fans in the group usually spent at least one afternoon or evening every March watching the New York Yankees getting closer and closer to being pennant-race ready.

Close by, too, just down Federal Highway in Pompano Beach, were the Texas Rangers. A bit farther north, in West Palm Beach, were the Atlanta Braves and Montreal Expos. And, not too far south of Ft. Lauderdale, in Bobby Maduro Miami Stadium, the Baltimore Orioles held forth.

The White Sox were in Sarasota, on the other side of the state, the Gulf Coast side. They made precious few trips to Florida's east coast, so when they did, attempts would be made to determine if tickets were still available, especially if they were coming to Ft. Lauderdale.

That happened just one time in all those years—1978, the year after the South Side Hit Men almost stole a division title without the aid of pitching or defense. It was a fun night at Ft. Lauderdale Stadium—Bobby Bonds drilled a couple hard-hit balls up the alleys, and Wayne Nordhagen hit a home run—until we heard from some vacationers from back home saying that the White Sox, just before the game began, had traded catcher Jim Essian and starting pitcher Steve Renko to the Oakland A's for lefty Pablo Torrealba. The deal left the Sox without a true big-league catcher, and there were fears that there was nothing special about Pablo Torrealba. Some language experts claimed that the word *torrealba* in Spanish meant "got all of it."

In later years, the family did indeed make the long drive across the state via Alligator Alley to see the Sox play in Sarasota, Port Charlotte, and Fort Myers. One of those years was 1989, when some people were excited about a new third baseman named Eddie Williams. It soon became apparent that Eddie just couldn't play.

It was during the Fort Myers visit that we read this rather surprising headline in a Chicago paper: "Jordan Cinch to Make Sox." The beat writer was as stunned as anybody—he hadn't written the story, which was totally bogus and made his paper look bad. He was not a happy camper.

There are lots of unhappy campers during the final week of March when final cuts are made and spring camps break in Arizona and Florida. But for the fans, a visit to those camps is invariably a fun time. So give Camelback Ranch in Glendale, Arizona, a visit one of these springs. Even if you miss the Sox, you can catch the Dodgers. Not a bad consolation prize.

99 "Brick" on the Call

During the 1950s and into the '60s, Chicago-area kids came home from school and turned on the TV to see the final inning or two of that day's baseball game, be it Cubs or White Sox. For whatever the reason, the Cubs' telecast was usually the one with the more triumphant ending.

There was the famous no-hitter by Sam Jones in May 1955, when the Cubs' right-hander walked the first three Pittsburgh batters in the ninth and then came back and struck out the next three. A few years later, the TV was turned on just in time to see Frank Bolling's ninth-inning, two-out drive to left hit the foul pole to give Detroit a 5–4 lead (and eventual win) over the Sox's Dick Donovan.

If you arrived home to see the Cubs' Walt Moryn single home the winning run against the Milwaukee Braves one week, rest assured you would be home in time a week later to see the Sox's Lou Skizas pop out to third to end the game with the tying and winning runs on base in a loss to the New York Yankees.

The man on the call for all those games, "capturing these baseball headlines as they're being made," as he used to say, was Jack Brickhouse, the man behind the WGN microphone for, oh, so many years. As time went by and the Sox ended their relationship with WGN, "Brick" became far more identified with the Cubs—who were still on WGN, after all—than with the Sox. Strangely, that caused some Sox fans to believe Jack, in all those years, had been a huge Cub fan and couldn't bear having to do the Sox telecasts.

That's silly, of course. To demonstrate Brick at his best, be sure to take a listen to his description of the Cleveland ninth on the night of September 22, 1959, the evening the Sox clinched their first pennant in 40 years. Copies are floating around, and you can always hear it by going to www.soxinteractive.com.

So you can get an idea, we now take you back 50-plus years, to Cleveland's Municipal Stadium, as the White Sox, seeking their first American League pennant since 1919, ran into some trouble in the last of the ninth inning. Woodie Held was the first Tribe hitter, facing Bob Shaw.

Brickhouse: "There's a high flyball, out into shallow right… Nelson Fox back on the grass, calls for the ball…He takes it… One out!"

Then came an infield hit by Jim Baxes, which brought up Jack Harshman, the former Sox pitcher and worrisome hitter, batting for himself. Ray Webster ran for Baxes.

Brickhouse: Ball two, strike one…There's a line drive base hit to right field!…Webster held up a moment, now advances to second…There are Cleveland runners on first and second with one out and Piersall is up…."

Into the game came Carroll Hardy, running for Harshman. Jimmy Piersall was the batter.

Brickhouse: "There's a ground ball, through Fox, into short right…the bases are full. A hard line drive handcuffed Nelson Fox…had he been able to make a clean pickup, it might have been a double-play ball…

"It goes as a base hit for Piersall, his third straight…and now, with the bases full and one out, here comes Al Lopez."

Sox manager Al Lopez had decided to yank Shaw at this point and go with 39-year-old sinkerball specialist Gerry Staley, his best reliever.

Brickhouse: "Coming in now is Staley. So far, Gerry has won 8 and lost 4 this year. He has been in 64 ballgames…this makes it his 65th relief appearance…A crowd of over 54,000 people, absolutely riveted to the edges of their seats at Cleveland…Webster on third, Hardy on second, Piersall on first, and the dangerous Vic Power is up…Here we go! Power is 1-for-4—an infield single…There's a ground ball…Aparicio has it! Steps on second, throws to first… The ballgame's over! The White Sox are the champions of 1959! The 40-year wait has now ended! The White Sox have won it! The White Sox have won it!"

It's a classic. You'll probably want to commit it to memory. In any case, after you hear it, go down to North Michigan Avenue, just a few steps south of Tribune Tower, and visit Jack's statue. It's a classic, too.

100 Go See the Sox Play on the Road

It's not much fun getting heckled while watching the White Sox lose another one on the road, and it's worse when the heckling comes after witnessing a devastating walk-off 10th-inning home run in Oakland followed by another in Anaheim. At least there were Carl Jr. burgers at Angels Stadium to assuage the anger.

It has been more than 40 years since that A's rookie outfielder, George Hendrick, batting .211 at the time, hit a hanging something from Steve Kealey way, way over the left-field wall at the Oakland-Alameda Coliseum. One of our number indicated the ball had reached the BART station on one bounce and was now on the train to Fremont. We had been told that Steve Kealey threw some long home runs, but this was ridiculous.

Chris Sale mows down the Yankees at Yankee Stadium in the Bronx.

Yet that is the fun and charm of seeing the White Sox away from home. (Games in Milwaukee and Wrigley Field don't count.) You learn a little more about your team, especially the younger players, when you see them in a different city and/or ballpark, away from their comfort zone. In most cases, they just don't seem to perform as well. Actually, neither do the older guys.

There was Toronto's Exhibition Stadium in 1986; even with the newly signed George Foster in the lineup, you knew there was no chance. The humidity that hung over old Memorial Stadium in Baltimore was stifling at that July 1988 twi-nighter, although Daryl

Boston, Gary Redus, and Harold Baines managed to hit home runs even though the rest of us could hardly breathe.

The heat was probably worse in Arlington, Texas, just before the 1994 strike, but that Sox team was so much fun to watch. Not that night, though: A chubby lefty named Brian Bohanan (1–1, 8.65 ERA) outpitched Black Jack McDowell and the Sox lost 4–1. The Sox have been losing at Kansas City pretty regularly the last several years, but being there in 1990 for Alex Fernandez's first big-league win was special…Interleague games in National League parks, however unfair they quite obviously are to the AL teams, still can be worth the drives to St. Louis or Cincinnati, for example. Jon Garland's home run at Great American Ballpark might still be going.

There have been a few trips to Detroit over the years, most ending in ignominious defeat—including Memorial Day, 1967, when 40,000-plus Tiger fans intimidated five college freshmen who, during final exams, had driven all the way from Holland on the other side of the state for a rather unique study break. The Tigers swept the Sox out of first place.

But the worst place of all has been Oakland, and not just because they sell foot-long hot dogs and then try to pile sauerkraut on them if you don't stop them in time. The author has seen 13 games at the Coliseum, starting in 1971. The Sox won the first two and have since lost 10 of 11—and the lone victory was the very strange no-hitter thrown by Blue Moon Odom and Francisco Barrios in July 1976. In that one, Odom and Barrios combined to walk 11 A's, but only one scored as the Sox romped 2–1.

Those two 1971 triumphs, by the way, were the ones that wrecked Oakland's home Opening Day and showed that happier days were ahead for a team that had lost 106 games the season before. It was quite the day by the Bay.

EXTRA INNINGS!

101 White Sox All-Time 25-Man Roster

(As Selected by the Author)

Pitchers (10)

*Eddie Cicotte
Years with White Sox (1912–1920)
His ERA was under 2.00 four years (1913, 1916, 1917, and 1919). Was 28–12 with league-best 1.53 ERA in 1917, 29–7 in 1919, and 21–10 in 1920, his last season. No-hitter in 1917.

*Urban "Red" Faber
(1914–1933: entire career)
Won 20 or more games four times, including three years in a row (1920–22). Lowest ERA in AL in 1921 (2.48) and 1922 (2.80). Career record of 254–213 with 273 career complete games. Hall of Fame, 1964.

20 Joe Horlen
(1961–1971)
Consistent starter had best year in 1967 when he went 19–7 with an AL-leading ERA of 2.06; also threw a no-hitter that year. Posted double-digit victory totals for seven straight seasons in the 1960s. Had 1.88 ERA in 1964.

16 Ted Lyons
(1923–1942, 1946: entire career)
Won 20 or more three times (1925, 1927, 1930). League-best ERA of 2.10 in 1942. Career record of 260–230 with 356 complete games. Hit .311 in 122 at-bats in 1930. Hall of Fame, 1955.

43 Gary Peters
(1959–1969)

Rookie of the Year in 1963. Went 19–8 in 1963 and 20–8 in 1964. Had lowest ERA in AL twice, 1963 (2.33) and 1966 (1.98). Career record of 91–78 with Sox. Good hitter had 19 career homers.

19 Billy Pierce
(1949–1961)

Back-to-back 20-win seasons in 1956–57. Won 14 or more games nine times for Sox. Led AL in ERA in 1955 (1.97) and strikeouts in 1953 (186). Sox record of 186–152; was 211–169 lifetime.

*Ed Walsh
(1904–1916)

Went 24–18 in 1907 with 1.60 ERA, then 40–15 record and 1.42 ERA in 1908. Had back-to-back 27-win seasons in 1911 and 1912. Led AL in strikeouts in 1908 (269) and 1911 (255). Hall of Fame, 1946.

*Guy "Doc" White
(1903–1913)

Went 27–13 in 1907. Won 16 or more games six straight seasons (1903–1908). AL ERA leader in 1906 at 1.52. Sox record of 159–123 with 262 career complete games.

31 Hoyt Wilhelm
(1963–1968)

Knuckleballer's six seasons on South Side were spectacular with ERAs of 2.64, 1.99, 1.81, 1.66, 1.31, and 1.73. Saved 20 or more games three straight seasons (1963–65). Most days, all but unhittable. Hall of Fame, 1985.

28 Wilbur Wood
(1967–1978)

Durable knuckleballer posted four straight seasons with 20 or more victories (1971–1974), including one in which he also lost 20 games (1973, when he was 24–20). Sox record of 163–148.

Catchers
72 Carlton Fisk
(1981–1993)

Played 24 years in majors, 13 with the White Sox. Hit 20 or more home runs four times for Sox, including career-high 37 in 1985. Hit for cycle in 1984. Hall of Fame, 2000.

10 Sherm Lollar
(1952–1963)

Just missed catching 100 or more games for 10 straight seasons (1952–1961) but was close: 93 in 1954 and 96 in 1957. Had back-to-back seasons of 20 and 22 home runs in 1958–59.

*Ray Schalk
(1912–1928)

Had 10 seasons in which he reached double digits in stolen bases, including career-best 30 steals in 1916. Played in two World Series for Sox. Hall of Fame, 1955.

Infielders
15 Dick Allen
(1972–1974)

Short but spectacular Sox career, starting with his AL MVP season in 1972 (37 HR, 113 RBIs, .308 batting average. Last Sox player to lead AL in homers (32 in 1974).

11 Luis Aparicio

(1956–1962, 1968–1970)

Rookie of the Year in 1956. Brilliant fielder. Had three straight seasons with more than 50 stolen bases (1959, 1960, 1961). Hit .308 in 1959 World Series. Hall of Fame, 1984.

4 Luke Appling

(1930–1943; 1945–1950: entire career)

Lifetime .310 hitter hit .300 or better for nine straight seasons (1933–41). In 1936, he won the first of his two AL batting titles, hitting .388. Hall of Fame, 1964.

*Eddie Collins

(1915–1926)

In 10 of his 12 seasons with the Sox, he hit .300 or better, including .372 in 1920. Stole 40 or more bases five times. Played in two World Series for Sox. Hall of Fame, 1939.

2 Nelson Fox

(1950–1963)

Won AL MVP award in 1959, first Sox player to do so. Batted .300 or better six times and was lifetime .288 hitter. Hit .375 in 1959 World Series. Hall of Fame, 1997.

35 Frank Thomas

(1990–2005)

From 1991 through 1997, never hit lower than .308. Hit 40 or more home runs five times. Drove in 100-plus runs 10 times. AL MVP in 1993 and 1994, batting champ in 1997.

23 Robin Ventura
(1989–1998)

Gold Glove 3B's best Sox season 1996: .287 with 34 homers. Drove in 90 or more runs six times and hit 10 of his career 18 grand slams for Sox. Named manager October 2011.

Outfielders
3 Harold Baines
(1980–1989, 1996–1997, 2000–2001)

Had six straight seasons with 20 or more home runs (1982–87). Batted .300 or better five times with Sox. Had four seasons with double-digit assists.

*Joe Jackson
(1915–1920)

Hit .300 or better in five of six seasons with Chicago. Played in two World Series for Sox. Best season may have been his final one, 1920, when he hit .382.

1 Jim Landis
(1957–1964)

Gold Glove center fielder could hit, too. Best season was 1961, when he batted .283 with 22 HR and 85 RBIs. Stole 20 bases and had on-base percentage of .370 in 1959.

9 Minnie Minoso
(1951–1957; 1960–1961; 1964; 1976; 1980)

Drove in 100 or more runs four times with Sox; also hit. 300 or better six times. Stole career-high 31 bases in 1951. Lifetime .298 hitter.

30 Magglio Ordonez

(1997–2004)

Hit .300 or better in five of his six full seasons with Sox. Drove in 100 or more runs four times. Hit 30 or more homers four times. Had 25 steals in 2001.

* Uniform numbers not used during player's career

102 20 Best Trades In White Sox History—and the 15 Worst

20 Best

1. Catcher Joe Tipton to Philadelphia (AL) for 2B Nellie Fox, October 19, 1949—A backup for an eventual All-Star and league MVP.
2. Catcher Aaron Robinson to Detroit for LHP Billy Pierce (21) and $10,000, November 10, 1948—Billy won 186 for the Sox over 13 seasons, twice won 20, and also started three All-Star Games.
3. OF Gus Zernial and OF Dave Philley to the A's, who sent LHP Lou Brissie to Cleveland; Cleveland sent LHP Sam Zoldak and C Ray Murray to A's and rookie OF-3B Orestes "Minnie" Minoso to Sox, who also got OF Paul Lehner, April 30, 1951—The Go-Go Era begins.
4. OF Bob Roth, OF Larry Chappell, RHP Ed Klepfer, and $31,500 to Cleveland for OF Joe Jackson, August 20, 1915—Thank you, Tribe.
5. OF Harold Baines and IF Fred Manrique to Texas for 2B Scott Fletcher, minor-league LHP Wilson Alvarez, and minor-league OF Sammy Sosa, July 29, 1989—Larry Himes' finest hour.

6. IF Fred Hancock, RHP Charlie Eisenmann, and $25,000 to Brooklyn Dodgers for minor-league SS Chico Carrasquel, September 30, 1949—Frank Lane puts one over on Branch Rickey.

7. RHP LaMarr Hoyt and minor-league RHPs Kevin Kristan and Todd Simmons to San Diego for 3B-OF Luis Salazar, LHP Tim Lollar, minor-league RHP Bill Long, and minor-league SS Ozzie Guillen—December 6, 1984—Roland Hemond's finest hour.

8. OF Jim Landis, OF Mike Hershberger, and RHP Fred Talbot to Kansas City A's for OF Rocky Colavito; Colavito and C Camilo Carreon then go to Cleveland for C John Romano, LHP Tommy John, and minor-league OF Tommie Agee, January 20, 1965—Sox will never be able to repay the Indians. Here comes another:

9. OF Minnie Minoso and IF Fred Hatfield to Cleveland for RHP Early Wynn and OF Al Smith, December 4, 1957—Without this one, Sox couldn't have won the pennant in 1959.

10. LHP Tommy John and IF Steve Huntz to L.A. Dodgers for 1B Dick Allen, December 2, 1971—The deal that electrified a franchise.

11. RHP Esteban Loaiza to New York (AL) for RHP Jose Contreras, July 31, 2004—The big Cuban won 17 straight during 2005–06.

12. SS Luis Aparicio and OF Al Smith to Baltimore for RHP Hoyt Wilhelm, SS Ron Hansen, minor-league 3B Pete Ward, and OF Dave Nicholson, January 14, 1963—It put Sox right back in contention.

13. LHP Juan Pizarro to Pittsburgh for LHP Wilbur Wood, October 12, 1966—Pizarro's arm was wearing out, a concept totally foreign to the knuckleballing Woodie.

14. RHPs Jaime Navarro and John Snyder to Milwaukee Brewers for SS Jose Valentin and RHP Cal Eldred, January 12,

2000—Deal won AL Central title for Sox: Valentin hit 25 HR and Eldred went 10–2.

15. IF Aaron Miles to Colorado for IF Juan Uribe, December 2, 2003—Kenny Williams at least should've been called in for questioning on this one.

16. RHP Stan Bahnsen and LHP Skip Pitlock to Oakland A's for LHP Dave Hamilton and minor-league 3B Chet Lemon, June 15, 1975—Chet, then 20, soon was playing center field and hitting .300.

17. Minor-league outfielder Mark Davis to the Angels for RHP Roberto Hernandez, August 3, 1989—Larry Himes knew where the players were: Roberto ranks third on the Sox's all-times saves list.

18. C Scott Bradley to Seattle for OF Ivan Calderon, June 26, 1986—Hawk Harrelson's finest hour.

19. RHP Jose DeLeon to St. Louis (NL) for LHP Ricky Horton and minor-league OF Lance Johnson, February 9, 1988—"One Dog" led AL in triples four straight years; led AL in hits in 1995, NL in hits in 1996.

20. OF Jim Rivera, 1B Gordon Goldsberry, IF Joe DeMaestri, C Gus Niarhos, and LHP Dick Littlefield to St. Louis (AL) for C Sherm Lollar, RHP Al Widmar, and IF Tom Upton, November 27, 1951—Frank Lane gets a No. 1 catcher; and by late July he also got Rivera back.

15 Worst

1. OF Sammy Sosa and LHP Ken Patterson to Cubs for DH George Bell, March 30, 1992—Cork and other stuff notwithstanding, an awful move.

2. OF Johnny Callison to Phillies for 3B Gene Freese, December 8, 1959—Within three years, Callison was in the All-Star Game; two years later, he was winning it—and he was still only 25.

3. C Earl Battey, minor-league 1B Don Mincher, and $150,000 to Washington Senators for 1B Roy Sievers, April 4, 1960—Two more future All-Stars are sent packing by Bill Veeck.

4. 3B Bubba Phillips, C John Romano, and 1B Norm Cash to Cleveland for OF Minnie Minoso, C Dick Brown, and LHPs Don Ferrarese and Jake Striker, December 6, 1959—Two years later, Minnie was 35 and Romano was an All-Star—as was Cash, who was hitting .361 with 41 homers.

5. OF-1B Bobby Bonilla, then 23, to Pittsburgh for RHP Jose DeLeon, July 23, 1986—Say it ain't so, Hawk.

6. LHP Eddie Lopat to N.Y. Yankees for C Aaron Robinson and two minor-leaguers: LHP Bill Wight and RHP Fred Bradley, February 24, 1948—Sox could lose badly to the Yankees off the field, too.

7. CF Tommie Agee and IF Al Weis to N.Y. Mets for OF Tommy Davis, C Buddy Booker, and RHPs Jack Fisher and Billy Wynne, December 15, 1967—Watch the 1969 World Series video if you disagree.

8. LHP Kevin Hickey and minor-league RHP Doug Drabek to N.Y. Yankees for IF Roy Smalley Jr., July 18, 1984—Even Roland Hemond wasn't always right.

9. C Jim Essian and RHP Steve Renko to Oakland A's for LHP Pablo Torrealba, March 28, 1978—A starting battery in exchange for Torrealba.

10. 2B Sandy Alomar (then 25) and RHP Bob Priddy to the Angels for 2B Bobby Knoop, May 14, 1969—Fans started figuring GM Ed Short was losing it.

11. RHP Bob Locker to Seattle Pilots for RHP Gary Bell, June 8, 1969—Fans knew Ed Short was losing it.

12. 3B George Kell, OF Bob Nieman, and RHPs Connie Johnson and Mike Fornieles to Baltimore for RHP Jim Wilson and OF-1B Dave Philley, May 21, 1956—Lots of quality for two guys in their mid-thirties.

13. Minor-league OF Ryan Sweeney and minor-league pitchers Gio Gonzalez (LH) and Fautino De Los Santos (RH) to Oakland A's for OF-1B Nick Swisher, January 3, 2008—Swisher stayed in Chicago one year and hit .219; Gonzalez was 21–8 in 2012; Sweeney is a lifetime .278 hitter.

14. 2B Nellie Fox to Houston for minor-league RHPs Jim Golden and Danny Murphy, December 10, 1963—Sox, hurt in 1964 by shaky 2B defense, would've been better off keeping Little Nell another year.

15. RHP Rich Gossage and LHP Terry Forster to Pittsburgh for OF Richie Zisk and RHP Silvio Martinez, December 10, 1976—There was nothing to show for Gossage and Forster by 1978.

103 The Nicknames Quiz

Here's a nicknames quiz for the real Sox fan: Who was…?
1. Art the Great
2. The Bandit
3. The Baylor Bearcat
4. Bee Bee
5. Beltin' Bill
6. Black Jack
7. The Blotter
8. The Big Hurt
9. Booter
10. The Brat
11. Bucketfoot Al
12. Bull

13. The Caracas Cat
14. The Cisco Kid
15. Citation
16. The Creeper
17. Cuban Comet
18. Cuban Missile
19. Daddy Wags
20. Deacon
21. Deacon
22. Donald Duck
23. Goose
24. Honey
25. Iron Mike
26. The Jet
27. Jungle Jim
28. Junior
29. The Mighty Mite
30. Moose
31. Moose
32. Moose (Can you name two out of three?)
33. No Neck
34. Ol' Aches and Pains
35. Old Blue
36. Ol' Gus
37. Ozark Ike
38. The Panther
39. Paw Paw
40. Pineapple
41. The Polish Prince
42. Psycho
43. Pudge
44. The Commander
45. Quick Draw

46. Spanky
47. Stanley Struggle
48. Suitcase
49. Tank
50. Wimpy

Answers:

1. Art Shires, 2. Ken Berry, 3. Ted Lyons, 4. Lee Richard, 5. Bill Melton, 6. Jack McDowell, 7. Floyd Baker, 8. Frank Thomas, 9. Marc Hill, 10. Eddie Stanky, 11. Al Simmons, 12. Greg Luzinski, 13. Chico Carrasquel, 14. Cisco Carlos, 15. Lloyd Merriman, 16. Eddie Stroud, 17. Minnie Minoso, 18. Alexei Ramirez, 19. Leon Wagner, 20. Grover Jones, 21. Warren Newson, 22. Eddie Fisher, 23. Rich Gossage, 24. John Romano, 25. Mike Hershberger, 26. Chet Lemon, 27. Jim Rivera, 28. Vern Stephens, 29. Nellie Fox, 30. Moose Solters, Bill Skowron, and Walt Dropo, 33. Walt Williams, 34. Luke Appling, 35. Ray Moore, 36. Early Wynn, 37. Gus Zernial, 38. Sammy Sosa, 39. Charlie Maxwell, 40. John Matias, 41. Richie Zisk, 42. Steve Lyons, 43. Carlton Fisk, 44. Carlton Fisk, 45. Tommy McCraw, 46. Mike Squires, 47. Stan Bahnsen, 48. Harry Simpson, 49. Dayan Viciedo, and 50. Tom Paciorek

104 Best of the White Sox... By the (Uniform) Numbers

Here are the best players to wear each uniform number, as selected by the author and a panel of trusted consultants. Remember that the Sox, like most teams, did not have uniform numbers until 1931. (Note: Longevity was often a factor in the decisions made.)

No. 1
Player: Jim Landis, CF, 1957–1964
Comment: Close race between Gold Glover Landis and fellow CF Lance Johnson, who led the AL in triples four years in a row.

No. 2
Player: Nelson Fox, 2B, 1950–1963
Comment: The Mighty Mite was a Hall of Famer and the 1959 AL MVP—plus, his number is retired and he has his own statue.

No. 3
Player: Harold Baines, RF/DH, 1980–89, 1996–97, 2000–01
Comment: Number's retired, has his own statue; those who laughed at Bill Veeck for drafting him No. 1 in 1977, where are they now?

No. 4
Player: Luke Appling, SS, 1930–1943, 1945–1950
Comment: "Ol' Aches and Pains," two-time AL batting champ and HOFer, left even Gene Freese (another No. 4) in the dust.

No. 5
Player: Ray Durham, 2B, 1995–2002
Comment: Only adequate defensively but hit as high as .296 in a season, stole as many as 36 bases, and hit as many as 20 homers.

No. 6
Player: Jorge Orta, 2B/3B/OF, 1972–1979
Comment: He never met a fastball he didn't like. Hit .316 in 1974 and .304 in 1975.

No. 7

Player: Jim Rivera, OF, 1952–1961

Comment: Not many .256 hitters were as popular as "Jungle Jim."

No. 8

Player: Albert Belle, LF, 1997–98

Comment: Not exactly a fan favorite, but it's tough to ignore those club-record numbers (49 HR, 152 RBIs).

No. 9

Player: Minnie Minoso, LF, 1951–57, 1960–61, 1964, 1976, 1980

Comment: You were expecting Danny Cater? Bee Bee Richard?

No. 10

Player: Sherm Lollar, C, 1952–1963

Comment: He was a Sox catcher when the author was a four-year-old and, also, when he was a sophomore in high school.

No. 11

Player: Luis Aparicio, SS, 1956–1962, 1968–1970

Comment: Little Looie, HOFer since 1984, squeezed past Dave Nicholson for No. 11 honors—only kidding.

No. 12

Player: A.J. Pierzynski, C, 2005–2012

Comment: A big favorite of Cub fans, A.J. beat out another Sox catcher, Ed Herrmann, a one-time All-Star (1974).

No. 13

Player: Ozzie Guillen, SS, 1985–1997 (Sox manager 2004–2011)

Comment: Ozzie sure made them forget the club's two previous 13s: Harry Chappas and Jamie Quirk.

No. 14

Player: Paul Konerko, 1B, 1999–Present

Comment: World Series hero, six-time All-Star, 15-year Sox stalwart beats out Bill Melton and Larry Doby—and Carl Sawatski.

No. 15

Player: Dick Allen, 1B, 1972–74

Comment: MVP in 1972 and league home run champ in 1972 (with 37) and 1974 (32). Remember those line-drive homers up "Allen's Alley"?

No. 16

Player: Ted Lyons, P, 1923–1946

Comment: Nope, not Ted Beard. HOFer Lyons won 260 games in his career, all of which was spent with the Sox.

No. 17

Player (tie): Chico Carrasquel, SS, 1950–55, and Carlos May, LF/1B, 1968–1976

Comment: No one could break the deadlock between the first Latino to start an All-Star Game and the man who hit .300 with one thumb.

No. 18

Player: Pat Kelly, RF, 1971–76

Comment: Longevity and an undistinguished field helped P.K. With Sox, hit as high as .291 and stole as many as 32 bases.

No. 19

Player: Billy Pierce, P, 1949–1961

Comment: 211–169 record, 3.27 career ERA, two-time 20-game winner, AL strikeout leader (1953), ERA champ (1955), three-time leader in complete games and three-time All-Star Game starter.

No. 20
Player: Joe Horlen, P, 1961–1971
Comment: His no-hitter vs. Detroit in final weeks of the 1967 pennant race was just one of his many contributions.

No. 21
Player: Gerry Staley, P, 1956–1961
Comment: Ninth-inning, bases-loaded, one-out, one-pitch hero of the 1959 pennant-clincher in Cleveland.

No. 22
Player: Dick Donovan, P, 1955–1960
Comment: Won 58 games his first four years in Chicago; out-polled Jose Valentin, Ivan Calderon, and Richie Zisk.

No. 23
Player: Robin Ventura, 3B, 1989–1998 (manager 2012—Present)
Comment: Solid candidates in Virgil Trucks and Jermaine Dye, but this Gold Glover hit for average and belted all those grand slams.

No. 24
Player: Joe Crede, 3B, 2000–2008
Comment: Back injury wrecked promising career; World Series hero had hit .283 with 30 HR and 94 RBIs in 2006, his fourth full year.

No. 25
Player: Tommy John, P, 1965–1971
Comment: Twice led AL in shutouts; had successive ERAs of 2.62, 2.47, and 1.98; and had the trade value to land Dick Allen from L.A.

No. 26
Player: Clint Brown, P, 1936–39

Comment: Meet the Sox's first relief specialist, who won seven games in relief and saved 18 games in 1937.

No. 27
Player: Thornton Lee, P, 1937–1947

Comment: Big lefty won 12, 13, 15, and 12 games (1937–40), then was 22–11 with AL-best 2.37 ERA in 1941.

No. 28
Player: Wilbur Wood, P, 1967–1978

Comment: Only No. 28 close is fellow knuckleballer Eddie Fisher. Woodie's best year was 1971 (22–13, 334 innings, 272 hits, 1.91 ERA).

No. 29
Player: Jack McDowell, P, 1987–88, 1990–94

Comment: Sox ace topped Jack Harshman, Keith Foulke, and Greg Walker by going 14–9, 17–10, 20–10, and 22–10 in successive years.

No. 30
Player: Magglio Ordonez, RF, 1997–2004

Comment: He automatically gave you 30 homers, 100 RBIs, and a .300 average. Won close race with Tim Raines and Bucky Dent.

No. 31
Player: Hoyt Wilhelm, P, 1963–68

Comment: Not to be confused with LaMarr Hoyt, also No. 31. "The Good Doctor" wins because he has a plaque hanging on the wall in Cooperstown.

No. 32

Player: Alex Fernandez, P, 1990–96

Comment: Edged out '60s fire-balling lefty Juan Pizarro with years like 18–9 in 1993 and 16–10 in 1996. Another Larry Himes pick.

No. 33

Player: Aaron Rowand, OF, 2001–05

Comment: Free-spirited sort edged two guys after his own heart: Steve Trout and Melido Perez. Wore No. 44 earlier.

No. 34

Player: Richard Dotson, P, 1979–87, 1989

Comment: Junior Moore? No, it's "Dot," if for no other reason than his 22–7 mark in the division title year of 1983. Also wore 49.

No. 35

Player: Frank Thomas, 1B/DH, 1990–2005

Comment: Earlier 35s Bob Shaw and Saul Rogovin were fine pitchers, but "the Big Hurt" was the greatest hitter in Sox history and is headed to Cooperstown.

No. 36

Player: Jim Kaat, P, 1973–75

Comment: Just when everyone thought he was through, "Kitty," out of Hope College in Holland, Michigan, posted back-to-back 20-win seasons in 1974 and 1975.

No. 37

Player: Bobby Thigpen, P, 1986–1993

Comment: Clinched this one with his then-record 57 saves in 1990 that helped the Sox to a surprising 94–68 season.

No. 38
Player: Frank Baumann, P, 1960–64
Comment: Lefty topped AL with 2.67 ERA in 1960, but had Norm Cash not been traded, this jersey would have been all his.

No. 39
Player: Roberto Hernandez, P, 1991–97
Comment: Closer for the 1993 and 1994 division champs, he still stands third in saves on the Sox's all-time list.

No. 40
Player: Britt Burns, P, 1978–1985
Comment: Big lefty went 18–11 in 1985, his finest season, then was forced to retire because of a congenital hip condition.

No. 41
Player: Tom Seaver, P, 1984–86
Comment: Was 15–11 with 4 shutouts in 1984 and 16–11 with a 3.17 ERA in 1985—at age 40. Hall of Fame, 1992.

No. 42
Player: Ron Kittle, LF/DH, 1982–86, 1989–90, 1991
Comment: Little competition here for the big man from Gary, 1983 Rookie of the Year and king of old Comiskey roof-shots.

No. 43
Player: Gary Peters, P, 1959–1969
Comment: Peters was one of the best pitchers—and likely the best-hitting pitcher—in club history.

No. 44
Player: Chet Lemon, CF, 1975–1981
Comment: He topped Phil Cavarretta, Connie Johnson, and Tom Paciorek, among other 44s. Sox fans were sad to see him go to Detroit for Steve Kemp in November 1981.

No. 45
Player: Carlos Lee, LF, 1999–2004
Comment: "El Caballo" hit for power and average and had a wonderful habit of hitting home runs, grand slams among them, against the Cubs.

No. 46
Player: Eddie Robinson, 1B, 1950–52
Comment: A leader of the original Go-Go Sox, he hit .314, .282, and .296 in his three years here with 71 homers and 294 RBIs.

No. 47
Player: Don Kolloway, IF, 1940–43, 1946–49
Comment: Chicago's very own—before there was a Channel 9. Born in Pilsen, lived in Blue Island. Dealt to Detroit in May 1949 and promptly hit career-best .292.

No. 48
Player: Ralph Garr, OF, 1976–79
Comment: Leadoff man came from Braves and hit .300 first two years here. Regrets to fans of Eddie Lopat and Rick Reichardt—and of Jose DeLeon, if any remain.

No. 49

Player: Smoky Burgess, C/PH, 1964–67

Comment: Smoky, pinch-hitter deluxe, wore No. 49 the final three weeks of the 1964 season after the Sox grabbed him from the Pirates. He switched to No. 2 the next spring.

No. 50

Player: Deacon Jones, 1B/PH, 1962–63, 1966

Comment: It's another pinch-hitter, Grover "Deacon" Jones, who in the minors had years of .343, .353, and .409 but due to a severe injury couldn't throw well enough to play regularly in the majors. Hit .321 with 8 RBIs as a 1962 September call-up.

No. 51

Player: Terry Forster, P, 1971–76

Comment: At age 20 in 1972 was the most overpowering reliever in the AL, with 29 saves, a 2.25 ERA, and 104 strikeouts in 100 innings.

No. 52

Player: Jose Contreras, P, 2004–2009

Comment: Hero of the glorious 2005 season had no challengers, unless you call Bill Gogolewski, Randy Wiles, Joel Davis, and Richard Barnes challengers.

No. 53

Player: Dennis Lamp, P, 1981–83

Comment: The most effective reliever on the 1983 division champs. Not much competition for this spot. Bert Roberge? Chris Tremie?

No. 54

Player: Rich Gossage, P, 1972–76

Comment: Hall of Famer spent his first five seasons with the Sox, who should retire No. 54 now so no more guys like Al Levine, Barry Lyons, or David Riske can wear it.

No. 56

Player: Mark Buehrle, P, 2000–2011

Comment: To beat out Bryan Ward and the immortal Ravelo Manzanillo to get the nod, "Burls" knew he'd need that perfect game.

No. 72

Player: Carlton Fisk, C, 1981–1993

Comment: He had to beat out Jim Cadile, "Refrigerator" Perry—oops, wrong sport. Pudge the First, like Gossage, had a spot on this list no matter what number he wore.

Sources

Newspapers
Baltimore Sun
Boston Evening Record
Boston Globe
Connecticut Post
Chicago's American
Chicago Daily News
Chicago Sun-Tmes
Chicago Tribune
Los Angeles Times
Miami Herald
New York Times
Pittsburgh Post-Gazette (East edition)
USA Today

Books

Allen, Dick, with Tim Whitaker. *Crash: The Life and Times of Dick Allen.* New York: Ticknor & Fields, 1989.

Asinov, Eliot. *Eight Men Out.* New York: Holt, Rinehart and Winston, 1963.

Boyd, Brendan C., and Harris, Fred C. *The Great American Baseball Card Flipping, Trading and Bubble Gum Book.* Boston and Toronto: Little Brown & Co., 1973

Condon, David. *The Go-Go Chicago White Sox.* New York: Coward-McCann, 1960.

Corbett, Warren. *The Wizard of Waxahachie.* Dallas: Southern Methodist U. Press, 2009.

Dykes, Jimmie, with Charles O. Dexter. *You Can't Steal First Base.* Philadelphia: Lippincott, 1967.

Helpingstine, Dan. *Through Hope and Despair.* Highland, Ind.: Helpingstine, 2001.

Kalas, Larry. *Strength Down the Middle.* Ft. Worth: Mereken, 1999.

Lindberg, Richard. *Total White Sox.* Chicago: Triumph Books, 2006.

Lindberg, Richard. *Sox: The Complete Record of Chicago White Sox Baseball.* New York: MacMillan, 1984.

Lindberg, Richard. *Stealing First in a Two-Team Town.* Champaign: Sagamore Publishing, 1994.

Minoso, Minnie, with Herb Fagen. *Just Call Me Minnie.* Champaign: Sagamore Publishing, 1994.

Reichler, Joseph L. *Baseball Encyclopedia*, 9th edition. New York: MacMillan, 1985.

Rogers, Phil. *Say It's So: The Chicago White Sox's Magical Season.* Chicago: Triumph Books. 2006.

Snyder, John. *White Sox Journal.* Cincinnati: Clerisy Press, 2009.

Vanderberg, Bob. *Sox: From Lane and Fain to Zisk and Fisk.* Chicago: Chicago Review Press, 1982.

Vanderberg, Bob. *Minnie and The Mick: The Go-Go White Sox Challenge the Fabled Yankee Dynasty, 1951 to 1964.* South Bend: Diamond Communications, 1996.

Vanderberg, Bob. *'59: Summer of the Sox.* Champaign: Sports Publishing Inc., 1999.

Vanderberg, Bob. *Frantic Frank Lane.* Jefferson, N.C., and London: McFarland, 2013.

Veeck, Bill, with Ed Linn. *Veeck As In Wreck.* New York: Putnam's, 1962.

Veeck, Bill, with Ed Linn. *Hustler's Handbook.* New York: Putnam's, 1965.

Publications

Baseball America (1987 to present)

Chicago White Sox Media Guides (1995, 2000-2013)

Chicago White Sox Scorebooks/Game Programs (1947 to present)

Chicago White Sox Yearbooks (1951 to present)

The Reader. "The Slugger." Michael G. Glab. Sept. 28, 2000.

The Sporting News (1936 to present)

SPORT magazine (July 1953, August 1954, May 1955, June 1955, August 1956)

Sports Illustrated (Aug. 1, 1960, April 19, 1965, June 7, 1965, Aug. 13, 1990.)

Street & Smith special commemorative. Champions: 2005 Chicago White Sox.

Web sites

AllSands.com

Baseball Almanac

Baseball Library

Baseball-Reference.com

Baseball Prospectus, "Wezen-Ball." Larry Granillo. May 6, 2011.

Beachwood Report, "White Sox Report," Roger Wallenstein. June 3, 2013.

Bleacher Report.

BrewersDepot.com. "The Story of Gabe and Walker."

ESPN.com.

Inkandescent.com. "From the Major Leagues to Award-Winning Artist." Michael Gibbs, June 4, 2013.

JockBio.com

Newspaper Archive

1919BlackSox@yahoogroups.com

1919Yahoogroups.com. "The Black Sox Trial: An Account." Douglas Linder, 2010.

Retrosheet.org

RobertEdwardAuctions.com

SABR BioProject: Bruce Nash, Bob Newlin, Dan Okrent, Saul Wisnia.

WhiteSoxInteractive.com. Mark Liptak, George Bova.